FIVE REASONS TO BELIEVE IN CALVINISM
AND FIFTY REASONS NOT TO

*An Examination of
Reformed Theology's Assumptions*

by

GIL VANORDER, JR.

SCHMUL PUBLISHING COMPANY
NICHOLASVILLE, KENTUCKY

All Scripture quotations, unless otherwise indicated, are taken from the Holy Bible, New International Version®, NIV®. Copyright © 1973, 1978, 1984, 2011 by Biblica, Inc.™ Used by permission of Zondervan. All rights reserved worldwide. www.zondervan.com. The "NIV" and "New International Version" are trademarks registered in the United States Patent and Trademark Office by Biblica, Inc.™

Cover image copyright: <a href="https://www.123rf.com/profile_stillfx">stillfx / 123RF Stock Photo</a>. Used by permission.

Published by Schmul Publishing Co.
PO Box 776
Nicholasville, KY 40340
USA

Printed in the United States of America

ISBN 10: 0-88019-626-2
ISBN 13: 978-0-88019-626-0

Visit us on the Internet at www.wesleyanbooks.com, or order direct from the publisher by calling 800-772-6657, or by writing to the above address.

Contents

Preface

I WAS ORIGINALLY GOING to title this book *Calvinism is Based on Assumptions* because that is true. After further consideration, I decided on the present title because I felt it was more likely to grab the attention of potential readers. I did not, however, change the original chapter headings (see the table of contents) because it was by examining the assumptions that I was led to the fifty reasons for rejecting Calvinism. If readers are unable to discover all fifty reasons while reading, they will ultimately find them listed in the last chapter. But in order to fully understand the reasons listed in that summary, readers will need to first read the book itself. I pray readers will not only be enlightened by these words but encouraged in their faith.

I've been told there is no point in even writing a book on this topic for several reasons. For one, the subject has been covered for hundreds of years, so you can't possibly have anything new to add to it. Secondly, few people read these kinds of books anymore. And finally, if someone should actually read the book, it won't make any difference because no one ever changes their views on this issue. Any *one* of these reasons should have been enough to discourage me from writing a book on Calvinism. When you consider all three reasons together, a person who writes such a book is qualified to be called arrogantly naive, stubbornly stupid, or certifiably insane. The reader is left with the task of deciding which of the three descriptions best fits.

My email address is given at the end of the book under the author bio. I listed it for the express purpose of allowing readers to contact me with their views on the book and on the subject of Calvinism in general. Readers may also decide to let me know which of the three descriptions they would most likely use in referring to me. I hesitated to give my email address for fear I wouldn't have the time to respond to every reader. Then I considered reason number two for not writing the book and became confident that would not be a problem. My desire is to respond to everyone interested enough to write.

Admittedly, my only qualification for writing this book is my time spent researching the topic and my time in prayer seeking God for discernment. I have no seminary degree or doctorate in theological studies. I am an unknown with no following or platform and I do not use any social media sites. So, why should anyone bother to read this book? They should because God is able to speak through anyone willing to be used of God for that purpose even if he is not a scholar. Jesus seemed to do all right with some common fishermen.

I have no desire to offend anyone but that is always a risk when writing on a subject that is so hotly debated. If I have written anything that is offensive, I apologize. At the same time, I desire to help fellow Christians whom hold to a theology that resulted from individuals who incorrectly interpreted the Scriptures. For that reason, I have written this book with the purpose of examining some of the more prominent assumptions held by Calvinists and explain why they are just that – assumptions. My hope is that readers will discover new reasons for questioning their theological views of Calvinism. More importantly, I hope readers will come to a better understanding of just how great and loving our awesome God really is for all people.

It is with a sincere heart, much study, and a great deal of prayer that I offer this book as the truth God has led me to.

Assumption #1
There are Five Good Reasons to Believe in Calvinism

REFORMED THEOLOGY IS EXTREMELY appealing to Christians because it offers many things the earnest believer desires in a theology. It is God-centered rather than man-centered, it is logical, it provides answers to many of the questions Christians want answered, it requires deep thought, and it is systematic. Many Christians are persuaded to become Calvinists for these reasons. What these sincere Christians do not realize is that Calvinism is not the only theology that offers these things. It may appear to be the only one that does to those being exposed to it for the first time, especially if they do not previously have a good theological background. For those who, earlier in their lives, have encountered only a simplistic faith or bad theology, Calvinism appears to be an extremely attractive alternative, if not a welcomed relief.

For example, Michael Horton, who authored the book *For Calvinism*, admits when he was young he was taught terrible things about God. He shares the story of his Christian school teacher saying to him, "If you have any unconfessed sin when you die – or Jesus returns – you'll probably go to hell."[1] Horton also tells how his "family attended regularly a house church where there were no sermons, no sacraments, and no formal officers. In fact, there was no membership. All of this was considered 'churchianity'."[2] In the afterword of his book Horton writes, "The church we were attending at the time was mostly of the 'doctrine divides, so let's not talk about those issues' school."[3] No wonder Horton became attracted to Reformed Theology. It was the first time he encountered a theology that seemed reasonable.

Calvinist Brian McLaren tells a similar story. He writes, "When I was growing up, there was anti-intellectualism rampant in Evangelical Christianity. At that time, it was mostly in the Reformed churches (Presbyterian, Christian Reformed, etc.) that one found much intellectual vigor and life of the mind."[4] Once again, it comes as no surprise that McLaren, like Horton, would become a Calvinist.

Christians who have not previously been exposed to sound theology are easily lured into thinking Calvinism is the only reasonable system of belief. If a theology presents itself as a big improvement over one's previous beliefs, it only makes sense to accept the new teaching even if one is merely turning from one bad theology to another. Nobody wants a theology that isn't well thought out or logical. But being systematic and logical does not guarantee a theology to be biblical. Just because a theology offers the brain a great deal of exercise does not mean it must be true. Nor should logic alone be the criteria one should use in determining the accuracy of a theology. This is especially true if the logic is based on mere assumptions, as much of Calvinism is, which will be demonstrated throughout this book.

Another reason Christians are drawn to Calvinism is because there are many scholarly theologians who have endorsed Reformed Theology. The thinking is that if intellectual giants believe in this theology then it must be true. Once again, the initiate is usually unaware that there have also been many intellectual giants who have rejected Calvinism. In addition, when listening to a Calvinist explain why he/she believes in Reformed Theology, the Calvinist comes across as more knowledgeable than the average non-Calvinist. This is because the average Calvinist is more steeply ingrained in their beliefs than are most non-Calvinists. But this too is insufficient reason to believe in a particular theology. Most cults (e.g., Jehovah's Witnesses or Mormons) are often more biblically literate than the average Christian. This is, unfortunately, because the cult member is painstakingly taught (indoctrinated) into the group's belief system while the average Christian is not. In that sense, it is an indictment on the church that there is so little discipleship and good teaching of the Word. Be that as it may, knowing the Bible and correctly interpreting it are two different things. One should never assume that a person is correctly dividing the Word of Truth simply because they can quote a great deal from it. It was reported that the former Soviet leader, Nikita Khrushchev, could quote whole sections of the New Testament, but his views hardly represented the beliefs of Christianity.

Obviously, the most important reason to accept a particular theology is because it agrees with what the Scriptures teach as truth. And, of course, Calvinists have their share of Bible verses that they point to as evidence for their beliefs. But, once again, non-Calvinists have their fair share of verses as well. There is, however, a big inequity in the two sets of passages. The verses that Calvinists proffer can easily be exegeted in a way that doesn't result in the same meaning that Calvinists give the verses.

By contrast, the verses proffered by non-Calvinists are extremely difficult to exegete in a different way. As a result, Calvinists are forced into being extremely creative in their interpretation of these passages.

Later in this book the reader may be surprised to discover the many contrived tactics Calvinists employ in their attempts to avoid the non-Calvinists' more sensible interpretation of certain passages. These tactics include convoluted thinking, creating things not found in the Bible, tacitly accepting two beliefs to be true even though it is impossible for both to coexist, alleging that God has a secret will that contradicts what He declares to be His will, claiming that blatantly obvious contradictions are a result of our inability to understand the Word of God, or by claiming God's ways are not ours, or when all else fails, simply calling the contradictions a mystery. These and other arguments offered by Calvinists will be shown to be less than stellar (if not disingenuous) defenses of Reformed Theology.

In summary, there are reasons that appear to justify a belief in Reformed Theology which, upon closer scrutiny, do not do so. Below are five more reasons why Calvinism is appealing:

1. Calvinism appeals to the Christian's desire to be humble.

Sincere Christians want to obey God. What does the Bible say God wants us to do? Micah 6:8 reads, "What does the Lord require of you? To act justly and to love mercy and to walk humbly with your God." James 4:10 instructs us to "Humble yourselves before the Lord, and he will lift you up." In the Old Testament as well as in the New Testament, there are commands to be humble. What could be more humbling than to realize, as Calvinists teach, that you were born into a state of total depravity? (See chapter 2.) You are so completely corrupted by sin that you hate God and your only desire is to sin. By accepting total depravity, one is certainly in no danger of becoming proud of oneself.

In addition, Calvinists teach that you are so sinful, God doesn't even ask you if you want to be saved because you can't answer in the affirmative. He simply saves you and He predestined whom He would save before the world began. Thus, salvation is unconditional. (See chapter 3.) Furthermore, if you believe that salvation is conditional, you cannot avoid becoming proud of yourself for saying "yes" to God's call. Christians, desiring to be humble before their God and not wanting to be full of self-conceit, are attracted to a belief that teaches both total depravity and unconditional election. Chapters two and three will reveal that these ideas are based on a number of false assumptions.

2. Calvinism appeals to the Christian's desire to grow deeper.

Sincere Christians are not satisfied with just the milk of the Word. They want to grow beyond being a baby and be fed with the meat of the Word. Calvinism seems to provide that by offering a theology that is often very tough to swallow. You are fed and must digest words and ideas that are not even found in the Bible. Reformed Theology can make your previous biblical literacy seem extremely shallow. As a result, sincere Christians are easily drawn to Calvinism.

3. Calvinism appeals to the Christian's desire to learn more about God.

For the Christian hungry to know more about God, Calvinism offers a feast of information about God and His nature. Learning what God is like, however, is not best undertaken by studying what Calvinists teach He is like, but by studying Jesus (God Himself). While on earth, Jesus did more than simply reveal what God was like. He Himself is God. John wrote, "In the beginning was the Word, and the Word was with God, and the Word was

THERE ARE FIVE GOOD REASONS TO BELIEVE IN CALVINISM | 13

God" (John 1:1). "And the Word was made flesh, and dwelt among us" (verse 14 KJV). Paul speaking of Jesus wrote, "The Son is the image of the invisible God" (Colossians 1:15). Jesus Himself said, "Anyone who has seen me has seen the Father" (John 14:9). Jesus said these words in response to Philip's request to see God.

Thus, to understand what God is like we have to look at Jesus, who is the exact representation of God (Hebrews 1:3). The Greek word used by the writer of Hebrews is *hypstaseos*, which means the "being, nature or essence" of God. Any theology of God, therefore, must begin with Jesus and move to God, rather than with what we may think God is like and then move that concept to Jesus. So, how does Calvinism's God compare to Jesus? Unfortunately, not very well. See chapter 4 to discover the many ways Jesus contrasts with the God of Calvinism.

4. Calvinism appeals to the Christian's desire to glorify God.

Because Christians desire to honor and worship God, Reformed Theology presents itself as an extremely attractive belief system. In fact, Calvinism teaches that glorifying God is the chief end of man. But as God-honoring as such an idea may sound, it is simply not true. Chapter 4 will demonstrate how false this idea is and reveal the true reason God created humans.

5. Calvinism appeals to the Christian's desire to grow in knowledge of spiritual things.

While Calvinism offers an enormous number of theological concepts, these concepts often require one to think counterintuitively in order to accommodate them. And when dealing with Scriptural passages that do not fit well into Reformed Theology, the believer is many times asked to simply trust that any normal understanding of the texts cannot be trusted. What appears to be obvious and straightforward really isn't. Again, all this will be shown later in this book.

Calvinism can be very attractive to those who enjoy thinking long and hard about what they believe, because Calvinism appeals directly to the intellect. Unfortunately, Calvinism can also appeal to the ego. It is a very short leap from believing in a theology that appeals to the intellect to becoming proud of one's scholarly beliefs. The intellectual prowess required to understand Reformed Theology can easily lead one to view anyone who follows an "inferior" theology with condescension. Sadly, in my experience, I have found Calvinists to be especially susceptible to this temptation.

Assumption #2
If You are Void of Something, Only the Opposite Can Be in You

FROM THE TIME OF John Calvin until today, followers of Reformed Theology have taught a concept of total depravity that is based on an assumption. That assumption claims that if the unregenerate are without any of God's righteousness, they must therefore possess only evil. In chapter VIII of the Second Helvetic Confession it states that man is "Full of all wickedness, distrust, contempt and hatred of God [not just indifference but hatred], we are unable to do or even to think anything good." In chapter 6 of *The Westminster Confession of Faith* it states that as a result of original corruption we are "made *opposite* to all good." (italics added)

Man is sinful, but is he by his very nature *"opposite* to all good" as the Confession claims? If a non-Christian rushes into a burning building and rescues a child from the flames is he doing something that is opposite to all good? Wouldn't throwing a child into the flames to be burned alive be more opposite to all good? Being sinful does not mean one cannot even "think anything good." For those who are demon-possessed that might be true, but it certainly isn't universally true. There are many non-Christians who think good things and act accordingly. Some do good due to their early childhood Christian training even though they themselves have never accepted Christ personally.

Calvinists argue that they are talking specifically about *spiritual* good, even though they will use the general term "good" without any such qualifications. They contend that only born-again Christians are capable of doing any good works. While the Bible makes it clear that we cannot be saved through good works because they accomplish nothing salvific unless perfectly performed (which is impossible for humans to do), that is not a reason to assume the unregenerate are incapable of doing any good works. In fact, the Bible tells us that is exactly what the unsaved (especially the Jews) do in their attempt to be righteous. How is that possible if the unsaved cannot do any good works? Furthermore, there is no Scriptural basis for assuming that all unbelievers hate God. There are unbelievers that don't even know there is a God to be hated. Others love God based on a misunderstanding of who He is. The Bible makes it clear that all are sinful and lost, but that does not warrant the assumption that all hate God or are incapable of doing anything but sin.

This is, nevertheless, the Calvinists' view of total depravity. Because the unsaved are unable to stop sinning, Calvinists believe sinning is all they can do. But that is a false assumption. Just because the unsaved cannot avoid sinning (which, incidentally, is true for the saved as well, according to Calvinists) does not mean that sinning is all they can do. The difference between the saved and the unsaved is not the amount of sin each one possesses, but the fact that one has their sins forgiven while the other does not. In some cases, the Christian behaves more sinfully than the non-Christian.

Obviously, there are verses that Calvinists claim support their view of total depravity, but such verses have been incorrectly interpreted and/or taken out of context (this will be shown later in the chapter). None of the verses Calvinists appeal to reveal humans to be filled only with evil. Not having something does not mean everyone must only possess the exact opposite thing.

Suppose every cherry in the world lacked the color white in its center. Would we then have to conclude that all cherries have only black in their centers? A sparrow has no loyalty to any particular country, but does that mean therefore that birds are, by their very nature, unpatriotic? A reindeer possesses no sense of morality. Must we assume then that such animals are full of nothing but immorality?[5] Non-Christians have no righteousness, but that does not justify the conclusion that they are full only of evil. Calvinism's concept of total depravity makes the assumption that if people are without one thing, they must possess only the opposite thing.

Calvinists view mankind as a monolithic group (i.e., constituting or acting as a single uniform whole). But people do not all act or think the same. For example, Abel was not like Cain. Their hearts were different and their attitudes toward God were different. When everyone else had become corrupt, Noah found favor in the eyes of the Lord because he "walked faithfully with God" (Genesis 6:9). Cornelius was "a devout and God-fearing" man even before he became a Christian (Acts 10:2). Why was Mary chosen to be the mother of Jesus if she "hated God" and was "opposite to all good?" People's hearts vary.

While all are sinful and separated from God, not all wish to stay that way. Like lost sheep, some run away from the fold as far as possible. Some even run when pursued. Others, however, only wander a short distance away. Fewer still are wise enough to realize when they become hungry that food can be found inside the pen. These sheep may even bleat in hope that the shepherd will open the gate and allow them to enter. While all are outside the safety of the fold not all are as eager to stay there. In the same way, not all humans hate God and are fighting to avoid Him. Some are mildly interested in Him. Others are very interested. A few are wise enough to recognize they are spiritually empty and actually seek after God. The prodigal son story illustrates this. While everyone lacks righteousness, not everyone's hearts are the same.

1 Chronicles 29:17 declares, "You test the heart and are pleased with integrity." According to Calvinists, God is never pleased when He tests men's hearts because none have any integrity. All members of the human race are the same. All are full only with evil. Yet, God examines the hearts of all men anyway. What point is there in doing so, if they are all the same? Why does Jeremiah 11:20 inform us that it is the Lord who judges righteously and tests the heart, if there is no difference between the hearts of sinners? God also knows some hearts will be open to the Gospel and some will not. Romans 10:10 tells us that it is with our heart that we believe and are justified. If all hearts are the same, then none will be justified despite what Paul claims.

Another Assumption

Calvinists insist the unregenerate are so full of evil that no one ever seeks after God. Quoting John Piper: "It is a myth that man in his natural state is genuinely seeking God."[6] Yet, over and over in the Bible, we find God admonishing the unregenerate to seek after Him. Why would God tell people to do something He knows they will never do? Certainly, God would be aware that seeking him is just a myth.

1 Chronicles 16:10-11, for example, assumes people will seek God. It reads, "Let the hearts of those who seek the Lord rejoice. Look to the Lord and his strength; seek his face always." Not only are unregenerate people told to seek God, but to do it always. How can they do that if total depravity prevents them from seeking God even one time? How can anyone's heart rejoice if they will never find the Lord by seeking Him because they have no desire to?

2 Chronicles 15:2 goes so far as to say we must seek first before we will be found by God. It reads, "The Lord is with you when you are with him. If ye seek him, he will be found by you, but if ye forsake him, he will forsake you." This makes it clear the choice to seek or not to seek is up to us – as are the consequences. Furthermore, we must seek first before we will be found by God.

"May all who seek you rejoice and be glad in you" (Psalm 40:16). Who are all those who seek God if no one does?

"Your heart shall live that seek God" (Psalm 69:32). If no one is willing to seek after God, who are *they* the Psalmist is talking about whose hearts shall live?

"Seek the LORD while he may be found; call on him while he is near. Let the wicked forsake their ways and the unrighteous their thoughts. Let them turn to the LORD, and he will have mercy on them, and to our God, for he will freely pardon" (Isaiah 55:6-7). There isn't even a hint here that such wicked and unrighteous people are unable to turn. The passage states it is possible to seek God, if you do it while He may be found. It would appear there will be a time when man cannot seek God, but apparently (if not obviously) it was possible when these words were spoken. Calvinists assume God cannot be sought at any time.

Lamentations 3:25 tells us, "The Lord is good to those whose hope is in him, to the one who seeks him." If no one seeks Him, then God is good to people who do not exist, making this verse nonsensical.

Both the Old and New Testaments tell us to seek God.

Not surprisingly, we find the New Testament to be consistent with the teachings of the Old Testament. We find similar admonitions to seek God throughout the New Testament.

Verses such as Matthew 6:33, "But seek first his kingdom and his righteousness, and all these things will be given to you as well." This passage comes from Christ's Sermon on the Mount where He is talking to as yet unbelievers. Why tell people to seek after the kingdom of God if they never will? Why tell the lost to vainly try seeking the kingdom of God if they will never find it? Why would Jesus give an injunction He knows the listeners might as well ignore because it serves no purpose? If you are one of the elect, God will give you the kingdom anyway, so Jesus should have told the people to simply wait for God to give it to you. Instead, He encourages them to waste their time seeking what they cannot find. Knowing the unregenerate will never seek God or His kingdom, it seems almost foolish of Christ to tell them to do so anyway. By saying what He said, He gives the impression it is possible to find the kingdom by seeking it. If it is not, then Christ's words are deceptive, if not ugly taunts.

"Ask and it will be given to you; seek and ye will find; knock and the door will be opened to you. For everyone who asks receives; the one who seeks finds; and to the one who knocks, the door will be opened" (Matthew 7:7-8). This passage is also part of the Sermon on the Mount preached to non-believers. Accepting Calvinism's definition of total depravity means Jesus is here promising unregenerate listeners they will find if they do something they will never do — seek. Why would Jesus do that? In fact, if no one ever sought Jesus, then no one would have even been on the mount listening to His sermon.

Proponents of Reformed Theology might argue that the only reason these people sought Jesus was for His miracles and not for Jesus Himself. Perhaps that is true initially, but in this case the people were willing to stay and listen to Jesus until it was evening even though it meant going without food. They knew there was no place nearby to obtain food, but they stayed anyway. Thousands were willing to ignore their physical need for food in order to be with Jesus. And they were unregenerate people. Although they may have come to Jesus for His healing touch (which is not a bad thing in itself but rather a wise thing to do), faith in Jesus was required for them to come. They believed Jesus cared enough and had power enough to rescue them from their condition. And Jesus rewarded them for their faith. The Bible says when Jesus saw the great multitude, He was moved with compassion toward them and healed their sick (Matthew 14:14). So, even if these people sought Jesus for the wrong reasons, they sought Him nonetheless because they had faith in Him and He rewarded them for doing so.

Hebrews 11:6 tells us, "He rewards those who earnestly seek him." According to Reformed Theology, no one will ever be rewarded for seeking God, because no one has a desire to seek God, especially not "earnestly." We must again conclude God is promising here to reward people who do not exist. Like Lamentations 3:25, this verse is nonsensical if we accept Reformed Theology's concept of total depravity.

Acts 17:27 entreats "all nations of men who dwell on all the face of the earth" [which would certainly include non-Christians] that "they should seek the Lord, if haply they might... find him, though he be not far from every one of us" (KJV). The reason non-Christians should seek the Lord is because in doing so they might find Him. In fact, the verse seems to imply that their chances are good because He is "not far from every one of us." Why promise people they might find the Lord if they do something they never will? Does God enjoy teasing people?

The unregenerate sought God.

The commands to seek God are evidence that sinners are able to do so, but there is an even more convincing refutation of John Piper's claim that people do not seek God. There are Biblical accounts of non-Christians who did so. There are numerous stories throughout both the Old and New Testaments of unregenerate men and women who sought God.

2 Chronicles 19:3 tells us King Jehoshaphat "prepared his heart to seek God." It doesn't say God prepared the king's heart to seek God. Jehoshaphat prepared his own heart.

Hezekiah prayed, "May the Lord, who is good, pardon everyone who sets their heart on seeking God" (2 Chronicles 30:18-19). Hezekiah didn't ask God to set everyone's heart to seek God. He asked God to pardon everyone who set their own hearts on seeking God. If no one has ever set his heart to seek God, then Hezekiah's prayer was senseless because none of those he prayed for would ever be pardoned by God.

King Josiah was sixteen years old (in the eighth year of his reign) when the Bible says, "he began to seek after God" (2 Chronicles 34:3). It doesn't say that at that age God caused Josiah to seek after Him. Like King Jehoshaphat, Josiah sought God of his own free will.

The New Testament tells of similar stories. Luke records, "A woman in that town who lived a sinful life learned that Jesus was eating at the Pharisee's house, so she came there with an alabaster jar of perfume. As she stood behind him at his feet weeping, she began to wet his feet with her tears. Then she wiped them with her hair, kissed them and poured perfume on them" (Luke 7:37-38). This woman did something Calvinists claim never happens. She sought Jesus and wept, probably in deep remorse for her sins.

Later, after some people complained, Jesus said this: "I tell you, her many sins have been forgiven—as her great love has shown. Then Jesus said to her, 'Your sins are forgiven.' Finally, Jesus said to the woman, 'Your faith has saved you; go in peace'" (Luke 7:47-48, 50). Wow, not only did the *sinful* woman seek Jesus, but her faith saved her. How can that be explained if Calvinism's concept of total depravity is true?

Luke chapter 7 has to be a nightmare for Calvinists. In another encounter, a centurion (not even a Jew) seeks Jesus for healing of his servant. In verse 9, Jesus says of the centurion, "I tell you, I have not found such great faith even in Israel." An unregenerate Roman soldier not only seeks Jesus but has such great faith that it amazes Jesus. You would have to remove a great deal of the Bible in order to say that nowhere in the Bible do you find a non-believer having sufficient faith to seek God. You find examples of them doing so over and over throughout the Bible.

In Acts 13:7 we read that a non-Christian named "Sergius Paulus, the proconsul, an intelligent man, sent for Barnabas and Saul because he wanted to hear the word of God." As a result of his desire to hear the Word of God, circumstances took place that caused him to believe (verse 12). He sought Saul and Barnabas because he wanted to hear the Word of God. He did this before he became a Christian. How was that possible if Calvinism's total depravity is true?

Many unbelievers sought Jesus (God) when He was here on earth, and they did not do so just for physical healing. Nicodemus comes to mind (John 3). If only the regenerated wish to seek Jesus, then Nicodemus must have been regenerated. But Jesus tells Nicodemus he must be born again. Obviously, Nicodemus was not regenerated (born again) even though he sought the Lord. How can this story be true if the unregenerate never seek the Lord?

What does it mean to be dead in sin?

Calvinists believe the natural man is incapable of seeking God because the Bible tells us that all men are dead in their sins as a result of the Fall. Based on that, Calvinists make another assumption. They assume "dead in sins" means the same as their concept of "total depravity." They assume the unregenerate can never do good, cannot understand the Gospel, and will never choose to respond positively to God. That's because Calvinists equate those described as dead in their sins to those who are physically dead even though Calvinists deny that they do so. For example, they frequently refer to the dry bones found in Ezekiel chapter 37 as evidence that people are so spiritually dead that only God can revive them. After all, Calvinists point out, a corpse cannot revive itself. But the unregenerate are not corpses. Nor are they brain dead. Furthermore, Ezekiel isn't even talking about individual salvation but the "whole house of Israel" (Ezekiel 37:11). God is promising to take the Jews out of the hands of the heathen and bring them (the two nations… divided into two kingdoms) together into one nation (vs. 21-22). Nowhere in the passage does is it say anything about total depravity or individual salvation.

Another story Calvinists claim demonstrates how spiritually dead the unregenerate are is the story of Lazarus. R. C. Sproul said, "Until God breathes new life into us, we are spiritually dead… a good illustration of monergistic, life-giving power is the raising of Lazarus from the dead."[7] But nowhere in Scripture does it say the story of Lazarus is an illustration of spiritual death. Again,

Calvinists are attempting to equate dead in sins with physical death despite there being no such comparison to be found anywhere in the Bible.

Ephesians 2:1 reads, "As for you, you were dead in your transgressions and sins." Edward White interprets verses like these to mean that sinners are, obviously, not literally dead, but are headed for eternal death. Such phrases represent the un-regenerate's future death based on their present sinful condition. It is similar to the phrase used when a lawbreaker receives the death sentence and is walking down the hall to the electric chair. We say he is a "dead man walking." He is still alive, but he is headed for certain death. White explains such verses as follows:

> An almost universal custom has affixed to these expressions what is termed a spiritual sense; namely, that of alienation from God, who is the highest life of the soul, "the strength of our life, and our portion forever." Hence have arisen the phrases, "spiritual death," and the "spiritually dead," both of them without example in apostolic usage.
>
> For there seems little doubt that the mode in which the Scripture terms here referred to are handled in the "apostolic fathers," more fully represents their real meaning than the modern application. That there is a figure in the Scripture use of the term the *dead,* cannot be disputed. But the question is: Are we to trace the figure in the *tense,* or in the *radical signification* of the terms? We submit that the figure is in the tense. The unregenerate men are described as *the dead,* and *dead in sins,* because they are *certain to die,* because they are under sentence of destruction, as men of mere *soul.* Thus, the figure of *prolepsis* is employed in Gen. xx. 3: "God said to Abimelech, *Thou art a dead man,* for Sarah, Abraham's wife." "The Egyptians said, We be all *dead men*" (Exod. xii. 33).

"All my father's house *were dead men* before the king" (2 Sam. xix. 28). The figure in each of these instances is that of using the present instead of the future tense. The unregenerate are "as good as dead."[8]

This interpretation explains why Adam and Eve did not die after eating the forbidden fruit even though God said, "You must not eat fruit from the tree that is in the middle of the garden, and you must not touch it, or you will die." Adam and Eve would never have tasted death if they had never eaten the forbidden fruit. But now they will experience death — not immediately, but in the future. This future interpretation of the words "dead in sins" also explains why the unregenerate are able to do things Calvinists insist are impossible. For example, even though doing good will not make a difference as to whether or not one remains dead in sin, good can still be done. Why else would the Bible warn those dead in sins that their good deeds will not save them?

The unregenerate can do good.

In the book of Acts, we read about a non-Christian man named Cornelius who was "devout and God-fearing; he gave generously to those in need and prayed to God regularly" (Acts 10:2). We learn Cornelius eventually becomes a Christian (Acts 11:14), but he is said to be a devout man who feared God before his conversion. Is praying and giving to the poor not good? Was unsaved Cornelius "*opposite* to all good" as Calvinists believe?

In Luke 16:19-31, Christ tells us about a rich man in hell who asks Abraham to send a beggar named Lazarus to his five brothers to warn them about hell, "so that they will not also come to this place of torment" (verse 28). You can't be any more spiritually dead than to be in hell itself; yet, even here a person is capable of caring about others and asking for the salvation of their souls. If that isn't a good thing, what is it?

It should be noted that Abraham told the rich man it would be useless to warn his brothers because they would not be persuaded even if someone rose from the dead to warn them. No amount of evidence would convince them. According to Reformed Theology, the reason they would not be saved is because they were not part of God's chosen elect. If ever there was a time to explain individual predestination this would have been the time. But predestination isn't even mentioned. Abraham doesn't say the brothers were not among those chosen by God. Instead, Abraham tells the rich man his brothers were bound for hell due to their unbelief. If individual predestination is true, why would Abraham fail to tell the truth about it at this time?

The unregenerate can understand the Gospel.

Calvinists maintain that those dead in their sins cannot even understand the Gospel. They quote 1 Corinthians 1:18 as evidence for their assumption, "For the message of the cross is foolishness to those who are perishing." In doing so, Calvinists fail to realize that viewing the Gospel as foolishness and misunderstanding it are two entirely different things. In fact, the unregenerate would have to understand the Gospel in order to judge it foolish. Otherwise, it would be a misunderstanding of the Gospel that they view as foolishness and not the Gospel itself. It is the Gospel, however, and not a misunderstanding of it, that the Bible says is viewed as foolish, so non-Christians must understand it. The Gospel is not that complicated or difficult to understand. According to Paul, it is simply that Christ died for our sins, was buried, and rose again the third day (1 Corinthians 15:1-4). What is there not to understand? Many non-believers completely understand the Gospel. They simply have chosen to reject it because they consider it foolishness. Furthermore, spiritual life is not required before one can understand the Gospel. If that were true, Satan himself, the first rebel to choose to sin and face death, would not understand the Gospel. It is because he does understand it, however, that he fights so hard to keep the Gospel from being preached. Being dead in sin does not mean one is unable to understand the Gospel. *Dead in sins* means one is not in the vine (Jesus) and so cannot grow spiritually. It does not mean that one cannot ask to be placed in the vine.

The unregenerate can choose to respond positively to God.

Calvinists also teach that the unregenerate will never choose to respond positively to God. Yet,, we find Abimelech, an unregenerate king of Gerar, did exactly that. Abimelech had taken Abraham's wife, Sarah, for himself because Abraham had told Abimelech Sarah was his sister and not his wife. When God told Abimelech that Sarah was Abraham's wife and that he should not keep her for himself, he responded positively to God and gave Sarah back to Abraham (Genesis 20).

Adam and Eve must have learned their lesson following their Fall. There is no indication they never again responded positively to God. They must have told their sons about God, as Cain doesn't appear shocked when God talked with him. Adam and Eve lost the most important thing they previously had, their intimate relationship with God, but it would be incredulous to believe they refused to ever again respond positively to God. Thus, they were not in a state of total depravity as Calvinists understand it.

Abel responded positively to God by offering the sacrifice God desired him to offer.

In the prodigal son story, after the son returns home,

the father says, "For this son of mine was *dead* and is alive again" (Luke 15:11-32). The "dead" son comes to his senses and returns on his own. Obviously, in this story Christ makes it clear that dead does not mean one is unable to choose to return to the father. Despite his horrible and sinful condition, the son was not in what Calvinists call total depravity or he would have been unable to make the choice he did. He had lost his relationship with the father and was "dead," but he was still able to return home without the father coming after him.

The unregenerate can believe spiritual truth.

Not surprisingly, Calvinists also claim sinners cannot accept spiritual truth. Yet there are many non-Christians who believe the earth was created by God and is a gift to mankind. Is that not a spiritual truth? Are these non-Christians believing an unspiritual truth? If an unregenerate person can believe that the world is a gift from God, why can't the same person believe the Gospel is also a gift from God? The Bible offers salvation to *"whosoever will."* It does not say "whosoever will, unless they are spiritually dead." God's gift of salvation is offered to all who are dead in sin (see Assumption #4). Salvation only becomes ours, however, when we accept it by faith. That is why Paul exhorts those dead in sin to "Wake up, sleeper, rise from the dead, and Christ will shine on you" (Ephesians 5:14). Notice Paul is exhorting people to do what Calvinists claim is impossible. Not only are people to wake themselves up from the dead but Christ will not shine on them until they do.

Where do Calvinists find Reformed Theology's concept of total depravity in the Bible?

So, where do Calvinists come up with their idea of total depravity? There are a number of Scriptures that Calvinists point to as evidence for their view. Consider some of the most often-quoted passages that Calvinists use as "prooftexts" for their belief in total depravity.

Genesis 6:5: "The LORD saw how great the wickedness of the human race had become on the earth, and that every inclination of the thoughts of the human heart was only evil all the time."

If everyone's thoughts are only evil all the time, they certainly are not going to choose to follow God. Having thoughts that are only evil all the time is almost Reformed Theology's very definition of total depravity. The problem is Calvinists fail to quote this verse in its context. The verse is not talking about all of humanity in general. The verse is referring only to the condition of people on the earth at that time – in Noah's day. Even then it was not inclusive of all men, as Noah's thoughts were not evil continually. It does not say this is the way all people have always been, are now, and always will be. It says "the human race had become" that way (i.e., over time). It was not that way previously. In fact, it is because of the way the people were then that God chose to bring the Flood upon the earth and destroy everyone. They were not always that way. Why did God choose to destroy them at this particular time? Something had changed.

Later in the chapter we read, "God looked upon the earth, and, behold, it was corrupt; for all flesh had corrupted his way upon the earth" (Genesis 6:12 KJV). Now, obviously, an all-knowing God would not be surprised by the corruption He saw. The passage indicates, however, there was something new on the earth as evidenced by the word "behold." If all mankind had already been corrupted from the time of Adam, there would be no need to tell the reader to "look what has happened." Why was there a need to look now at a condition that has always been there? The verse suggests that something had changed from the way it was.

We learn what that new something was from the words "all flesh had corrupted his way." God destroyed the people of that time because they had corrupted themselves beyond whatever depravity the Fall caused. If their condition was the same condition all humans are in at all times, why did God single them out for destruction and not other generations? The reason is because their sinful condition was worse than previous generations. So, their corruption was not due to Adam's sin but their own.

The story of the Flood brings up an interesting question. If people are hopelessly lost in their sins and can only be rescued by God, why didn't He rescue more people at that time instead of destroying them all? If God chooses who is saved and who is not on some basis other than a person's ability to respond positively to His call, why did He only save Noah? Verse 9 tells us why, "Noah was a righteous man, blameless among the people of his time, and he walked faithfully with God." How was Noah able to do that, if everyone desires only to sin as a result of total depravity?

Though the passage doesn't say it, one might suggest that God made Noah that way. But if that is true, then the question remains, "Why only him and not others?" Verse 6 tells us, "The LORD regretted that he had made human beings on the earth, and his heart was deeply troubled." Why would the heart of God be troubled with man's condition, if He could change it any time He willed? It seems far more plausible that He was grieved by the behavior of the people and their unwillingness to turn to Him by their own free will.

And why start over with Noah and his family, knowing nothing is going to change? Man is still going to be totally depraved according to what Calvinists believe. So what is the point of destroying everyone and beginning again if there is no hope of man being any different? If man will continue to choose only sin and not God, nothing will be changed as a result of the mass destruction. So, why the Flood?

Calvinism's total depravity is not in there.

Jeremiah 13:23: "Can an Ethiopian change his skin or a leopard its spots? Neither can you do good who are accustomed to doing evil."

If a person is no more able to do good than a leopard is to change its spots, then the Reformed view of total depravity must be true. Once again, however, Calvinists ignore the context of this verse. In context, those being spoken of (actually, spoken to) are the habitually disobedient people of Jerusalem who had, during this period of their history, forgotten God (verse 25). If the verse is referring to all non-believers at all times, then these people would not have "forgotten" God because they would have never known Him in the first place. The unregenerate have never known God. How could they be the ones who have forgotten someone they never knew?

Furthermore, those being described (actually, spoken to) are those *who are accustomed to doing evil*. In other words, these people are unable to do good because they have been sinning repeatedly for so long, they are now addicted and cannot stop. They are not that way because of one sin (Adam's). The passage is referring to a specific group of people, not all of humanity.

Jeremiah 17:9: "The heart is deceitful above all things, and desperately wicked: who can know it?" (KJV)

Calvinists assume that the verse is saying that *"a deceitful and desperately wicked heart* is not capable of seeking after God and everyone has such a heart." To determine if this verse is saying that no one's heart will ever seek God, one must include the very next verse to see the entirety of what Jeremiah is saying. Jeremiah goes on in verse 10 to say, "I the LORD search the heart and examine the mind, to reward each person according to their conduct, according to what their deeds deserve." Unless God only rewards evil things (which we know He does not), the heart must be capable of good as well as bad. If total depravity is true, then God would never reward anyone, making this verse meaningless.

It is also worth noting that prophets like Jeremiah often used hyperbole in their attempts to convince people of the truth. This verse cannot be ruled out as an example of that.

Psalm 51:5: "Surely I was sinful at birth, sinful from the time my mother conceived me."

Calvinists take this verse literally, which means an egg is sinful when a sperm enters it. The problem is the book of Psalms and all the poetic books, like Jeremiah, make use of hyperbole. This verse is an example of that. The Psalmist (David) here is using hyperbole to express how sinful he believes he is. He is not talking in literal terms. We can see the verse is hyperbolic by reading the verse that follows (verse 6): "Yet you desired faithfulness even in the womb; you taught me wisdom in that secret place." You cannot literally be taught wisdom in the womb because your brain isn't sufficiently developed. The Psalmist is using hyperbole.

Even if this poetic verse was meant literally, David is saying he was born sinful, not that he was born into total depravity. Being sinful does not mandate that you also be in the state of total depravity that Calvinists believe in. Sinful people can repent of their sins as this Psalmist does.

Matthew 7:18: "A good tree cannot bear bad fruit, and a bad tree cannot bear good fruit."

Calvinists assume this verse means that sinners are all bad trees unable to bear good fruit. Once again, Calvinists take the verse out of context in order to claim it supports the Reformed concept of total depravity. When read in context, you find Christ is not describing the condition

of the unregenerate. He is explaining how to recognize
false prophets by their fruits. To understand the context,
one simply needs to read the three verses that come before verse 18. The only ones being described here are false
prophets, not all mankind. Nor is total depravity the issue being discussed.

It's not found here either.

John 6:44: "No one can come to me unless the Father
who sent me draws him."

This is one of the most often-used verses by Calvinists
to defend their belief in total depravity. The reason they
so often quote it is because they assume it teaches that
man is in a state of inability that only God can overcome.
The "drawing" is assumed, without any exegetical necessity, to be the work of efficacious grace renewing the
sinner so he can—and ultimately will— believe the gospel. Calvinists make much of the Greek word *helko,* which
they claim conveys the idea of "dragging." R. C. Sproul
claimed that the word draw (*elko* in the Greek) means by
force. Sproul wrote, "*Elko* is far more than simply wooing. The meaning of *elko* is 'to compel by irresistible superiority' according to Gerhard Kittel's *Theological Dictionary of the New Testament.*"[9] "We are so depraved that
God must drag us to himself."[10]

The problem is that what Sproul claimed is simply not
true. Nowhere in Kittel's dictionary do the words "compel by irresistible superiority" even appear. In fact, referring to the word *elko* or *helko,* Kittel actually refutes his
claim by stating, "there is no thought here of force or
magic."[11] Thus, Sproul's definition of the word *elko (helko)*
is based on a definition he himself made up.

Besides that, if John wanted to record Jesus saying that
God must "drag" us to Himself, he would have used the
Greek word *suro. Suro* in the Greek New Testament is
used for "dragging in a more violent and aggressive

sense." It never means "'draw." John used both terms. For example, he used both terms in John 21:6 (*helko*) and John 21:8 (*suro*). When the disciples could not draw (*helko*) their net into the boat (because their drawing failed) they instead dragged (*suro*) the net behind the boat as they made their way to shore. Looking at John 6:44, we see that John did not use the word *suro* (aggressive dragging) but the word *helko,* which means the drawing is not definitive. We know this because the verb "draw" in John 6:44 is in the subjunctive mood, which is not the mood of reality (indicative mood), nor the mood of command (imperative mood), nor the mood of desire or wish (optative mood), but instead it is the mood of potential, which indicates the verb could potentially happen. So, the draw is not a definite occurrence.[12]

Furthermore, John 6:44 must be understood in the light of verse 45 which reads: "It is written in the Prophets, 'They will all be taught by God.' Everyone who listens to the Father and learns from him comes to me." Thus, the sinner comes to Christ by listening to the Father and learning from him, not by passively experiencing "efficacious grace." Neither here nor anywhere else do we find a text that necessitates an "effectual call" on a totally disabled unbeliever in order for salvation to take place.

Look for a moment at the parallels in these two verses. Verse 44 says that no one can come to Christ unless drawn by the Father. Verse 45 says that all who listen to the Father and learn from Him come to Christ. It would seem clear that the teaching ministry of God through His Gospel and Word is the means by which God draws people to Jesus. But we must listen to His Word and learn (believe) in order to be saved. This is confirmed by Peter (1 Peter 1:23), James (James 1:18), and Paul (2 Timothy 3:15), all of whom declare that *the Word of God* is an agency of the new birth. Quoting the writer of Acts, "Now the Berean Jews were of more noble character than those in Thessalonica, for they received the message with great eagerness and examined the Scriptures every day to see if what Paul said was true. As a result, many of them believed" (Acts 17:11-12).

Yes, God must initiate salvation, but He does so through revelations of Himself, especially through His Word. If there is no evidence of God's existence, then there is no reason to believe in Him. Nor can we place our faith in the Gospel if we have never heard the Gospel. As Romans 10:14 states, "How can they believe in the one of whom they have not heard?" God must first reveal Himself to us, so we can see our sinfulness compared to His holiness. We will not repent of our sins until we realize our sinful condition. Thus, God the Holy Spirit must first convict us of our sinful state. But that is not the same as God dragging us to Himself. In fact, faith in God must precede God's conviction. If we don't first believe in God, then we will fail to recognize any conviction of sin is from Him. Without a belief in God, we will see conviction as nothing more than a feeling of guilt over our bad behavior. We must realize we are accountable for our sins to someone greater than ourselves or other people. We must believe in God before we will seek His forgiveness.

God has revealed Himself in many ways, including through His creation, which leaves us without excuse (Romans 1:20). Arminians call this *prevenient grace.* God has also revealed Himself through His Word, the Holy Scriptures. Romans 10:17 declares that "faith comes by hearing and hearing by the word of God." What is heard is the message that "God has raised him [Jesus] from the dead" (verse 9). Verse 9 also says that if we believe in our hearts that God has done this and shall confess with our mouths the Lord Jesus, then we will be saved. Nothing is said about total depravity preventing anyone from doing these things. Repeatedly, we find the writers of the

New Testament explaining the need for people to place their faith in the Gospel in order to be saved and none of them say anything about total depravity or a person's inability to believe.

For example, Paul explains that the Gospel of Christ results in "salvation for everyone who believes" (Romans 1:16). It's that simple.

Paul also explains that the Scriptures "are able to make you wise for salvation through faith in Christ Jesus" (2 Timothy 3:15). If we are wise, we will place our faith (the faith we already have) in the Savior rather than in our works or anything other than Christ. When confronted with the Gospel and the conviction of the Holy Spirit there are those who do repent of their sins and place their faith in the Lord Jesus Christ. They are the ones who receive eternal life as a result. Those who refuse to repent and believe do not receive eternal life.

The author of Hebrews writes, "For we also have had the gospel preached to us, just as they did; but the message they heard was of no value to them, because those who heard did not combine it with faith" (Hebrews 4:2). Was God the one who failed to combine the Gospel with faith or was it those who heard the Gospel? The verse makes it clear that the reason the gospel is of no value to some people is because they fail to combine it with faith. The onus to believe the Gospel is not on God but on us.

Other verses Calvinists claim demonstrate total depravity.

Romans 3:10-12 reads: "As it is written: There is no one righteous, not even one; there is no one who understands; there is no one who seeks God. All have turned away, they have together become worthless; there is no one who does good, not even one."

If there is not a single person (*not even one*) who seeks after God, then everyone must be in a state of total depravity, reasons the Calvinist. R. C. Sproul points out that "the qualifying phrase, 'no, not one,' makes it clear that the universal judgment is not hyperbole."[13] Unfortunately, this is yet another example of how Calvinists take passages out of context in their attempt to prove the existence of total depravity. As in the Genesis passage, the reference here is not to all humans everywhere and under all conditions. Those being referred to are those (a specific group of people) who are attempting to get to heaven through following the law.

Paul is talking specifically about those who try to be justified by doing good or keeping the commandments rather than through faith in Christ. In verse 20, he makes this clear when he says, "Therefore, no one will be declared righteous in God's sight by the works of the law." Paul wants to emphatically inform us that not one person who attempts to keep the law is righteous or even seeking after God. Every single person who tries to gain acceptance with God through personal effort lacks understanding, and their efforts are unprofitable – no exception.

Paul wants it perfectly understood that from the very beginning ("As it is written" refers back to Genesis) no one is justified, except through faith. He states in verse 28, "For we maintain that a person is justified by faith apart from the works of the law." When placed in context, the passage does not exclude anyone from seeking God, only from seeking Him through works rather than through faith. Whether you are a Jew or a Gentile, you are not seeking God if you attempt to do so through your own efforts. If this passage is wrongly interpreted (as Calvinists do) to mean no one at any time can ever seek God in any way, period, then how does one understand all the passages throughout the Bible that tell of non-Christians who sought God or all the admonitions to seek God? Such an incorrect interpretation of this passage in Romans 3 makes the Bible contradict itself.

In Chapter 11 of *Exegetical Notes on Calvinist Texts,*
Grant R. Osborne comments on the first three chapters
of Romans as follows:

> The entire section deals with the pagans (1:18-32),
> the moral Jew (2:1-16), Jewish guilt (2:13-3:8) and
> concludes by bringing together both Jew and Gentile
> under one roof—universal guilt. Therefore, we must
> conclude that the universality here deals with the
> quantity (all people) rather than quality (total sin)
> regarding depravity. There is no hint that depravity
> means man cannot accept Christ.[14]

What Osborne points out is that chapter 1 is talking
about pagans in general, chapter 2 is talking specifically
about the Jews, and chapter 3 informs both Jews and
Gentiles that they cannot seek God through works. Chapter 3 is not saying God cannot be sought in other ways
(e.g., through faith).

Romans 7:18: "For I know that good itself does not
dwell in me, that is, in my sinful nature. For I have the
desire to do what is good, but I cannot carry it out."

If this verse is proof of total depravity, then Paul is saying as a Christian he is in a state of total depravity, because Paul says this about himself following his conversion. In context, Paul is explaining the battle he has as a
Christian in trying to avoid sin. He makes this clear in
verse 25 where he says, "I myself in my mind am a slave
to God's law, but in my sinful nature a slave to the law of
sin." Only those who ignore the context of this verse see
evidence for total depravity.

1 Corinthians 2:14: "But the natural man receiveth not
the things of the Spirit of God: for they are foolishness
unto him: neither can he know them, because they are
spiritually discerned" (KJV).

In this verse, Paul is not talking about whether or not
the natural man can become a Christian, but whether or

not he can understand *the things God has prepared for those who love him* (see verse 9). In context, Paul is explaining that it is the Holy Spirit who enables Christians to comprehend *the deep things of God* (verse 10) given to us as a result of our love for Him. Verse 14 does not say the natural man cannot receive the Holy Spirit, but that he cannot receive the things of the Spirit. Obviously, the natural man cannot receive the things of the Spirit until he first receives the Spirit Himself. Only then can the Spirit of truth guide one into all truth. But being unable to understand the deep things of God is not the same as being unable to receive the Holy Spirit.

The New International Version of verse 14 makes this point even more obvious: "The person without the Spirit does not accept the things that come from the Spirit of God but considers them foolishness, and cannot understand them because they are discerned only through the Spirit." You must first have the Spirit before you can understand *the things that come from the Spirit*. Such an obvious fact does in no way give credence to Calvinism's concept of total depravity.

John 12:39-40: "For this reason they could not believe, because, as Isaiah says elsewhere: 'He has blinded their eyes and hardened their hearts, so they can neither see with their eyes, nor understand with their hearts, nor turn—and I would heal them.'"

Using this verse to "prove" that sinful man cannot respond to the Gospel ignores a number of things. For one, the verse is referring to an Old Testament passage (Isaiah 44:18). Isaiah is talking specifically about Jews who had made idols for themselves and not mankind in general. Secondly, God blinded the eyes of these Jews because of *their* sin, not because of Adam's sin.

Christ quotes a similar verse (Isaiah 6:10) and explains why the Jews will not see, understand, or be converted. He says, "For this people's heart has become calloused;

they hardly hear with their ears, and they have closed their eyes. Otherwise they might see with their eyes, hear with their ears, understand with their hearts and turn, and I would heal them" (Matthew 13:15).

Notice that, in this case, Christ says the Jews have closed their own eyes. God only closes the eyes of those who deserve to have their eyes closed due to their previous sin. Even so, the verse says God would heal them if they would open their eyes.

The writer of Acts also quotes Isaiah 6:10: "For this people's heart has become calloused; they hardly hear with their ears, and they have closed their eyes. Otherwise they might see with their eyes, hear with their ears, understand with their hearts and turn, and I would heal them" (Acts 28:27). The reason the eyes of the Jews (not the eyes of all mankind) were closed was because they had hardened their hearts and had willfully chosen not to listen to God. Even so, God says He would have healed the Jews if they had not become calloused.

None of these verses, which are quotes from the Old Testament, can be used as evidence for universal total depravity. Not only do the verses apply specifically to the Jews alone, but the verses are not even talking about man's ability or inability to accept the Gospel. The Gospel was unknown to the Jews at the time. The verses refer to the consequences of the sins the Jews had committed, not original sin. Whether the closing of their eyes was done by God or the Jews themselves, it is always the fault of the people involved. We find God doing a similar thing to a group of people during the latter days. We find it in 2 Thessalonians 2:11: "For this reason God sends them a powerful delusion so that they will believe the lie."

For what reason? The previous verse (verse 10) tells us for what reason God did this: "They perish because they refused to love the truth and so be saved." They had previously refused to receive the truth, so after that God sends them "powerful delusion" so they will "perish." This brings up a hard question to be asked of Calvinists, "If these people were already deluded and damned from the Fall, why would God need to send them an additional delusion so they might perish?" In the King James Version, the verse says God *shall* send them powerful delusion. The word "shall" means it will happen in the future. The delusion caused by original sin took place in the past. So, why are two delusions necessary to insure damnation? If these people are not going to be saved due to total depravity, why would an additional delusion be needed to keep them from being saved? It would appear the Fall alone did not guarantee they would be lost.

Look, again, at Isaiah 44:18: "They know nothing, they understand nothing; their eyes are plastered over so they cannot see, and their minds closed so they cannot understand."

The previous verse (verse 17) tells us these Jews were in the situation they were in because they were praying to a wooden idol, saying, "Save me! You are my god!" These Jews' eyes were shut because of their own sin (idolatry), not because of Adam's original sin. Knowing that, the same difficult question faces the Calvinist, "If everyone's eyes are already shut and everyone's hearts and minds already lack understanding as a result of Adam's sin, what is the need for any additional shutting of the eyes or lessening of the understanding?" If blindness and lack of understanding of spiritual things is a result of total depravity, what transpired when God caused it to happen a second time? Did people become even blinder or more ignorant? If so, how and for what purpose?

We see the same situation in Isaiah 29:10: "The LORD has brought over you a deep sleep: He has sealed your eyes (the prophets); he has covered your heads (the seers)."

Like the previous verse, this verse does not apply to all mankind but to the Jewish prophets and seers at that time.

Even so, how is it possible for God to close the eyes of people whose eyes were already closed due to the Fall? Verse 13 tells us why God closed their eyes. The Lord says, "These people come near to me with their mouth and honor me with their lips, but their hearts are far from me." The Jewish people themselves had removed their hearts from God. It is in response to Israel's turning from God that He blinds them, not because of Adam's sin. God is always justified for closing the eyes of sinners. It is never something He does without cause or explanation. He never says He does it because of the Fall.

Likewise, Romans 11:8 cannot be used to support universal total depravity because it is quoting Isaiah 29:10. The verse in Romans reads, "As it is written: 'God gave them a spirit of stupor, eyes that could not see and ears that could not hear, to this very day.'" The words, "*as it is written*" refer to the verse in Isaiah 29 and not to the Fall of man. Calvinists who claim this verse evidences total depravity fail to understand its original historical context. Like all the other verses, Romans 11:8 refers neither to the whole population of humanity nor to total depravity.

By using the words "*to this very day*" Paul is saying that from the time of Isaiah right up to the time of his writing that the Jews were continuing to harden their hearts against God. Paul is not talking about mankind in general from the time of the Fall. Elsewhere Paul writes, "Even to this day, when Moses is read, a veil covers the hearts of Jews" (2 Corinthians 3:15). There is good news for them, however, as we read in the next verse (verse 16), "Nevertheless when it [Israel's heart] shall turn to the Lord, the veil shall be taken away" (KJV). Notice it says, *when it* [the nation's heart] *shall turn to the Lord*, not when God turns their heart to Himself.

There is one final verse offered by Calvinists as a prooftext for their belief in total depravity that must be considered due to its frequent use. It is Ezekiel 36:26: "I will give you a new heart and put a new spirit in you; I will remove from you your heart of stone and give you a heart of flesh."

Calvinists argue, "If our hearts are stone, it is obvious that God has to give us a new heart and put a new spirit in us. We ourselves can't change our stone hearts into hearts of flesh." It should come as no surprise that Calvinists are here, once again, taking this verse out of its context. A careful contextual study of this passage and related verses shows that the passage is not addressing individuals and the manner in which they are to be saved, but rather the prophetic *house of Israel*. The thrust of the prophet's argument is to show what God in His grace will do to restore Israel to her land in a future day. Regeneration of the individual unbeliever is not the subject. In context, it is the nation of Israel which itself does not include all of humanity.

Furthermore, in an earlier passage Ezekiel writes, "Cast away all your transgressions… and make yourself a new heart and a new spirit" (Ezekiel 18:31 KJV). Here, the responsibility is placed in the hands of the people for a new heart and a new spirit. So, even if the subject was individuals, it is they that must cast away their hearts of stone. But again, the gift of a new heart signifies the new birth of the nation of Israel, not of any individual. However, Ezekiel also conditions the reception of the new heart for the nation upon repentance of the people by saying, "Cast away all your transgressions."

All of the above verses have been used by Calvinists at various times to support their view of total depravity. But none of them do. While some of the verses may make it clear that all are sinners, none of them say sinners will always refuse salvation. There simply is no biblical support for Reformed Theology's concept of total depravity.

A belief in Reformed Theology's total depravity isn't necessary.

Sinning does not mean one must be in a state of total depravity. Adam and Eve were not in a state of total depravity before they sinned, but they still sinned. As a result, they were driven out of the Garden of Eden. Because God is perfectly Holy, just that one act of disobedience caused them to be separated from God's presence. The Bible says, "Whoever keeps the whole law and yet stumbles at just one point is guilty of breaking all of it" (James 2:10). So, we don't have to be in a state of total depravity to be out of relationship with the Lord. A condition of total depravity (even if it existed) isn't necessary to be dead in sin, because just one sin keeps us from God.

Somebody once asked Dallas Willard if he believed in total depravity.

"I believe in sufficient depravity," he responded immediately.

"What's that?" the inquirer asked.

"I believe that every human being is sufficiently depraved that when we get to heaven, no one will be able to say, 'I merited this.'"

Even one sin means we stand before God as sinners deserving eternal separation from the One who is Holy. This is all we need to know to understand we need forgiveness and redemption. Calvinists disagree. Calvinist Lorraine Boettner stated that until we accept total depravity (not just our sinful condition) "we shall never be able properly to appreciate our real condition or our desperate need of a Redeemer."[15]

That is yet another assumption Calvinists make that is not supported by anything found in Scripture. Total depravity isn't even a biblical term. By placing so much emphasis on their concept of total depravity, Calvinists seem more concerned with the *condition* of man (how thoroughly infected by sin he is) than they are with the *position* of man (lost and separated from God). God's emphasis, on the other hand, is not on how extensive or intensive sin is but on how it has broken our relationship with Him. He is far more concerned (due to His great love for us) with restoring our relationship with Him than He is in pointing out how terribly sinful we are or how thoroughly sin has affected us. John 3:17 tells us, "God did not send his Son into the world to condemn the world, but to save the world through him."

Jesus never used the term "total depravity." He did use the word "lost" but His emphasis was on our being separated from God rather than on how sinful we are. If you look at His parables, you see Him comparing the unsaved to a lost sheep and a lost coin (the sinful condition of a coin or a sheep certainly wasn't His point). Christ's emphasis was not on the degree to which sin had corrupted man but on how lost man was. He understood that the real tragic consequence of the Fall was not our depravity (total or otherwise) but our separation from God. Everything else that resulted from original sin pales in comparison to our lost relationship with Him.

Calvinists put a great deal of emphasis on understanding something (total depravity) that doesn't even need to be understood in order for someone to realize their need for forgiveness and salvation. In doing so, Calvinists minimize the greatest loss that resulted from sin, which is to love and be loved in relationship.[16]

Assumption #3
God Saves us Even Though We have no Desire to be Saved

THE ASSUMPTION OF UNCONDITIONAL election is based on the previous assumption regarding total depravity. If we will never believe the Gospel or repent of our sins because we are spiritually dead, then God must do more than just call for our response. He must make the response for us. We are not involved. Our salvation is unconditional. We don't even want to be saved, but God saves us anyway if we are one of His elect. If the unregenerate are incapable of making a positive response to God's call on their own, the only logical conclusion one can draw is that God must do so for them. Thus, logic requires unconditional election be accepted if one accepts the total depravity assumption. Indeed, the entire balance of the TULIP acrostic must be accepted on the basis of logic if Calvinism's concept of total depravity is true.

Sproul wrote, "If one embraces this aspect of the T in TULIP, the rest of the acrostic follows by a resistless logic.

One cannot embrace the T and reject any of the other four letters with any degree of consistency."[17]

Sproul is correct. If you believe total depravity (T) means man will never accept Christ by faith, then logic demands that election be unconditional (U). And, if salvation is unconditional then Christ must have died only for the elect, so limited atonement (L) has to be true. Likewise, if God chooses who is saved even though they have absolutely no desire to be saved, then irresistible grace (I) must be accepted. And finally, it only makes sense that eternal security, or perseverance of the saints (P), be true if irresistible grace is true. Why would God elect and then unelect people? Systematically, each point's veracity is built logically upon the validity of the previous point. Conversely, if one of the points is false, one must then question the veracity of the other four points. Thus, the entire foundation upon which Calvinism rests is their concept of total depravity. If the "T" has been incorrectly interpreted, then all the rest of Reformed Theology comes crumbling down. While the logic may be flawless, it is useless if it is based upon a false premise.

If total depravity is incorrectly interpreted by Calvinists (as chapter 2 demonstrates), then one is not required by logic to believe the other aspects of the TULIP theology. One is then free to interpret each concept based on what the Scriptures actually say rather than on a constrained bias that is demanded by logic and not by good exegesis. For example, one can accept without difficulty or confusion Christ's words regarding conditional election just as they are written. Again and again, Jesus taught that salvation was conditioned upon our repenting (Luke 13:3) and believing in Him (John 3:16). He constantly stressed the need for us to meet God's conditions, especially in His parables. Consider, for example, the following:

In the parable of the ten virgins (Matthew 25:1-12), five

virgins did not bring enough oil for their lamps and so missed out on the bridegroom. All ten could have gone with him, but only five did what was needed to be ready. The bridegroom could have taken in the other five but didn't (verse 12), because they did not adequately prepare for his arrival. They did not meet the necessary conditions to be ready. If Calvinism is true, the story should have ended with the bridegroom choosing the ones he wanted and leaving those he did not want without giving any explanation as to why. The parable makes it clear it was the decisions made by the virgins that determined their fates. A belief in Calvin's total depravity makes it impossible to interpret this passage as written.

In the wedding invitation parable (Matthew 22:1-14), everyone is invited, but not all come. And even among those who do accept the invitation there is one who is not accepted, because he did not dress appropriately. Could not the king have accepted him anyway? The king could have simply given the man a wedding garment whether the man wanted one or not. Instead, the king threw the man outside, into the darkness, where there will be weeping and gnashing of teeth (verse 13). Why did the king do this? It was because the man (not the king) failed to meet the conditions required for the occasion.

Jesus ends the parable by saying, "Many are invited, but few are chosen" (verse 14). Was the man not chosen because the king did not invite this particular man to be at the wedding? No, the king wouldn't have invited him if He didn't want him at the wedding. The man was not chosen because the man did not meet the conditions necessary for being at the wedding. As in the parable of the ten virgins, the offer is universal, but it is only the person who meets the required conditions that is accepted.

In the prodigal son story (Luke 15:11-32), it was only after the boy *came to his senses* (vs. 17) and decided to return to his father, and actually returned, that he was accepted back. The father did not go out after him and force him to return. The choice was the son's. The reunion with his father was conditioned upon the son walking back home.

If salvation is unconditional, why did Jesus use parables that clearly indicate there are conditions? Was Jesus trying to confuse or, worse, deceive us? Or was Jesus trying to explain that salvation is conditional? The answer should be obvious. Yet, Calvinists reject the obvious answer because it would not follow logically from their form of total depravity.

God provided the means for all Jews to avoid death by the blood of the Passover Lamb, but it was only effectual for those who applied it to their doorposts (Exodus 12). In the same way, God provided for everyone the blood of Christ, our Passover Lamb (1 Corinthians 5:7), but it is only effectual for those who apply the blood.

Just as God intended the serpent lifted up in the wilderness to be effectual for those who looked to it in faith (Numbers 21), so Christ, our Serpent in the wilderness (John 3:14-15), is only effectual for those who look to Him in faith. Healing was available to all, but it was effectual only for those who believed. It was conditional.

In the same way, God intended the cities of refuge to be available to all but effectual only for those who entered them and stayed within (Numbers 35). So too, Christ, our City to whom we have fled for refuge (Hebrews 6:18), is only effectual for those who enter into union with Him and remain in union with Him. Christ's atonement accomplished exactly what God intended. God intended it to save those who by faith believe the Gospel (1 Corinthians 1:21).

Thus, faith is a condition of salvation. Wherever God's Word tells of God's deliverance or salvation, faith is always a condition for it. This is true in both the Old and New Testaments.

The Passover

Look, again, at the Old Testament story which most closely represents how salvation works – the Passover (Exodus 12). The Israelites were told they had to put lamb's blood on the doorposts of their homes if they were to avoid having their firstborn destroyed. No one was required to do so. It is obvious from the wording the choice to do so was up to each individual household. God didn't put the blood on anyone's doorpost. Nor does the passage say anything about God giving anyone the faith they would need to put the blood on their doorposts. Only those who decided on their own to believe the blood over the doorpost was required for salvation acted accordingly and only they were the ones spared.

Not only did they have to act in faith, but this story makes it abundantly clear that God's offer of salvation was to any and all who met the required conditions. This is particularly noteworthy. God did not predestine certain ones to be spared based on some reason known only to Him. He gave everyone a chance to avoid death by choosing of their own free will to put the blood of the lamb on their doorposts. God spared them based on their decision to trust in the plan God provided for their deliverance.

Nothing in the Old Testament more closely foreshadows salvation through the blood of Christ (the Lamb of God) than the Passover. It is critical then to realize that the Israelites had to first meet God's conditions before being spared.

The Old and New Testaments agree.

In the same way faith is found to be a pre-condition for salvation in the Old Testament, faith is also found to be a pre-condition for salvation in the New Testament. Consider the following:

John 3:14-15: "Just as Moses lifted up the snake in the wilderness, so the Son of Man must be lifted up, that everyone who believes may have eternal life in him." Just as the Israelites had to look to the snake to be healed, the same condition is required for eternal salvation. We must look to Jesus.

John 6:40: "Everyone who looks to the Son and believes in him shall have eternal life."

Romans 1:16: "I am not ashamed of the gospel, because it is the power of God that brings salvation to everyone who believes."

Romans 10:9: "If you declare with your mouth, 'Jesus is Lord,' and believe in your heart that God raised him from the dead, you will be saved."

1 Corinthians 1:21: "God was pleased through the foolishness of what was preached to save those who believe."

Ephesians 1:13: "After you believed, ye were marked in him with a seal, the Holy Spirit."

None of these passages say anything about God having to give people faith in order for them to believe. If such is required, why is something that important not even implied? As they stand, all these passages can only lead one to infer that a person's own faith is a pre-condition to salvation.

From Genesis to Revelation the Bible emphasizes the importance of humans placing their faith in God. Abraham's faith was counted unto him for righteousness (Genesis 15:6, Romans 4:3). Rahab the harlot's life was spared when Jericho fell because she had faith that God was on the side of the Israelites (Joshua 2, Joshua 6:23, and Hebrews 11:31). Joshua and Caleb entered into the *Promised Land* because they were the only ones who had faith God could defeat the giants (Numbers 13:30 and Numbers 32:11-12). We read of Daniel in the lions' den; Shadrach, Meshach, and Abednego in the fiery furnace; David against Goliath; and Old Testament reference after reference that tells of great men and women who put their faith in God. People we should both honor and emulate. In none of these situations, is there any mention of total depravity preventing them from trusting God. Nor do the passages say anything about God suddenly giving them a special faith that enabled them to trust God. No, it was the individuals' own faith that was being described. Most revealing of all is the fact it was their personal faith that determined their fates. God's rescues and rewards were conditioned upon their faith.

In the New Testament, Christ actually told people it was their faith that resulted in their salvation. Luke records the story of "a woman in that town who lived a sinful life" but came and washed Jesus' feet. Afterwards, Jesus tells her, "Your sins are forgiven. Your faith has saved you; go in peace" (Luke 7:37-50). Jesus didn't say, "I give you the faith you need to be saved." Nor did He say anything about God the Father giving the woman the needed faith. No, it was the woman's own faith that He said saved her. Obviously, Jesus saved her, but it was her faith that made it possible.

After the four men let the man sick of the palsy down through the roof to Jesus, Mark 2:5 reads, "When Jesus saw their faith, he said to the paralyzed man, 'Son, your sins are forgiven.'"

It was after seeing their faith that Jesus said, "Your sins are forgiven." Forgiveness was conditioned upon the faith Jesus saw in the men.

If *our* faith is not a condition for salvation, why would Jesus be pleased with great faith (Luke 7:9) and disappointed with little faith (Matthew 6:30). What difference does it make how much faith people have if no one has sufficient faith to be saved? If God saves us unconditionally, the amount of faith we have prior to His saving us is insignificant.

If salvation is unconditional, why does Paul tell the

Corinthians to "examine yourselves to see whether you are in the faith" (2 Corinthians 13:5)? What possible good would that do? Suppose, after examining yourself, you found you were not in the faith. There is nothing you could do about it according to Reformed Theology because it is all of God. So, there would be no point in examining yourself unless there is something you could do about it.

So, Paul thought salvation was conditional. He even thought the number of people he could reach was conditioned upon his becoming a servant to all (1 Corinthians 9:19). Peter thought salvation was conditional. He believed a husband's salvation could be conditioned upon a faithful wife's manner of living (1 Peter 3:1).

God's actions are often conditioned upon ours.

In 2 Chronicles 7:14 God says, "If my people, who are called by my name, will humble themselves and pray and seek my face and turn from their wicked ways, then I will hear from heaven, and I will forgive their sin and will heal their land." God will not forgive their sin nor heal the land unless the people pray. His forgiveness and healing are conditional.

2 Chronicles 12:7: "When the Lord saw that they humbled themselves, this word of the Lord came to Shemaiah: 'Since they have humbled themselves, I will not destroy them but will soon give them deliverance. My wrath will not be poured out on Jerusalem through Shishak.'"

2 Chronicles 12:12: "Because Rehoboam humbled himself, the Lord's anger turned from him, and he was not totally destroyed."

James writes, "You receive not because you ask not." We pray so that we might receive. God's giving is conditioned upon our prayers.

1 John 1:9 states, "If we confess our sins, he is faithful and just to forgive us our sins and to cleanse us

from all unrighteousness." Forgiveness and cleansing come after we confess our sins. God's actions are conditioned upon ours.

When the jailor asked what must "*I* do to be saved," he wasn't told there is nothing you can do. He was told he must "Believe on the Lord Jesus Christ." His salvation was based on him believing. It was conditional.

Nowhere in the Bible is there found a single writer making the statement, "salvation is unconditional." Unconditional election, if true, is too important a truth not to be stated outright. Yet, such a statement is absent from the Scriptures. Instead, you find statement after statement to the contrary. Why then do Calvinists believe in unconditional election? As was stated earlier, the primary reason is because logic requires it. A belief in unconditional election is demanded if one believes in total depravity as understood by Calvinists. Logic requires such a belief even if the Scriptures teach otherwise.

Appeals to Scripture

Obviously, Calvinists do not rely on logic alone for their belief in unconditional election. For certain, there are Scriptures that Calvinists point to as evidence for their belief. But once again, as with total depravity, the verses they appeal to do not teach the concept Calvinists claim they do. These passages include the following:

2 Thessalonians 2:13: "God hath from the beginning chosen you to salvation" (KJV). This verse means, according to Calvinists, that we were not involved in our salvation because it happened before we were even born. The problem is Calvinists are assuming that God did not use His foreknowledge when choosing whom He did. That might be understandable until you read the remainder of the verse which reads, "through sanctification of the Spirit and belief of the truth." In other words, God decided from the beginning that one of the conditions for

His choosing to save a person would be their faith (*belief of the truth*). Obviously, a person cannot believe the truth before he is even born, so this verse is not saying certain individuals are unconditionally elected from the beginning. It is explaining that from the beginning God decided how a person would be chosen to salvation. Salvation would require the sanctification of the Holy Spirit and faith in Christ (belief of the truth). God would not know if someone put their faith in the truth (met this condition for salvation) unless He used His foreknowledge. So, rather than supporting a belief in unconditional election, this verse actually supports just the opposite.

John 6:37: "All those the Father gives me will come to me." The question is, "Who does the Father give to Christ?" Calvinists assume it is those whom God has unconditionally predestined to salvation because they all come to Christ. It does not occur to Calvinists that the reason they all come to Christ might be because they are the ones who have met the conditions for salvation. Another equally valid interpretation would be that the ones God chooses to give to Jesus are those He foreknows will respond positively to His Son. That is why they come to Christ. Why would God bother to give Christ those He knows will refuse His offer of salvation? Either of these interpretations better synchronize with the rest of Scripture than does the assumption that God gives the Son the ones He has chosen to be elect. The verse does not say God gives the predestined to Christ. That is an assumption not found in the words themselves.

John 6:44: "No one can come to me unless the Father who sent me draws them." Jesus says these words only seven verses after verse 37. Like verse 37, Calvinists assume those being drawn by God are those He unconditionally predestined to salvation. But, again, that is not what the passage says.

As was pointed out in chapter 2, the verb "draw" is in

the subjunctive mood, which is the mood of potential. Thus, it may or may not happen. If the *draw* is not a definite occurrence, it cannot be talking about the elect.

Chapter 2 also explained how John 6:44 must be understood in the light of verse 45 which reads: "It is written in the Prophets, 'They will all be taught by God.' Everyone who listens to the Father and learns from him comes to me." Verse 44 says that no one can come to Christ unless drawn by the Father. Verse 45 says that all who listen to the Father and learn from Him come to Christ. It would seem clear that the teaching ministry of God through His Gospel and Word is the means by which God draws people to Jesus. But they must listen to His Word and learn (believe) in order to be saved. God's drawing requires a response before salvation occurs.

Later in the chapter, Jesus tells us why He said what He did to this particular group of people. In verse 64 Jesus said, "There are some of you who do not believe." Then in verse 65 he said, "This is why I told you that no one can come to me unless the Father has enabled them." In between these two statements by Jesus the Bible says, "For Jesus had known from the beginning which of them did not believe and who would betray him" (verse 64). Knowing ahead of time who would betray Him requires foreknowledge. The reason Jesus said what He did to these individuals was because He fore-knew they would not be drawn by God because it would be useless due to their unreceptive condition (they *did not believe* and would not believe). They were planning to betray Christ and so were not open to being drawn to Him. There would be no point in God drawing them to Jesus because He knew "from the beginning" they would not be drawn due to their unbelief. In verse 47 of the same chapter, Jesus tells them, "The one who believes has eternal life." The people Jesus was talking to did not believe. It could be that it was for that reason (and that reason alone) they would not be drawn by God and thus not have everlasting life. People are not saved because God predestines them to eternal life, but because they have faith in Jesus. These people did not.

Why would Jesus even mention their foreknown condition if it makes no difference as to whether they are drawn by God or not? If God predestines people, their foreknown condition of not believing would be irrelevant. But Jesus said their foreknown condition was relevant. Jesus said their foreknown condition was the very reason why He told them they would not be drawn. They would not be drawn because He fore-knew they were not open to it. That's a reasonable interpretation. If nothing else the text tells us is that God foreknows who will put their faith in Jesus and who will not, which aligns with Romans 8:29, Galatians 3:8, and 1 Peter 1:2.

Ephesians 2:8: "For it is by grace you have been saved, through faith—and this is not from yourselves, it is the gift of God." Calvinists argue that we are not saved through *our* faith but through the faith that God gives only to the elect. The condition for faith is met by God and not us. Calvinists claim this verse makes that idea obvious. That may seem obvious until you realize their exegesis of the verse is faulty. Dr. Jerry L. Walls and Dr. Joseph R. Dongell point out in their book, *Why I Am Not a Calvinist* the following:

> ...the terms (faith, this, it) that seem so clearly linked in English are not so clearly connected in Greek. The English ear depends largely on word order for making sense of language, and so automatically presumes that this (which "is not from yourselves") must obviously refer back to faith, since faith immediately precedes this in the word order of the text. But Greek, being an inflected language, actually depends on "tags" that are attached to words for guiding the reader. If our writer had desired readers to connect

faith directly to this, these two words should have matched each other as grammatically feminine. We find, however, that this, being neuter in gender, likely points us back several words earlier – to the idea of salvation expressed by the verb. Accordingly, we should read the text with a different line of connections as follows: "For it is by grace [a femi-nine noun] you have been saved, through faith [another feminine noun]; – and this (salvation is) not from yourselves, it (this salvation) is the gift of God."[18]

The "gift of God" is *salvation* [a neuter pronoun] accepted through faith. The grammar will not permit "faith" to be the antecedent of "it."

In other words, the verse is saying salvation (not faith) is the gift of God. Nowhere in the Bible does it say God has to give us another special kind of faith to believe. The Bible tells us to believe. It never says we must wait for God to give us the needed faith. God asks us to trust in His Son, Jesus. If God asks this of us, He must think it is possible for us to do it. Would He ask us to put our faith in Christ if we don't have the faith to do so?

Faith is not limited to the elect.

There is no biblical reference that says the Fall removed faith from anyone. Nor does the Bible say that as a result of Adam's sin, God has to give humans a second, different (more spiritual?) kind of faith in order for them to believe. There is only one kind of faith found in the Scriptures. In the book of Hebrews we learn that "faith is confidence in what we hope for and assurance about what we do not see" (Hebrews 11:6). By that definition, everyone has faith. Faith is innate to every human being. Even atheists have faith there is no God. Believing there are extraterrestrials somewhere in outer space requires faith. Faith is demanded of every religion, and in most cases, that faith is in God (at least some interpretation of Him). Mormons, Jehovah's Witnesses, and many others believe in God. You don't have to be a Christian to believe in God, as evidenced by the Jews' belief in Yahweh or the Muslims' belief in Allah.

According to Calvinists, however, the faith we were born with is insufficient for salvation. God must give us a second kind of faith before we can be saved. What two kinds of faith are there? The Bible doesn't say there is innate faith and then there is some other kind of faith (a more spiritual faith?) that God gives us. The Bible only gives one definition of faith.

Calvinists do not accept the idea that the unregenerate are able to have faith in the Gospel because of the Fall. As was pointed out earlier, that is because Calvinists equate spiritual death with death itself. Dead people can't speak, think, feel, or even breathe. But *spiritually* dead people can do all these things including believe.

Calvinists disagree. They maintain that an unregenerate person is incapable of putting his faith in Jesus. They quote *The Westminster Confession* which says that natural man is unable "to convert himself, or to prepare himself thereunto." While it is true we cannot convert ourselves, we can ask God to convert us.

Calvinists don't believe we can do that, either. They contend that we are unable to ask for anything spiritual because we are so morally corrupted by sin. Calvinists believe that original sin resulted in moral inability, and so faith is impossible for the unregenerate. Such a deduction is based on the assumption that faith is a moral ability. But faith is no more a moral ability than is the ability to speak. Faith is a universal ability. Both pagans and priests have faith and can exercise it even if they are radically corrupt.

That doesn't mean everyone will put their faith in the right place. The Bible records all kinds of places where people put their faith, including idols such as the golden calf (Exodus 32:8), oneself (Luke 18:9), others (Micah7:5), riches (Mark 10:24), chariots and horses (Psalms 20:7), power (Psalms 62:10), one's righteousness (Ezekiel 33:13), works of the law (Romans 8:3), one's Jewish heritage, etc. What people place their faith in varies, but everyone has faith. Obviously, where everyone needs to place their faith (the faith they already have) is in the Lord Jesus Christ. That's what the Bible calls us to do.

Calvinists object by saying unbelief is a sin and the unregenerate reside in a state of sinful unbelief. As a result, they are incapable of faith. But unbelief itself is not a sin. Unbelief in aliens from outer space is not sinful. Unbelief is only a sin if it is God whom we fail to believe. We sin if we place our faith in anything or anyone other than God. The unregenerate can choose what or whom they will put their faith in.

Psalms 118:8 reads, "It is better to trust in the Lord than to put confidence in man." Albert Barnes states in his commentary that "This is the Hebrew form of comparison."[19] In other words, the kind of faith placed in man is the same kind of faith placed in God. Only where the faith is placed is different.

Do non-Calvinists teach Pelagianism?

Calvinists insist that such statements about faith demonstrate that Arminianism is clearly a variety of Pelagianism (salvation by works) or, at the very least, semi-Pelagianism (partly by our works). The reason Calvinists say that is because they fail to differentiate between faith and works. Unlike works, faith is not part of salvation.

By itself, faith accomplishes nothing to save a person. God must save us. While God requires faith before He saves that doesn't mean the saving is partly done by us. Thus, trusting God to save us does not mean our theology is semi-Pelagian. If it does, then Christ taught a semi-Pelagian theology. In the prodigal son story, for example, the father was the one who alone determined whether or not the son could enter into his home. Prior to making that decision, however, the son had to return to the father and trust the father to forgive him. Seeking the father's forgiveness does not mean the son was the one who determined his ultimate fate. The father could have refused to forgive the son even after he sought the father's forgiveness. Nevertheless, the son had to make a decision to return before the father allowed him to enter into his home. Only if the son had *not* sought the father's forgiveness would the son have determined his ultimate fate of never again being with the father. Deciding to return to the father was required for restoration, but the son didn't restore himself. In the same way, faith is required for our restoration with God, but we can't restore ourselves or even partially restore ourselves. Faith is not works. Again, if Calvinists are correct in saying that Arminianism teaches a semi-Pelagian theology then Calvinists must also say Christ taught a semi-Pelagian theology.

Faith is not a form of works.

To demonstrate how Calvinists equate faith with works, consider a statement made by J. I. Packer: "To rely on oneself for faith is no different in principle from relying on oneself for works, and the one is as un-Christian and anti-Christian as the other."[20]

Really? Where in the Bible does it declare that relying on faith is un-Christian and anti-Christian? Calvinists like Packer fail to understand that works is relying on oneself, while faith is relying on God. They are not the same. The Bible makes it clear that relying on faith and relying on works are mutually exclusive (e.g., Galatians 3:12).

Grant Hawley, in his book *The Guts of Grace*, says this:

> Phrases like, "For by grace you have been saved through faith… not of works…" (Eph 2:8-9), and, "to him who does not work but believes" (Rom 4:5), are complete nonsense, if works are part of the definition of the words faith and believe. If a woman at a wedding reception said, "The one who does not move, but dances, enjoys the reception," you would wonder if she had had too much to drink because moving is part of the definition of the word *dances*.[21]

It is equally nonsensical to say you are not saved through works but through faith (as the Bible declares) and also claim that faith and works are the same (as Calvinists contend).

Again, quoting Dr. Jerry L. Walls and Dr. Joseph R. Dongell, "The Bible itself does not describe faith as a work that accomplishes a task, or as a deed that establishes merit, or as a lever that forces God to act."[22] Walls and Dongell further state, "Since by its very nature faith confesses the complete lack of human merit and human power, it subtracts nothing from the Savior's grace or glory. By its very nature, faith points away from all human status and looks to God alone for rescue and restoration."[23]

You can't partially save yourself.

Recognizing my need as one who is sinful and lost does not mean I have taken part in my own salvation. Such recognition saves no one. Nor have I done anything to partially save myself by recognizing that only Christ can save me from my lost and sinful condition. Putting my faith in Christ to save me only means that I have met a condition necessary for the salvation process to take place. My faith is not part of the process itself. It is like the alcoholic who finally admits he/she has a problem and needs help. This, in itself, does nothing to change an alcoholic's situation, but it is necessary before any recovery steps can be undertaken.

Calvinists think like this: "If salvation doesn't happen until I decide to accept it, then I make salvation happen." Wrong. Salvation happened a long time ago when Christ died on the cross and rose again. His salvation does me no good, however, until I ask to have it applied to me.

Calvinists fail to separate the acceptance of salvation from the salvation itself. Accepting a gift does not mean you had any part in creating the gift, purchasing the gift, delivering the gift, or even determining who the gift would be made available to. Only the giver does that. Likewise, the gift of salvation is all of God. Deciding to accept the gift, however, is up to us.

Deciding is not doing.

By itself, deciding you want something done does not make anything actually happen. For example, you may decide you want a new house built on your property. You can want that to happen until the day you die, but that does not make it happen. Added to your dilemma is the fact you have no carpentry skills. You have no knowledge of plumbing or electrical work. You can't even mix or pour cement for a foundation.

Now suppose a master builder comes along with blueprints for how the house should be built, all the materials needed for the house to be built, the knowledge and ability to build the house, and the willingness to build it for free. But he will not build on your property until you say you want the house there. You believe the plans are perfect for you, so you decide to trust the builder and accept his offer. After the house is built, do you conclude that you built the house yourself? Do you even think that you partially helped build it? Not if you are honest. Just because you chose to accept the builder's offer does not mean you had any part in the actual construction. Deciding is not doing. The builder did it all. All you can do is be grateful he did.

The same is true of salvation. Just because you have to trust Jesus before God saves you does not mean you saved yourself or even partially saved yourself. The reason Calvinists call Arminianism semi-Pelagian is because they see faith as a part of God's salvation, which it is not. Salvation is all God's doing.

And, just as a reminder, God does not have to get permission to build any house He wants, anywhere He wants, any time He wants, but He will not take over your property and build a house there just because He can. He does not force you into a house (see Assumption #5). He gives you a choice as to whether or not you want His *house* built in you. Obviously, His heart seeks a positive response to His offer.

Faith doesn't save anyone, but it is required.

Suppose a man falls off a cliff and lands on a ledge with no way to climb back up. Another man comes along and lowers a rope to the man stranded on the ledge. The man must put faith in the rescuer and his rope when he grabs it and hangs on in order to be saved. If he is brought to safety, does the man claim that it was his faith that saved him? What if the rope broke, or the would-be rescuer didn't have the strength to pull up the weight of the stranded man, or the rope slipped out of the rescuer's hands or he deliberately let go of the rope? The man on the ledge would be lost. The man's faith is the same in all these situations, but in only one case is it not misplaced. He does not need a different (more powerful) faith in order to be saved. Faith must be placed in the right place, in a real rescuer (Savior) and his rope (the atonement) and not in a false one. So, it is not faith that saves the stranded hiker even though he must have faith in order for his rescue to take place. Faith itself saves no one, but it is required (is a pre-condition) before the actual rescue (salvation) itself can take place. The assumption that a person who puts faith in Christ (i.e., the rescuer) has partly saved himself is total fiction. Nevertheless, it is one of the most deeply held assumptions of Calvinists.

Regeneration → Conversion (faith and repentance) → Justification

Because Reformed Theology teaches that the unregenerate do not have the faith needed to believe the Gospel, Calvinists assume that God must regenerate a person before faith is even a factor. R. C. Sproul states, "When speaking of the order of salvation (*ordo salutis*), Reformed Theology always and everywhere insists that regeneration precedes faith."[24] The Bible, on the other hand, always and everywhere insists that faith precedes regeneration. Later, the abundant Scriptural references showing the correct order will be examined. Before that is done, however, there are some problems with the construct generally that should be pointed out.

One problem is that salvation is not a series of events with several time lags in between the various events. Regeneration, conversion, and justification all transpire at the same time – all three occur instantaneously at salvation. Even well-known Calvinist John MacArthur admitted this. He said, "From the standpoint of reason, regeneration logically must initiate faith and repentance. But the saving transaction is a single, instantaneous event."[25] Biblically, salvation is a single instantaneous event, yet it is also a series of events with a specific sequential order. How can MacArthur not see there is more than just a paradox in what he is saying but a glaring contradiction? Notice that MacArthur says from "the standpoint of reason" and "logically must." Faith must follow regeneration because logic demands it (even though the Bible does not). The only reason logic demands it is because of Reformed Theology's concept of total depravity.

Another Problem

A second problem with the Reformed *ordo salutis* is that the word regeneration means rebirth. When you are reborn you have new life. Thus, you must have Christ (who is life) when you are reborn. If you have Christ you have His righteousness, you have His justification, and you have eternal life. John the apostle writes, "Whoever has the Son has life; whoever does not have the Son of God has not life" (1 John 5:12). Christ does not give you faith so you can have eternal life. He Himself is life and He enters your life at regeneration. Christ did not say, "I have the way, the truth, and the life." He said, "I am the way and the truth and the life" (John 14:6). Christ is not merely an agent who gives faith for life, He is the life. Before raising Lazarus from the dead, the Lord said, "I am the resurrection, and the life" (John 11:25). He did not say, "I have life to impart."

Furthermore, when you are regenerated you become a newborn son or daughter of God. You cannot be regenerated and remain unborn. They are one and the same. So where does faith fit in? According to the actual words of the Bible, faith always comes *before* rebirth (regeneration). The correct order is repeatedly given in the Bible.

Galatians 3:26 states, "you are all children of God through faith." You become a child of God (born again, regenerated) through faith in Christ Jesus. You do not receive faith by regeneration. You receive regeneration by faith. Faith comes first.

John 1:12 says the same thing: "To those who believed in his name, he gave the right to become children of God." God gives rebirth (regeneration) to those who believe. You do not become a child of God (are reborn) so you can believe. You believe so you can become a child of God (be reborn or regenerated). Again, faith must come first.

John tells us he wrote about the signs Jesus did "that ye may believe that Jesus is the Christ, the Son of God, and that by believing you may have life in his name" (John 20:31). How do you have life? By believing. Believing comes before life (regeneration).

Colossians 2:12: "Having been buried with him in baptism, in which you were also raised with him through faith." You were raised to new life (regenerated) through faith. You were not given faith through new life (regeneration). The *ordo solutis* is crystal clear. Faith occurs before regeneration. The Reformed *ordo salutis* contradicts every one of these verses.

Yet Another Problem

Not once in either the Old or New Testament is the word "regeneration" found preceding the word "faith." In fact, the Greek word for regeneration *(palingenesias)* is only found two times in the entire Bible (Matthew 19:28 and Titus 3:5). In neither case does the passage say faith comes after it.

Nevertheless, Calvinists have a couple of prooftexts that they claim teach that faith comes after regeneration. One is the same verse they routinely appeal to as proof of predestination which was referenced earlier – John 6:44. Jesus said, "No man can come to me, except the Father which hath sent me draw him." Calvinists point out the parallelism in verse 35 which makes the words "come to me" mean the same as "believe in me." Based on that, they contend verse 44 means faith (coming to Jesus) follows God's drawing. That is not the issue, however. The two things at issue are:

1) Is the faith that follows God's drawing mandated or optional? As previously stated, the verb "draw" is in the subjunctive mood, which is the mood of poten-

tial. It is not mandated. So, faith may or may not follow God's drawing.

2) The second question that must be answered before one can correctly interpret the verse is, "What does God's drawing involve (mean)?" Calvinists assume that the Father's drawing is the same as His regeneration of a person. That is not, however, what the verse says. Drawing and regenerating are not the same. Calvinists redefine the word *regeneration* in order to make this verse fit their theology. Daniel D. Musick wrote about this when responding to Sproul:

In order to establish credence for their *ordo salutis*, many Calvinists broaden the theological definition of regeneration. According to Scripture, regeneration is God's transformation of the sinner from death to life. But the Father's drawing to Christ is not regeneration. Dr. Sproul evidently quotes this passage because he equates the Father's drawing to Christ with regeneration, hence altering the definition. If we broaden the definition of regeneration to include the father's drawing, everyone would agree that regeneration precedes faith. In like manner, if we broaden our definition of cheese to include sand and rocks, everyone would agree that the moon is made of cheese.[26]

One other verse Calvinists appeal to for their *ordo salutis* is 1 John 5:1. It reads, "Everyone who believes that Jesus is the Christ has been born of God." Calvinists argue that the word "believes" means it is happening now in the present, while the words "has been born of God" means it happened in the past. Thus, faith is shown to follow regeneration.

The problem is John isn't even addressing the order of salvation here. In the passages where he does address the issue, he makes it clear that faith comes before regeneration. So, at best, the verse is saying the two things (belief and rebirth) occur simultaneously. Even if the verse is incorrectly interpreted (as Calvinists do) to mean faith follows regeneration, there is no reason to conclude prior faith is excluded. Faith is required both before and after one is born again. The one thing the verse does not do is preclude faith from coming prior to regeneration. (For a more complete exegesis of 1 John 5:1 see Appendix A).

Does the Bible declare that regeneration comes before faith and repentance?

Examine the following verses to see which comes first— regeneration or repentance and faith:

Ezekiel 18:31-32— "Why will you die, people of Israel? For I take no pleasure in the death of anyone, declares the Sovereign LORD. Repent and live!"

The order clearly laid out is as follows:
1. "Repent"
2. "...live!"

Life comes from repentance, not the other way around. The order is unambiguous.

Acts 11:18— "So then, God has granted even the Gentiles repentance unto life."

The order clearly laid out is as follows:
1. "Repentance unto..."
2. "...life"

The Gentiles were not granted life unto repentance, but just the opposite according to the text.

John 5:40— "You refuse to come to me to have life."

The order clearly laid out is as follows:
1. "Come to me..." (through faith)
2. "...to have life."

John 6:53— "I tell you the truth, unless you eat the flesh of the Son of Man and drink his blood, you have no life in you."

The order clearly laid out is as follows:
1. "Unless you eat...drink" (by faith)
2. "...you have not life in you."

John 6:57 — "So the one who feeds on me will live because of me."

The order clearly laid out is as follows:
1. "the one who feeds on me…" (by faith)
2. "…will live"

John 20:31 — "But these are written that you may believe that Jesus is the Christ, the Son of God, and that by believing you may have life in his name."

The order clearly laid out is as follows:
1. "these [scriptures] are written that you may believe…"
2. "…by believing you may have life…"

It couldn't be stated any more definitively. Life is the result of faith, not the other way around.

Acts 15:9 — "He made no distinction between us and them, for he purified their hearts by faith."

The order clearly laid out is as follows:
1. "He purified their hearts…"
2. "…by faith."

It does not say He purified their hearts by regeneration so they would have faith.

John 1:12 — "To those who believed in his name, he gave the right to become children of God."

The order clearly laid out is as follows:
1. "…to all who believed…"
2. "…he gave the right to become children of God…"

The right to be born of God is given only to those who first believe. The order can't be reversed.

John 12:36 — "Believe in the light while you have the light, so that you may become children of light."

The order clearly laid out is as follows:
1. "Believe in the light…" (belief must come first, before anything else takes place)
2. "…so that you may become children…" (born again, given new life, regenerated)

Colossians 2:12 — "…having been buried with him in

baptism, in which you were also raised with him through your faith in the working of God, who raised him from the dead."

The order clearly laid out is as follows:

1. "...baptism, in which you were also raised..."
2. "...through your faith..."

You were raised to new life (regenerated) through faith. You were not given faith through new life (regeneration). The *ordo solutis* could not be more obvious. Faith occurs before regeneration.

James 1:18 — "He chose to give us birth through the word of truth, that we might be a kind of firstfruits of all he created."

The order clearly laid out is as follows:

1. "...give us birth..."
2. "...through the word of truth..."

Faith in God's word results in birth (regeneration), not the other way around. How is it possible to even suggest that the order is the opposite of what is manifest in Scripture after Scripture?

Galatians 3:26 — "You are all sons of God through faith in Christ Jesus..."

The order clearly laid out is as follows:

1. "You are all sons of God..."
2. "...through faith in Christ..."

You do not become a son of God (become reborn, regenerated) so you can later obtain faith.

Now, you have to ask yourself: "Are all these verses wrong or do Calvinists incorrectly interpret John 6:44 and 1 John 5:1?" The Bible doesn't contradict itself, so the answer is obvious.

Faith comes before regeneration.

God does not give us some kind of special faith before we can believe. The obligation to have faith and believe is ours. In fact, we can be slow to believe, as Jesus points out in Luke 24:25. If God has to first give us faith before we can believe, why would He give us slow faith? Jesus scolds people for having little faith (e.g., Matthew 6:30; 8:26; 14:31; 16:8). How can you blame people for having little faith if you are the one who gave them that amount? Is little faith enough for salvation? If not, why give some people a useless amount of faith and then scold them for having it? In truth, Jesus should scold Himself for giving such little faith that a person cannot believe the Gospel. If God ordains everything, including how much faith a person is given, He cannot blame anyone for not being given enough faith. It's God's fault, not the unbeliever's.

When the prison keeper asked Paul and Silas, "What must I do to be saved?" (Acts 16:30), they did not tell the jailor to wait until God regenerates you so you can believe. They simply told the jailor to "Believe in the Lord Jesus, and you will be saved" (verse 31). If regeneration comes before faith, why give the man the impression he could believe and be saved? Didn't they know it was impossible for the prison keeper to believe until after he was regenerated? Or did they somehow know God had already regenerated the man when they told him to believe? If so, how did they know? If they did know, why is there no mention of this regeneration taking place in the jailor prior to his believing? Indeed, why is there not a single instance from Genesis 1:1 to Revelation 22:21 where regeneration is said to have taken place before someone was able to place their faith in God?

Following the jailor's inquiry, he was told only one thing – believe. If Paul and Silas were Calvinistic they should have replied, "You can do nothing to be saved. You were born corpse-like dead in your sin and a dead man can do nothing. If God makes you alive (regenerates you) then you will be convinced to believe our gospel." They failed to explain anything like that. Instead, they did not hesitate to simply say, "Believe on the Lord Jesus Christ and you will be saved" (Acts 16:31). Believe so as to have new life. That is the gospel appeal sent for all to hear and respond to.

What else does the Bible teach about faith?

Consider some other things the Bible declares about human faith.

"This is what the ancients were commended for. By faith we understand that the universe was formed at God's command, so that what is seen was not made out of what was visible. By faith Abel brought God a better offering than Cain did. By faith he was commended as righteous, when God spoke well of his offerings. And by faith Abel still speaks, even though he is dead. By faith Enoch was taken from this life, so that he did not experience death: 'He could not be found, because God had taken him away.' For before he was taken, he was commended as one who pleased God. And without faith it is impossible to please God, because anyone who comes to him must believe that he exists and that he rewards those who earnestly seek him" (Hebrews 11:1-6).

We see that a person's faith is commended by God. If the faith a person has is not his own, but faith given to him by God following regeneration, shouldn't God commend Himself for such faith rather than the person who merely receives it?

We also see that faith pleases God. Is God pleased with the person who has faith, or is He simply pleased with Himself for giving faith to people? According to verse 5, God was pleased with Enoch and not Himself.

We also find that God rewards those who earnestly seek Him. Calvinists say no unregenerate person ever seeks God. Perhaps then, God should reward Himself for causing people to seek Him rather than rewarding the seeker.

The Bible tells us that God seeks faith (Luke 18:8). Why, if no one has any? Additionally, the Bible tells us that when God finds faith, He is pleased and rewards it. How can God find faith if no one has any?

The Bible also tells us that faith is counted for righteousness (Genesis 15:6; Psalms 106:31; Romans 4:3; Galatians 3:6). How is that possible if man is without any faith to be counted for righteousness? If the Bible is talking about the faith that comes after regeneration then, according to Reformed Theology, we do not receive righteousness with rebirth but later after we believe. We remain unrighteous even after being born again. Is that what the Bible teaches?

It should also be noted that there is no mention of Abraham being reborn or regenerated prior to his faith being counted for righteousness. That same absence is true throughout the Scriptures. Abraham was not unique in having his faith counted for righteousness. Righteousness can be credited to anyone who believes in Jesus. This is evidenced by Paul's words to the Romans: "The words 'it was credited to him' were written not for him [Abraham] alone, but also for us, to whom God will credit righteousness—for us who believe in him who raised Jesus our Lord from the dead" (Romans 4:23-24). Earlier, Paul wrote these words: "To the one who does not work but trusts God who justifies the ungodly, their faith is credited as righteousness" (Romans 4:5). There is no mention here of regeneration being required before faith is counted for righteousness. Earlier still, Paul wrote, "This righteousness is given through faith in Jesus Christ to all who believe" (Romans 3:22). Again, there is no mention of regeneration being required first.

Later, Paul writes, "What then shall we say? That the Gentiles, who did not pursue righteousness, have obtained it, a righteousness that is by faith; but the people of Israel, who pursued the law as the way of righteousness, have not attained their goal. Why not? Because they pursued it not by faith but as if it were by works" (Romans

9:30-32). How can anyone obtain righteousness through faith if they have none? If righteousness comes after faith and faith comes after regeneration, then those who are regenerated are still unrighteous? If Paul thought faith comes after regeneration, he surely would have stated that several times, but he doesn't say that even one time. Instead, he wrote that "faith comes by hearing" (Romans 10:17). He didn't say faith comes by regeneration. Paul also believed that justification comes immediately after faith. He wrote, "Therefore, we conclude that a man is justified by faith" (Romans 3:28). Again, if regeneration comes before faith and faith comes before justification (as this verse says) then the regenerate remain unjustified until God gives them the faith they need. Thus, according to Calvinists, people are not immediately justified even though they are born again.

If a person receives faith only after God regenerates them, why is there no mention of that happening to anyone in the book of Romans, or anywhere else for that matter? The wording in this passage of Romans indicates that people can try to save themselves through works or they can put their faith in Christ to save them. A simple reading implies that humans are capable of doing either one. Only if they choose to do the second one, however, do they obtain righteousness. The choice is theirs.

Summary

To summarize what has been said in this chapter: We are not saved by our decision to trust Jesus. We do not even partially save ourselves by placing our faith in Him. God does all the saving. It is like a man who decides to have open heart surgery to save his life. The surgeons and support staff save the man while he is unconscious. A person consenting to such a surgery could be a bad man or a good man. What saves him is not his character or even his decision. He is saved by the surgical team alone. Likewise, we can decide to trust the Lord to save us, but He alone can save a person. Faith in a physician adds nothing to what the physician does. Faith is not works.

Also discussed in this chapter is the fact that unconditional election is believed to be true by Calvinists primarily because it logically must follow their concept of total depravity. The idea that regeneration precedes faith must also be believed by Calvinists because it too is demanded by logic if one believes in total depravity. In truth, almost everything Reformed Theology holds to be true is built logically on their particular understanding of total depravity. If the Bible teaches a different understanding of what it means to be "dead in sin," then Calvinism should be completely rejected. One can then build a theology based on what the Bible says rather than on a theology that relies so heavily on the logic that must follow its foundational concept.

The key question then is, "What happened as a result of the Fall?" All Christians agree that Adam sinned and was separated from God as a result. Nor is there any argument against the belief that Adam's sin affected and infected all mankind. The debate is whether or not man was never again willing or able to respond positively to God or His calling. Calvinists say, "Everyone lost their ability to respond to God after the Fall. As a result, God must regenerate people before they are able to place their faith in Him." Logic requires Calvinists to believe regeneration comes before faith despite the voluminous number of verses declaring just the opposite. The few verses Calvinists look to for support of their belief that regeneration comes first aren't even dealing with the subject of the *ordo salutis*. At best, one can only assume they allude to it. That assumption can only be made, however, if one's exegesis is influenced by a Reformed theological bias. In some cases, even such an assumption cannot be made. Looking at John 6:44, for example, Calvinists assume the word *draw* means *regeneration* even though *helko* never does.

By contrast, multiple verses state outright that regeneration follows faith. That fact alone should be conclusive enough to believe faith comes first, but there are additional reasons to reject the belief that regeneration comes first. With all the accounts of people placing their faith in God (in both the Old and New Testaments), there is not a single mention of regeneration being involved first. In fact, the word regeneration *(palingenesias)* isn't to be found anywhere in any of these accounts. If regeneration is the first critical requirement for salvation, does it make sense that the Bible never mentions it even once when telling of people who placed their faith in God? Nor is there ever a mention of God giving anyone some form of special faith in order for them to believe. The faith people exercised in the Bible is said to be their own.

Finally, faith is shown to be a condition for salvation. Christ Himself makes that clear in many of His parables. All that to say, unconditional election may logically follow Calvinism's understanding of total depravity, but it is not taught in the Bible.

Assumption #4
If Christ Died for All Then He is not a Real Savior— Only a Potential One

CALVINISTS BELIEVE IN a limited atonement because they assume God designed the atonement to be effectual only for those He predestined to save. Christ is not the whole world's Savior because not all are saved. This sounds logical until you realize there is a difference between the provision of the atonement and the application of the atonement. In other words, Christ's death provided salvation for the whole world, but only those individuals who accept Christ's atonement for their sins benefit from it. Like the blood of the Passover lamb, the blood of Christ is available to all, but only those who apply the blood for themselves are saved. Christ is the true Savior of the world (John 4:42), but unless we are willing to accept Him for who He is (the Savior), His death does not save us. He is still the world's Savior, however, even if few accept Him as such.

The Bible also calls Jesus the *King of kings* (e.g., 1 Timothy 6:15). Does the fact most people do not bow down to Him or recognize Him as such make Him only a potential king? No, if not a single person accepted Him as King, He would still be the King of kings. Jesus is not a potential anything. He is King of kings and Lord of lords and Savior of the world regardless of who people may believe He is. John tells us Jesus "was the true Light, which lighteth every man that cometh into the world" (John 1:9 KJV). Christ is the light for *every man* born and not just for the elect. In the very next verse, however, John points out that "the world knew him not" (verse 10). If the world didn't recognize Jesus as the Light, does that mean Jesus isn't really the Light but is only a potential light? If so, verse 10 is making a false statement because it says that Jesus is the light that lights everyone born whether they recognize Him as such or not. Isn't Jesus still the Word (John 1:1) even if "his own received him not" (verse 11)? Yes, Jesus is everything the Bible tells us He is, even if some do not accept Him as the Light, the Word, the King of kings, the Lord of lords, or the Savior of the world. As has been said, "If Christ is not the Savior of all, He cannot be the Judge of all."[27]

Because all are not saved, Calvinists reason then that Christ's atonement was designed to be ineffectual for the majority of mankind. This reasoning leads Calvinists to assume that the atonement was designed to be a limited one. As Christians, however, we must not rely on our limited reasoning ability when creating our theology but on what the Bible declares to be true. The Bible tells us Christ died for everyone in the world which means the atonement is unlimited. It is effectual for everyone, but only those who choose to appropriate it are saved. The Bible declares that Christ died for sinners (1 Timothy 1:15). That includes everyone unless only the elect are sinners. You cannot find a single Scripture that claims Christ died for some sinners but not all. Romans 5:6 states that Christ died for the ungodly. Again, unless the elect are the only ones who are ungodly, then Christ died for all of mankind including the non-elect. In addition, the Bible tells us that God is "the Savior of all people, and especially of those who believe" (1 Timothy 4:10). Notice that believers are only one portion of those God is the Savior of and not the sum total. God is also the Savior of non-believers even if they refuse to accept Him as such. Hebrews 2:9 reads, "Jesus should taste death for everyone." It does not say, "Jesus should taste death for everyone who is of the elect." 1 John 2:2 declares that Jesus Christ is "the atoning sacrifice for our sins, and not only for ours but also for the sins of the whole world." Christ atoned for the elects' sins as well as the whole world's sins. Christ's atonement is unlimited.

Double Indemnity

R. C. Sproul argued that "If Christ died for everyone's sins then no one should go to hell. If the payment for sin was made on the cross for everyone, then no further payment should be required. No law court allows payment to be exacted twice for the same crime, and God will not do that either.[28] If God accepts payment of one person's moral debt from another, will he then exact payment of the same debt later by the person himself? The answer is obviously no."[29]

The answer is "no" only if the person accepts the payment from the other person and presents it to the judge. If the guilty person refuses the other person's offer, the guilty person remains responsible for the payment. The judge doesn't choose who pays. The person does. Imagine you had a neighbor who was starving. So, you kill one of your lambs and give it to him to eat. Then imagine that he refuses to eat the lamb and dies of starvation as a result. Does the fact that both he and the lamb died mean the lamb was not killed for your neighbor? No, the lamb died for your neighbor, but the neighbor also died because he refused to appropriate the lamb that died for him. In the same way, Christ died for everyone (including our neighbors) but unless our neighbors accept Him, it doesn't do them any good. One might even suggest that the unregenerate end up in hell, not only for their sins, but also for refusing to accept Christ's payment for their sins.

Christ's atonement is available to all.

Calvinists have their proof-texts which they are convinced demonstrate the atonement to be limited. For example, John 10:15: "I lay down my life for the sheep." The verse doesn't say Jesus died for everyone. It says He died for His sheep. Acts 20:28: "Be shepherds of the church of God, which he bought with his own blood." Again, this verse says He bought the church with His blood and not all humanity. Ephesians 5:25: "Husbands, love your wives, just as Christ loved the church and gave himself up for her." Based on these verses, Calvinists are convinced Christ's atonement was limited to His sheep or His church (i.e., the elect).

Yes, the verses tell us that Christ died for His sheep or His church. But none of these verses say that the church or His sheep are the only ones He died for. As Millard Erickson, himself a Calvinist, points out:

> Statements about Jesus loving and dying for his church or his sheep need not be understood as confining his special love and salvific death strictly to them... It does not follow from a statement that Christ died for his church, or for his sheep, that he did not die for anyone else, unless, of course, the passage specifically states that it was only for them that he died... Certainly if Christ died for the whole, there is no problem in asserting that he died for a specific part of the whole. To insist that those passages which focus on

his dying for his people require the understanding that he died only for them and not for any others contradicts the universal passages.[30]

Contradiction or Harmony

How, for example, do Calvinists explain universal passages like Romans 5:6, 1 Timothy 1:15, 1 Timothy 4:10, Hebrews 2:9, and 1 John 2:2 noted previously? These verses are in direct contradiction to the verses Calvinists claim support limited atonement. The only way to harmonize the two sets of verses is by realizing that one set has been incorrectly interpreted. So, who has come to the wrong conclusion regarding the verses they proffer as evidence for their position regarding atonement? Honest scrutiny of the verses shows it is far likelier that Calvinists are mistaken in their interpretations. As Professor Robert Lightner has stated:

> The task of harmonizing those various Scriptures poses a far greater problem for those who hold to a limited atonement than it does to those who hold to an unlimited position. Those who hold to an unlimited atonement recognize that some Scriptures emphasize the fact that Christ died for the elect, for the church, and for individual believers. However, they point out that when those verses single out a specific group they do not do so to the exclusion of any who are outside that group since dozens of other passages include them. The "limited" passages are just emphasizing one aspect of a larger truth. In contrast, those who hold to a limited atonement have a far more difficult time explaining away the "unlimited" passages.
>
> The fact is, the Scriptures do not always include all aspects of a truth in any one passage. If these texts are used in isolation to "prove" that Christ died only for the elect, then it could be argued with equal logic

from other isolated passages that Christ died only for Israel (cf. John 11:51; Isa. 53:8), or that He died only for the Apostle Paul (for Paul declares of Christ, *"Who loved me, and gave himself for me,"* Gal. 2:20). As well might one contend that Christ restricted His prayers to Peter because of the fact that He said to Peter, *"But I have prayed for thee"* (Luke 22:32).[31]

Just because one group or individual is said to have been died for, bought, or prayed for does not mean one should assume they are the only ones. A particular group can be a subset of the whole group. Additionally, one should not consider only one or two verses in isolation as being the whole truth. We must consider the Bible in its entirety. If any of our assumptions from one verse is discredited by other Scriptures, then such assumptions must be discarded. This is the case for assuming the atonement is limited because there are too many verses that tell us it is not.

Romans 14:15 and 1 Corinthians 8:11 both warn believers against flaunting their freedom in Christ in front of brothers and sisters of weaker conscience because this might cause one for whom Christ died to be "destroyed." The Greek word translated "destroyed" always means utterly destroyed; it cannot mean "damaged." Because Calvinists believe in eternal security, they must assume that those destroyed were never really Christians. But if that is the case, then limited atonement cannot be true because these passages say those destroyed are those "for whom Christ died." Either Christ died for these non-elect (i.e., everyone) or eternal security isn't true. These passages require Calvinists to reject one, if not both, of their TULIP theologies.

Few, Many, or All?

There are three other verses that Calvinists claim teach limited atonement. All three verses are very similarly worded. Hebrews 9:28 is one of those verses: "So Christ was sacrificed once to take away the sins of many people." Another is Matthew 20:28: "The Son of Man did not come to be served, but to serve, and to give his life as a ransom for many." And finally, Matthew 26:28: "This is my blood of the covenant, which is poured out for many for the forgiveness of sins." Calvinists conclude that because the word "many" rather the word "all" is used in these verses, the verses are obviously teaching a limited atonement.

Even if you set aside the possibility that the verses might say "many" rather than "all" because not *all* believe, Calvinists are still making an assumption in their exegesis. They assume the word "many" is meant to express the opposite of the word "all" indicating the verses support limited atonement. The reference to "many" in these verses, however, can just as easily be used to support unlimited atonement.

Earlier in Matthew Jesus had said that "few" find eternal life (Matthew 7:14) and "few" are chosen (22:14). It is reasonable to assume He used the word *many* in Matthew 26:28 to contrast them with the *few* He had referenced earlier, those who are actually saved. Christ did not say His blood was poured out for a "few" (those who find eternal life), but for "many" suggesting the word *many* was used as an opposite to the word *few* rather than opposite to the word *all*.

This is the same meaning as in Romans 5:15: "For if the many died by the trespass of the one man, how much more did God's grace and the gift that came by the grace of the one man, Jesus Christ, overflow to the many!" The word "many" in this verse is clearly defined later in verse 18 as "all men." It reads, "Just as the result of one trespass was condemnation for all men, so also the result of one act of righteousness was justification that brings life for all men." We also know the word *many* in verse 15 means "all men" because all men die as a result of Adam's sin (not just *some* or *a few* but *all*). Likewise, the word *many* means Christ's atonement was for *all men* (not just *some* or *a few* but *all*). In the same way Adam's sin resulted in the death of all men, Christ's atonement offers life to all men. Even John Calvin himself declared, "By the word many He means not a part of the world only, but the whole human race."[32]

What do the Scriptures teach?

Patently, what Calvin (or anyone else) believes about the atonement is not what matters. It is, obviously, what the Scriptures teach that is of consequence. So, does the Bible state that the atonement is limited or unlimited? In addition to the many verses previously mentioned (e.g., 1 Timothy 1:15, Romans 5:6, 1 Timothy 4:10, Hebrews 2:9, 1 John 2:2), consider the following:

In the very first chapter of John (verse 29), when John the Baptist saw Jesus coming, he declared, "Look, the Lamb of God, who takes away the sin of the world." The word "world" is not used in the Bible to refer to the elect – just the opposite. The word *world* is used to refer to sinful, unsaved mankind, as in 1 John 5:19, "The whole world is under the control of the evil one."

The Bible declares that "Jesus is the Savior of the world" (John 4:42, 1 John 4:14). He is "the bread of God which gives life unto the world" (John 6:33). And He is "the light of the world" (John 8:12). Again, the world does not refer to the elect but to the lost. John 1:9 makes that fact even clearer, when John states, "Jesus is the true Light, which lighteth every man that cometh into the world" (KJV). Obviously, the elect are not the only ones who come into the world. So, Jesus is the light of every human being who was ever born or ever will be. That means He is also the Savior of every person born. The only limitation on Christ's atonement (if one wishes to argue for one) would be that Christ is not the Savior of those who were never born. In that sense only, could one say the Bible teaches a limited atonement.

Jesus Himself said He was the light of salvation. "I have come into the world as a light, so that no one who believes in me should stay in darkness" (John 12:46). Nowhere in the Scriptures does it say that Jesus died only for the elect. If he didn't come to die for the whole world, why didn't He make that clear? If limited atonement is true, why didn't Jesus teach anything about it?

First Timothy 2:4-6 is talking about "our Savior" and reads, "who wants all people to be saved and to come to a knowledge of the truth. For there is one God and one mediator between God and mankind, the man Christ Jesus, who gave himself as a ransom for all people." The passage doesn't say He gave Himself a ransom only for "those He chooses to save" but for "all people." Furthermore, His desire is that "all people" be saved."

Calvinists attempt to avoid the obvious by claiming these verses aren't talking about "all people" but "all kinds of people" from all over the world. They contend the idea being conveyed is that the elect are not just Jews from Israel but are people elected from all over the world.

While "all kinds of people" are included in "all people" they are not synonymous. Nor are the verses dealing with the Jewish elect as well as other elect. The verses are talking about all "mankind." Verse 5 does not say there is "one mediator between God and the elect." It says there is one mediator between God and all of mankind. Any exegesis that claims otherwise reveals serious Reformed Theological bias.

There are too many verses that support unlimited atonement. Consider some additional ones.

Even More Biblical Support

Acts 17:30: "In the past God overlooked such ignorance, but now he commands all people everywhere to repent."

It appears that prior to this particular time God over-looked those who, in ignorance, did not repent, but now he expects everyone ("all people everywhere") to repent. *All people everywhere* cannot legitimately be interpreted to mean the elect from everywhere. There is no such re-striction given. Furthermore, a previous verse talks about the "God who made the world and everything in it" (verse 24). That would include "all people everywhere" and not just the elect. Verse 26 tells us, "From one man he made all the nations, that they should inhabit the whole earth." All the inhabitants of the whole earth came from Adam and not just the elect.

1 Timothy 4:10: "That is why we labor and strive, be-cause we have put our hope in the living God, who is the Savior of all people, and especially of those who believe." He is not just the Savior of the elect but of everyone else ("all people"). He is especially the Savior of the elect be-cause they have chosen to believe and apply His atone-ment to themselves.

Hebrews 2:9: "Jesus, who was made lower than the angels for a little while, now crowned with glory and honor because he suffered death, so that by the grace of God he might taste death for everyone." Here again, the verse does not say "taste death for the elect." Instead, it says "taste death for everyone."

2 Peter 2:1: "But there were also false prophets among the people, just as there will be false teachers among you. They will secretly introduce destructive heresies, even denying the sovereign Lord who bought them— bring-ing swift destruction on themselves." If the price Jesus paid for salvation was only for the elect, how could He have "bought" false prophets and teachers who deny the Lord? Perhaps the false prophets were part of the elect. But then why would they be swiftly destroyed if eternal security is true? If they were not of the elect, then there is only one reasonable explanation for how Christ could

have bought them. Christ paid the price for these individuals just as He died for every other person in the world, saved or unsaved. Any attempt to interpret this verse otherwise is a desperate attempt to avoid the obvious.

John tells us that "Jesus is the atoning sacrifice for our sins, and not only for ours but also for the sins of the whole world" (1 John 2:2). John uses the words "the whole world" to explain that Jesus is not just the Savior of the elect, but He is the Savior of the non-elect as well (the whole world). John didn't use the words "but also for the sins of other believers" or "but also for the sins of the elect in other parts of the world." No, he said "but also for the sins of the whole world." The whole world in general includes everyone.

R. C. Sproul disagrees. He wrote the following:

> On the surface this text seems to demolish limited atonement. We must ask, however, "What does *our* mean here?" *Our* could refer to Christians as distinguished from non-Christians, believers as opposed to nonbelievers. If this interpretation is correct, then Christ is a propitiation not only for Christian believers, but for everybody in the whole world.
>
> On the other hand, *our* could refer specifically to Jewish believers as opposed to believers of the whole world. One of the central questions of the church's earliest formative period was whether or not Gentiles could be included in the body of Christ.[33]

That may have been a central question Paul addressed, but it wasn't John's central question. It certainly wasn't the question he was addressing in this passage. Furthermore, the question of who could be saved was being asked by the Jews, not the Gentiles. As such, John's letter would have been addressed to Jews, but it wasn't. It was addressed to Gentiles who were not asking if they could be in the Body of Christ. If the word "our" refers to Jewish believers who doubted Gentile salvation, then John would be writing to Jews. As Ernest DeWitt Burton points out in commentary of 1 John, it "seems likely that its audience was largely gentile rather than Jewish, since it contains few Old Testament quotations or distinctly Jewish forms of expression."[34]

Calvinists must reject the universal meaning of the word "world" because of their theological presupposition that the atonement is limited to the elect. Thus, Calvinists change the obvious definition of the word "world" and claim it refers to other non-Jewish believers or the remaining elect around the world or anything other than what the word "world" actually means. But the word John uses for "world" is the word *kosmos*. He uses the same word (*kosmos*) twenty-three times in the same letter. Not once does he use the word *kosmos* to describe other believers or others (e.g., Gentiles) found throughout the world. In fact, in every case, John uses the word to describe unbelievers, forces opposed to Christianity, or literally the whole world. For example, 1 John 2:15-17, 3:1, 3:13, 4:4-5, 4:9, 4:14, 5:4-5, and 5:19. Substituting the word "believer" or "elect" for the word "world" in any of these passages would be absurd. Consider how a couple of these passages would read if the word *kosmos* is translated in the way Calvinists claim it should be translated.

1 John 2:15-17 would read, "Do not love the [elect] nor the things in the [elect]. If anyone loves the [elect], the love of the Father is not in him. For all that is in the [elect], the lust of the flesh and the lust of the eyes and the boastful pride of life, is not from the Father, but is from the [elect]. The [elect] is passing away…"

1 John 3:13 would read, "Do not be surprised, brethren, if the [elect] hates you."

1 John 5:4 would read, "For whatever is born of God overcomes the [elect]; and this is the victory that has overcome the [elect] – our faith."

Translating the word *kosmos* the way Calvinists do results in nonsensical verses.

Calvinists claim that despite John's use of the word *kosmos* in nearly two dozen cases to connote one thing, John used the word in an entirely different way just one time in the same letter. Even though there is zero evidence to support such an anomaly, Calvinists still insist that it is the sole exception of John's undeviating meaning of the word "world." The only reason for making this one verse a lone exception in John's letter is because, as it stands, it contradicts the theology of limited atonement. Any honest observer would view such exegesis as being riddled with theological bias, especially when you consider all the other verses that support unlimited atonement.

Created for Hell

A belief in limited atonement not only contradicts the Scriptures, but it creates a big problem for those who believe in it. It forces them to face a very harsh reality. If Jesus only died for the elect, then God intentionally creates people in order to send them to hell. After all, who creates people? God does. Who determines whether the people God creates go to heaven or hell? According to Reformed Theology, God does. Thus, God creates some people for the purpose of sending them to hell? God could create only those people whom He sends to heaven, but He doesn't. Calvinists claim God has good reasons for creating people for hell. For Calvin, God's end not only justifies the means, but God actually takes pleasure in creating people for hell. Calvin wrote,

> Scripture clearly proves… that God by his eternal and immutable counsel determined once for all those whom it was his pleasure one day to admit to salvation, and those whom, on the other hand, it was his pleasure to doom to destruction.[35]

Again, quoting Calvin, "Those, therefore, whom God passes by he reprobates, and that for no other cause but because he is pleased to exclude them from the inheritance which he predestines to his children."[36] The God that Calvin believed in creates people for the purpose of sending them to hell, and He is pleased to both create them and to damn them eternally.

The *Westminster Confession of Faith* (chapter 3) reads, "By the decree of God, for the manifestation of His glory, some men and angels are predestinated unto everlasting life, and others foreordained to everlasting death."[37] This sounds like God is more interested in manifesting His glory than He is in showing love for His lost sheep. Despite His claim that He desires all to be saved (2 Peter 3:9), Calvin's God desires to save only a small minority.

A Good or Bad Shepherd?

During His earthly ministry, Jesus told many parables to help us understand the kingdom of God. In one story Jesus used the illustration of a man with a hundred sheep who goes out and rescues just one that goes astray (Matthew 18:12-13). In the very next verse (verse 14) Jesus, the Good Shepherd, says, "In the same way your Father in heaven is not willing that any of these little ones should perish." Jesus was saying God loves and seeks after every one of His lost sheep. Calvin, on the other hand, believed the Good Shepherd takes pleasure in the destruction of the majority of His lost sheep. Calvin turned the Good Shepherd into a very bad one.

Elsewhere, the Bible says, "we all, like sheep, have gone astray" (Isaiah 53:6). So, we all need to be rescued. But Calvinists believe Jesus only wants to rescue a small minority of His lost sheep. The rest can go to hell – literally. Despite the Bible making it very clear that Christ loved and died for the whole world (all His lost sheep), Calvinists believe He really only died for a few (the elect). Good shepherds want to rescue all their lost sheep.

Luke 19:10 reads, "For the Son of Man came to seek and to save the lost." According to Reformed Theology, the Son of Man came only to seek and to save some of the lost.

Isaiah 53:6 ends by saying, "The Lord has laid on him the iniquity of us all." God placed the sins of the whole world on the Good Shepherd who died for all of His lost sheep – not just a select few. God cares for every single one of His lost sheep and desires to rescue them all. To say otherwise is to portray God as less than the loving God He is and Christ as a very poor shepherd.

Calvinists believe that Arminian theology faces the same quandary as Reformed Theology. If God foreknows that a person will reject Christ and He creates that person anyway, He is just as culpable as the Calvinists' God. In making such a statement, Calvinists demonstrate that they misunderstand the meaning of *foreknowledge*. God's foreknowledge is foreknowledge of what *will* happen, not what *might* happen. So, God can't use his foreknowledge to see what is going to happen and then act to make sure it doesn't happen, for then God's foreknowledge would have been incorrect (i.e., not foreknowledge). God can foreknow events without being responsible for their occurring. Calvin's God doesn't just foresee what is going to happen. He ordains what happens. Foreknowing evil will occur is not the same as causing evil to occur.

On Top of the Mountain

To illustrate, suppose a man is sitting on top of a mountain. From his lofty perch he can see two cars below speeding along the narrow road that winds around the mountainsides, one driving down the mountain road and the other up. The person sitting atop the mountain can also see that the two speeding cars are about to come around a blind corner at the exact same time. Sure enough, they have a terrible head-on collision.

Did the fact the viewer knew ahead of time the two cars would crash mean he caused it? Of course not. It may even have been possible for the person on the mountain to have known both drivers and have previously warned them about speeding on the mountain road. What if the person was the owner of both vehicles and owned the mountain as well? Would this mean the viewer made the decision for the drivers to choose to speed in such a dangerous way? Once more, the obvious answer is no. So, we cannot hold God responsible for our bad choices simply because He knows ahead of time what they will be.

Auto Makers

To have the ability to stop something from happening doesn't mean you caused it to happen. If such reasoning were true, we could blame automobile makers for all accidents. After all, they have the ability to prevent accidents from happening by simply not making cars. But we all benefit from the creation of the auto. We do not blame the maker of the car for the alcoholic's decision to drink and drive, even if he or she kills an innocent family while driving drunk. We do not wish that automobiles had never been invented. We are grateful for the freedom to drive across country or just across town to visit a friend or relative. We are glad we can drive to the ocean or to a picnic. We do not ask for the removal of all autos because people abuse the privilege of driving.

In the same way, we should be grateful God created us and gave us the gift of free choice, even if we abuse it through disobedience. Yes, sin's existence could have been avoided if God hadn't created other beings or given them the ability to choose to sin. But He Himself didn't sin by creating two good things: people and their gift of choice.

Nor can we blame God if we make the wrong choices, even though He knows ahead of time that we often will.

While God did not stop anyone from abusing His gift of free choice by choosing to sin, He didn't just ignore it, either. Fortunately, because God foreknew we would all fall into sin, He made a plan to rescue us. He chose Christ to be our Savior even *before the foundation of the world* (1 Peter 1:20). God saw that we would sin and become lost, so He made a way for us to be found and rescued. He loved us so much, even as sinners, that He gave His only begotten Son, Jesus, who died for us all.

Why did God create humans?

Love was the reason Jesus died for us (all of us). Indeed, love was the primary reason God created us in the first place. Calvinists disagree. They believe everything God does is for His own glory, including the creation of humans as well as His condemning of them. Calvinists believe that the primary reason God created people was so they would glorify Him. God's major motivation for creating man was not love but His desire for self-glorification. *The Westminster Confession of Faith* declares, "The chief end of man is to glorify God." John Piper said it this way, "The chief end of man is to glorify God and enjoy displaying and magnifying his glory forever."[38]

Jonathan Edwards also taught that the ultimate reason God created the world was to fully manifest His glory. He wrote:

> Thus it appears reasonable to suppose, that it was God's last end, that there might be a glorious and abundant emanation of his infinite fullness... and that the disposition to communicate himself, or diffuse his own fullness, was what moved him to create the world.[39]

The Reformed argument is that by creating man, God

was able to show both His justice (by sending sinners to hell for all eternity) and His mercy (by electing some for eternal life).

Notice that Edwards used the word "reasonable" rather than "biblical" for his supposition. While glorifying God is extremely important, the Bible doesn't assert that man's primary purpose is to glorify God. When asked what the greatest commandment was, Jesus (God) did not say it was to glorify Himself or to glorify God the Father. He said it was to "Love the Lord your God with all your heart and with all your soul and with all your mind" (Matthew 22:37). Loving God is the most important thing man can and should do. The second most important thing is to "love your neighbor as yourself" (verse 39). Thus, glorifying God can, at best, only be the third most important thing man can do. It certainly isn't "the chief end of man."

The Father did not send His Son to die because He wanted more glory for Himself. It was done because of God's great love for His lost sheep. John 3:16 tells us why Christ died. He sacrificed His life because He so loved the world. Nowhere in the Bible does it say that God so desired the manifestation of His glory that He gave his only begotten Son. God should be glorified for offering redemption to sinners (all sinners everywhere), but that was not the primary reason He did so. Love was. Love was also the reason He created humans (all humans) in the first place. God is not self-centered. He is selfless.

According to Reformed Theology, however, God created certain people whom He ordained for hell primarily so He could display His wrath and justice. Thus, these humans are pawns God uses for the purpose of furthering His self-glorification at the expense of human suffering. He cares more about being able to display the fullness of His glory than He does about the eternal torment of people.

We are to believe that the primary reason God created

some humans was in order to display His justice and He created others in order to display His mercy. If that's true, wouldn't you think displaying His love would be more important given 1 Corinthians 13? At the very least, you would expect God to show both equally. But He doesn't. He displays far more of his wrath and judgment by condemning the overwhelming majority of His creations. And displays His mercy to only a minority of them. It wouldn't take very many to display His judgment, but He eternally torments most of the people He creates while showing mercy to only a few.

Does God deserve more glory for giving or for receiving?

Jesus said, "It is more blessed to give than to receive" (Acts 20:35). If gaining glory for Himself is the primary reason God created people then He is more interested in taking from others than in giving. As children of God, we should seek to be like Jesus. That's also what God wants (for us to be conformed to the image of Christ). So, the obvious question is this: What is Jesus like? Is He primarily glory seeking or loving? The obvious answer is He is love. So, do we become more like Him by glorifying Him or by loving Him? God doesn't need more glory or love. He doesn't need anything. What He wants most, however, is not more self-glorification in the world but more love. If man was created in the image of God and the best image of God is love, then man was created to love like He does. God's desire in creating humans was primarily to provide God more opportunities to *give* love, not to *get* more glory for Himself. God is a giver, not a taker. That's also what He desires for us to be like. It follows then that the chief end of man is to love and be loved.

Where is the love?

Sadly, love is not the primary emphasis of Reformed Theology. Consider, for example, the contents of *The*

Westminster Confession of Faith. While a whole chapter of the *Confession* is dedicated exclusively to the *providence* of God, not one of the thirty-three chapters is dedicated to the *love* of God. The Bible teaches that our number one priority is to love God with all our hearts, souls, and minds (Matthew 22:37). When reading the works of most Reformed theologians, one comes away thinking that understanding God's sovereignty and our total depravity is our number one priority. While *grace* (love?) is a recurring theme, it is very exclusive unless you believe sending the lost to hell is an act of love.

While it is merely anecdotal to say what I have observed, I have often been shocked by the cavalier attitude some Calvinists have toward salvation. Love does not respond with more joy over one's own good fortune than sorrow over those not so fortunate. Being more concerned with one's own privileged status than with the lost condition of others is not love but selfishness. At the very least, such a tragic situation should not be viewed with mere academic acceptance. If I am no different than every other sinful human being on the earth, yet am one of the lucky few who are not punished for it, real love would result in great mourning for those who were not so lucky. I have not found this to be the case, however, among most of the Calvinists I have known or read. I have found that a belief in Reformed Theology more often leads to self-satisfaction and pride than to weeping over the lost. In a way, their attitudes make sense, because Calvinists see no reason for weeping because God is glorified by sending people to hell. We should rejoice that God's will is being accomplished.

Can we blame Calvin?

Perhaps this lack of emphasis on love goes back to Calvin himself. If it is true that "whoever does not love does not know God" (1 John 4:8), then a strong argument could be made (based on his behavior) that Calvin did not know God. At the very least, he had a poor understanding of God's love. History tells us he was arrogant, bad tempered, demanding, and cruel. He even had people killed who did not agree with his theology. For example, when a man named Jacques Gruet placed a placard in a church that challenged Calvin, he was tortured and eventually beheaded.

Another opponent of Calvin, a Spanish physician and theologian named Michael Servetus, attended a Sunday church service where Calvin was in the pulpit. When Calvin saw him, he had him arrested. Calvin charged him with heresy and urged the city council to execute him by beheading him. On October 27, 1533, the city council burned Servetus at the stake. These and others were killed with Calvin's approval, despite his personal conviction that such acts were both inhumane and criminal. In his first edition of *The Institutes of Christian Religion*, 1536, Calvin wrote the following: "It is criminal to put heretics to death. To make an end of them by fire and sword is opposed to every principle of humanity."[40] Calvin later removed this line from all subsequent editions of *The Institutes of Christian Religion*. One need not guess why.

No Excuse

This kind of information about Calvin is rarely exposed when writers praise Calvin for his great theology. Some have tried excusing Calvin's behavior by pointing out that the death penalty for heresy was the common practice of the day. That would be like excusing Lot, if he had indulged in homosexual behavior, because it was the common practice of his day in Sodom and Gomorrah. No, Calvin cannot be excused for his behavior, because he himself knew it was wrong, as evidenced by his own writing. Calvin showed no love for his enemies despite the fact Jesus told him he should (Matthew 5:44-45).

People who know Jesus love others. What about those who encourage people to kill others simply because they disagree with their beliefs? Do they know Jesus? At the very least, it would seem wise to question any theology of God they espouse. An editor once wrote me a note reminding me that David was a sinner and then asked, "Do we stop reading the Psalms?" He said such thinking was a "logical fallacy." He also told me he was a Calvinist (no surprise there). The logical fallacy, however, was the editor's. There is a huge difference between sinning and teaching that sinning is what everyone should do. David never taught that his sins were acceptable behavior. If he had, then I would have to question his theology as well.

John Wesley often argued with his wife; thus, he too was at times lacking in love. The difference is that Wesley never preached that what he did was right or that all men should fight with their wives. He recognized it was wrong, even if he did it himself. Calvin, on the other hand, advocated the murdering of those who disagreed with him. He was not only all for it, but taught others they should do so as well.

Anyone who says evil is a good thing that Christians should practice does not have a correct theology. You can't even give Calvin the benefit of the doubt and assume that what he did was done in ignorance. He was fully aware that what he did was wrong as evidenced by his own writings. There is no escaping the fact Calvin held a theology that demonstrated a tremendous lack of understanding of the heart of God.

First Corinthians 13:13 tells us that love is the greatest of the three things that endure. In light of this truth, one has to wonder why Calvin did not give more attention to the subject, particularly in describing God. Not once in his *Institutes of the Christian Religion*, a 1,500 page summary of Christian doctrine, did Calvin even mention 1 John 4:8 that declares, "God is love." Obviously, one cannot quote every verse in the Bible in a theology book (even one that is 1,500 pages), but this declarative verse is absolutely essential in explaining who God is. Calvin completely ignored a verse that does not just say, "God is loving," but describes the very essence of who God, is as evidenced by His being a Triune God (Father, Son, and Holy Ghost) in loving relationship.

Even with his brothers and sisters in Christ, Calvin had little interest in loving relationships as expressed in his view of heaven. "To be in Paradise and live with God is not to speak to each other and be heard by each other, but is only to enjoy God, to feel his good will, and rest in him."[41] Paradise for Calvin was a place where no one ever speaks to him and he never has to speak to another human being. If love is expressed through communication, then Calvin did not wish to love other Christians. He didn't even want to talk to them. It is also interesting to note that Calvin does not even say it is God's love that we will feel in Paradise, but his good will. Calvin, apparently, thought the idea of enjoying God's love wasn't worth mentioning when describing heaven. It would appear that Calvin viewed heaven as a place for the enjoyment of rest rather than a place for the enjoyment of relationships.

God is passionless.

In addition to a lack of emphasis on God's love, Calvin taught that God was passionless. He got this idea from Augustine, who got the idea of impassibility from the Gnostics, who were considered heretics by the Early Church. In *The Westminster Confession of Faith* (II.1.) we find the following: "There is but one... true God, who is infinite in being and perfection, a most pure spirit, invisible, without body, parts or passions."[42] Calvinists explain that this statement refers to God not having sexual passions. For Calvin, however, God not only lacks sexual passions, but He is void of any emotions.

Genesis 6:6 tells us God was "grieved at His heart" (KJV) over the sin in Noah's day. According to Calvin, however, He was not really grieved. Because God is without passions, He cannot grieve even though the Bible says God was grieved. Commenting on Genesis 6:6, Calvin says that "since we cannot comprehend [God] as he is, it is necessary that, for our sake, he should, in a certain sense, transform himself [by using figures of speech about himself]... Certainly, God is not sorrowful or sad; but remains forever like himself in his celestial and happy repose."[43] Thus, the words *grieved at His heart* do not mean what they say; they are merely a figure of speech. Without any explanation as to what the figure of speech stands for, we have no idea what was actually going on with God, making the words meaningless to us. Rather than revealing what God is like, the phrase offers no understanding of God. Why would God use words about Himself that are not actually true? Why would He use figures of speech that are confusing, if not deceptive, rather than clarifying?

How can we know?

Even worse, how can we know if any of the descriptions of God in the Bible are genuine rather than simply imagery? Did Calvin believe the Bible is not to be taken literally when it tells us that God was angry with Moses (Exodus 4:14) or with His people many times throughout the Old Testament? If God was not angry, what was He? Why does the Bible not only talk about the wrath of God, but give examples of God demonstrating His wrath? How is it possible to conclude from all these descriptions of God showing His anger that He remains "forever like himself in his celestial and happy repose?"

Throughout the Bible God is portrayed as having passions. Yet, Calvin would have us believe none of them are real. They are merely figures of speech. Calvin's theology seems to teach that the Bible was not written to reveal God as much as it was written to show us God is unknowable. It would appear God desired to make Himself even more mysterious than He already is by giving descriptions of Himself that are misleading. If we are unable to know which descriptions of God are real and which are figurative, we are left uncertain as to what God is really like. Rather than understanding more about God from reading the Bible, we become even more confused.

The Bible says God made man in His own image. According to Calvin, the emotions man was endowed with were not part of God's image. Calvin's God gave man something extra that He Himself did not have – passions. Calvin's God created man with emotions such as sorrow, anger, joy, and sadness, even though He Himself has none of these emotions. In this way, man was *not* made in the image of God.

Where did the idea of an unemotional God come from? Not from the Bible but from Aristotle's theory of an immutable God who is without feelings. Chapter 11 will explain the historical development of Calvinism and how Augustine and, later, Calvin got many of their ideas from pagan Greek philosophers.

So how do we best determine what God is really like? God can best be known by studying what the Bible says about Jesus, who is the exact representation of God (Hebrews 1:3). The Greek word used by the writer of Hebrews is *hypostaseos* which means the "being, nature, or essence" of God. Any theology of God, therefore, must begin with Jesus and move to God, rather than with what we may think God is like and then move that concept to Jesus. As Austin Fischer has written, "When we fail to let God define himself in Jesus because we think we know better, we commit idolatry."[44]

So, how does Calvinism's God compare with Jesus?

Calvinism's God and Jesus

Sadly, there are numerous dissimilarities. For example: Calvinism's God doesn't look for faith in anyone because, according to Reformed Theology, there is none to be found, as a result of total depravity.

Jesus, on the other hand, found people with faith and encouraged them to place it in Him.

Calvinism's God determines how much faith a person has.

Jesus, on the other hand, was pleased when He found great faith (Luke 7:9) and disappointed when He found little faith (Matthew 6:30). Apparently, Jesus was disappointed with the amount of faith He (God) gave people.

Calvinism's God ordains sin (See Assumption #12).

Jesus, however, forgives sin.

Calvinism's God ordained everything before the foundations of the world without the use of His foreknowledge. Thus, His decisions were not affected by human prayers, or human desires, or human needs. If that is the case, He should never have told us to pray, because our prayers accomplish nothing. Our prayers come too late because God has already determined everything.

Jesus, by contrast, feels our pain (Hebrews 4:15) and responds to human needs. He teaches us to pray and promises to hear our prayers and to answer them.

Calvinism's God captures our hearts through His irresistible grace.

Jesus, on the other hand, captures our hearts through His wondrous love.

Calvinism's God glorifies Himself by sending people to eternal torment for committing sins that He preordained them to commit.

Jesus, on the other hand, weeps over Jerusalem because the people would not let Him gather them under His wings.

Calvinism's God wills suffering.

Jesus removes suffering.

Gregory Boyd stated it this way: "Without exception, when Jesus confronted the crippled, deaf, blind, mute, diseased, or demon possessed, he uniformly diagnosed their affliction as something that God did not will... Jesus consistently revealed God's will for people by healing them of their infirmities."[45]

Austin Fischer points out that:

> This sets up a rather awkward dilemma in Calvinism wherein God the Father is making people suffer and God the Son (Jesus) is healing people of the suffering the Father is inflicting... For me this was neither mystery nor paradox, but sheer divine schizophrenia. It opened up a fissure in the very heart of God by splintering the Trinity, setting up Father and Son in opposition to one another — the Father crucifies sinners while the Son is crucified for sinners.[46]

Again, quoting Fischer:

> In the crucified Jesus, we learn that the God who pours out wrath is the God whose hands are nailed to the cross. The God who punishes sin is the God who takes the punishment. The God who judges is the God who looks upon those crucifying him and says, "Forgive them" (Luke 23:34). I found the crucified God very difficult to square with the God of Calvinism.[47]

Calvinism's God decided who would be saved before humans existed and his foreknowledge was not involved. So, obviously, human faith was not a factor in making his decisions. His sovereignty means He does not respond to human faith.

Jesus, on the other hand, looked into a person's heart and if He found faith there, He responded to it. Luke recorded the story of "a woman in that town who lived a sinful life," but came and washed Jesus' feet. Afterwards, Jesus tells her, "Your sins are forgiven. Your faith has saved you; go in peace" (Luke 7:37-50). The woman's own faith saved her. Jesus said the same words to a leper whom He healed: "Rise and go; your faith has made you well" (Luke 17:19).

In Matthew 9:22, Jesus said to the woman with the issue of blood, "your faith has healed you." A blind man shouted to Jesus with the words, "Jesus, Son of David, have mercy on me" (Mark 10:47). Jesus asked the man, "What do you want me to do for you?" (verse 51) The blind man said, "Lord, that I might receive my sight" (verse 51 KJV). Jesus then said to him, "Go, your faith has healed you," and immediately he received his sight (verse 52).

After the four men let the man sick of the palsy down through the roof to Jesus, Mark 2:5 reads, "When Jesus saw their faith, he said to the paralyzed man, 'Son, your sins are forgiven.'" Any unbiased reading of this story would lead one to believe that sins were forgiven as a result of Jesus seeing human faith. I'm sure that is what the men heard Jesus say. Jesus was moved to both heal and forgive based on the faith He witnessed.

In at least one case, Jesus even asked the seekers about their faith before He healed them. Matthew 9:28-29 records Jesus asking two blind men who sought Him for healing, "Do you believe that I am able to do this?" They said, "Yes, Lord." Then Jesus touched their eyes and said, "According to your faith let it be done to you." It was their faith Jesus responded to.

Notice that in none of these situations is there any mention of God giving these people the faith they needed to believe. Nor is there any mention of God regenerating any of them before they could believe. If what Calvinists believe is true, why is there never any mention of regeneration taking place prior to someone putting their faith in Christ?

And Jesus did not discriminate. He healed everyone who sought Him by faith for healing from all manner of sickness and disease. Matthew 4:23-24 tells us, "Jesus went throughout Galilee, teaching in their synagogues, proclaiming the good news of the kingdom, and healing every disease and sickness among the people. News about him spread all over Syria, and people brought to him all who were ill with various diseases, those suffering severe pain, the demon-possessed, those having seizures, and the paralyzed; and he healed them."

Jesus could have healed everyone on the planet. But He didn't do that. What Jesus did was heal everyone who had faith to come to Him for healing. No one was rejected. At the same time, no one was healed who had no desire to be healed through irresistible grace. The choice was always in the hand of the one seeking healing. Only those who believed in Jesus came to Him to be healed.

Calvinism's God would have selected to heal just a few out of the crowds (for reasons known only to him) and would have ignored all the others, leaving them to die. People's faith would have no influence on whom He healed because He decided who they would be long before they were even born. They could only hope that they were one of those God predestined to heal. They would have no choice in the matter.

There is a very stark difference between the way Calvinism's God and Jesus interact with people. Jesus demonstrates more love. Below is an illustration which demonstrates the difference between what Calvinism's God is like and what Jesus is like.

The Gift of Healing

Imagine you knew someone who had the gift of healing and this person could heal anyone he chose to. Suppose you discover, however, this person was very selective in the way he used his gift. Without telling anyone why, he would enter a cancer ward where everyone had been diagnosed as terminal and heal only a small minority of the patients he encountered. There were no differences in the two groups. Everyone was in the same condition. Those healed didn't even know why they became so lucky and the others did not.

All the cancer victims not only smoked but had inherited the cancer genetically and through the second-hand smoke they inhaled from their smoking parents. So, they not only caused the cancer by their own behavior, but they could not avoid it anyway because it was passed down from one generation to another (like original sin). Thus, they not only deserved to die, but they could do nothing to avoid it because of their parents' genes or their parents' earlier behavior.

The Compassionate Healer

Now suppose another healer enters the cancer ward and offers to heal anyone willing to trust him and give up smoking. One might think everyone would do so, but that would not be true. Some people just aren't willing to let go of their smoking (sins), even if they know it will end in their death. There are even people who have been diagnosed with lung cancer who continue to smoke. I knew a lady who had to be on oxygen to breathe and smoked right next to the oxygen tanks. Others are diagnosed with diabetes but are unwilling to give up their sweets. Others have heart conditions but are unwilling to see a physician. As absurd as it might appear, many people make such foolish choices every day. But some do make the right choice and their lives are spared as a result. The same is true when it comes to salvation. Though all can decide they want to be saved, most prefer their sinful lives to the offer of healing that Jesus gives.

The pertinent question here, though, is this: Which of the two healers is more compassionate? Is it the one who selects to heal only the few he likes or the one who offers to heal all who are willing to be healed? The answer is obvious. If the first healer announced that he loves all the patients, but has a special love only for those he heals, would that make him more caring? What kind of love could the healer have for those he leaves to die? Only the second healer possesses unconditional love for all the patients.

Nor would it help to learn the first healer is unwilling to divulge his reasons for showing favoritism. Such secrecy might suggest the first healer has something ugly to hide. Concealing His true motives evokes a sense of mistrust, rather than trust. At the very least, such secrecy keeps people at a distance by not allowing them to learn anything about the first healer's heart. Instead of revealing himself to people so they can know him better and relate to him more easily, he deliberately keeps people away behind a wall of ignorance. One has to wonder why he does not want anyone to know what motivates him to act the way he does. Is he afraid of disclosure or is he afraid of being that intimate?

The God of Calvinism

Calvinism's God is the first healer. He only loves a small minority of the patients enough to heal them, but he doesn't tell them why he loves them more. Even worse, he tells the other patients they too can be healed if they will seek his healing because he loves the whole world. He offers them healing knowing full well He has no intention of healing them. He tells them to repent (give up their smoking), trust him and be healed, while he is totally aware they can't do any of these things on their own. Such behavior can, at best, be described as cruel taunting. It is a huge understatement to say this healer is less compassionate – he is incredibly malevolent. How can you avoid seeing the dishonesty in a God who offers something to people He has no intention of giving them?

John Wesley had no problem seeing the situation for what it is. He said this of Calvinism:

> A doctrine full of blasphemy, representing our Lord as a hypocrite, a deceiver of the people, a man void of common sincerity, as mocking His helpless creatures by offering what He never intends to give, by saying one thing and meaning another. It destroys all the attributes of God, His justice, mercy, and truth, yea, it represents the most holy God as worse than the devil, as both more false, and more unjust.[48]

Unlike the God of Reformed Theology, Jesus sets free from sin anyone and everyone who trusts Him to do so. He said, "Come to me, all you who are weary and burdened, and I will give you rest" (Matthew 11:28). Notice that Christ said people must first come to Him. That was required of anyone seeking to be healed when Jesus was on earth, and it is still required today. Most importantly, He said these words to "all [who] are weary and burdened." This would include the non-elect, unless you believe only the elect are "weary and burdened." Jesus also said, "Let anyone who is thirsty come to me and drink" (John 7:31). The word "anyone" means the offer is not restricted to the elect only. The offer is unlimited but is given only to those who come to Christ and drink. Jesus' love is inclusive while the love of Calvin's God is exclusive.

Calvinists assume that God has two kinds of love.

If God sends people to hell, one might conclude that He only loves the elect. The Bible is clear, however, that this is not the case. If God loves only the elect, then Mark 10:21-22 would have to be taken out of the Bible because it tells us God loved a non-elect person. The rich young ruler did not follow Christ (the ruler *went away sad*), yet the Bible says, "Jesus looked at him and loved him." John 3:16 would also have to be removed from the Bible as it tells us God loves the whole world. Jesus said, "If you love those who love you, what credit is that to you? Even sinners love those who love them" (Luke 6:32). By contrast, God's love is all inclusive. He even loves those who do not love Him (the non-elect).

Given that God loves everyone, how does one explain a theology which teaches God treats people differently when it comes to salvation? Calvinists have an answer that is based on yet another assumption (no surprise there). Their answer is to assume God has two kinds of love, even though there is no biblical statement telling us that. If the love that caused Christ to die on the cross for sinners is only given to the elect, what is the other kind? God is love. What two kinds of love is He? According to Reformed Theology, God has (and *is*) a general kind of love that includes sinners (expressed through what Calvinists call *common grace*). At the same time, God has (and *is*) another, more exclusive, kind of love that is only for the elect (expressed through what is termed *effectual grace*). Thus, Calvinists believe God has (and *is*) both a perfect agape love, as well as some other less than perfect (semi-agape?) and less effective kind of love (less effective because it is not enough to save the non-elect). Where does one find a God with two kinds of love (agape and ?) taught in the Scriptures? It is an assumption that must be made, however, if one believes in Reformed Theology. It appears obvious that Calvinists have created a God with two kinds of love in an attempt to justify a God who doesn't practice egalitarian fairness. (Assumption # 10 addresses the issue of egalitarian fairness.)

Imagine a father who says he loves all five of his children but gives an allowance to only two of them. His explanation for doing so is to tell his children that he has a different kind of love for the two who are given special treatment. All five are equally behaved but only two are selected to receive an allowance. Even worse, the father tells the other three to ask for an allowance, knowing full well he never intends to give them one. Furthermore, he informs them that when he dies, he will leave all his wealth only for the two chosen to receive an allowance. Again, he gives no real explanation as to why. How is it possible to view such a father as loving?

A Calvinist once told me this analogy fails because God is not the father of the non-elect. That thought is even worse because it means God brings children into the world with absolutely no intention of fathering them.

Calvinists try to justify this belief in two kinds of love by using the analogy of a man who loves all women but has a special kind of love only for his wife. This analogy makes sense only if the man's love for other women means he has a desire for their well-being and good. As Austin Fischer points out in his book *Young, Restless, No Longer Reformed*, if the man really loves other women, at the very least,

We would expect him to be kind and help them out. And we would certainly expect him to help them avoid some sort of terrible pain and suffering if at all possible. But this is an exceedingly misleading way to speak of God's "love" for the reprobate, for far from helping them avoid terrible pain and suffering, he brings the most terrible pain and suffering upon them (hell).

As such, it would be more truthful to say something along the lines of, "I love my wife by being kind, compassionate, and sacrificial towards her, but I love all other women by doing something far worse than raping, torturing, or murdering them – I ordain their eternal damnation in hell." [49]

What kind of love is this?

If that is what God considers love, why would anyone be interested in knowing such a God? How can anyone trust a God who claims to love people, but treats them so horrifically? Jesus told us to "Love your enemies, bless them that curse you, do good to them that hate you, and pray for them which despitefully use you, and persecute you; That you may be the children of your Father which is in heaven" (Matthew 5:44-45). According to Calvinism, however, God Himself does not do this even though He commands His children to do so. He may say He loves His enemies, but His actions speak louder than His words. Honesty demands one admit He really loves only His family members. It is not unlike a mafia boss who takes care of his own but kills off those who go against him. No sane person would believe the mafia boss if he said he loved his enemies despite treating them the way he does. Anything can be called love if you totally redefine the word.

Calvinists protest and point out that God shows love to the non-elect in many ways other than salvation. The death of Christ, they say, has secured many non-redemptive benefits for mankind in general. Boettner writes, "God makes His sun to shine on the evil and the good, and sends rain on the just and the unjust. Many temporal blessings are thus secured for all men, although these fall short of being sufficient to insure salvation." [50]

Where do the Scriptures ever state that temporal blessings in the natural realm—sunshine, rain, etc.— were secured for mankind by Christ's death? There is not a shred of evidence for this idea; it is entirely philosophical and conjectural. More to the point, how does treating someone nice in this life justify torturing them for all eternity? Rapists often take their victims out for a nice dinner before raping them. Does that excuse the rapist for his horrible conduct?

No, try as they will to sugar coat it, the universal love Calvinists believe in isn't really love at all. It's far more like anti-love. The Bible tells us that God is love. Calvinists assume that He is actually two kinds of love, of which one is not love at all.

Assumption #5
God's Saving Grace Cannot be Resisted

IF TOTAL DEPRAVITY MEANS no one desires to be saved, then it *logically* follows that God must save people by His irresistible grace. Irresistible grace is yet another belief Calvinists are required to accept on the basis of logic rather than on God's Word. Arminians read the Bible and find a God who pours out His love in order to woo the lost to Himself. His desire is that none be lost, but He doesn't force anyone to respond positively to His imploring love. He knows that true love is a volitional decision. Therefore, He does not demand love but desires that we love Him because He first loved us.

Calvinists, on the other hand, look at their doctrine of total depravity and conclude that no one will ever respond to God's love. So, logic requires God to do more than simply woo us to Himself. He must draw us to Himself irresistibly. Dr. Sproul states it this way: "While wooing is a necessary condition for coming to Christ, it is not a sufficient condition. It is necessary but not compelling."[51]

But that is not what Romans 2:4 indicates. Paul asks the question, "Do you show contempt for the riches of

115

his kindness, forbearance and patience, not realizing that God's kindness is intended to lead you to repentance?" It appears that God, at least, expects His love and kindness (wooing) to lead to repentance. Why would God need to be patient and kind if He knows such kindness will not lead to repentance? God doesn't appear to understand that He needs to do more than just show His kindness. In fact, God is just wasting His time wooing if wooing is insufficient to bring anyone to Himself. If God must save by His irresistible grace, why bother with wooing at all?

Arminians see irresistible grace as God forcing people to come to Him. If the unsaved have no desire to come to God on their own due to total depravity, then God must bring them against their wills. For the Arminian this means God's gift of salvation is not only given to people who don't want it, but it is given with the requirement that the people take it. Requiring someone to accept something they do not want is not a loving act of giving, but an act of sheer brutishness.

Calvinists counter by saying God does not force anyone to accept Him. They claim that God changes people's desires so that they end up wanting to come to Him. The same Dr. Sproul who claimed that the Greek word *helko* means God drags us to Himself, also said the following:

> Reformed theology does not teach that God brings the elect "kicking and screaming, against their wills," into his kingdom. It teaches that God so works in the hearts of the elect as to make them willing and pleased to come to Christ. They come to Christ because they want to. They want to because God has created in their hearts a desire for Christ.[52]

Does God force us to choose Him against our wills?

Seriously? If it is God who causes us to turn from hating Him to loving Him, how can such love be genuine? If

God reprograms a person (as we reprogram a computer) to make a person want God, wouldn't that make man more of a robotic machine than a human being? How is changing a man's will without his consent any different from forcing him to change? How can anyone seriously claim that people do not become Christians against their wills because God reprograms their wills? Only those convinced that Reformed Theology is true could accept such thinking. Calvinists have to accept it because it logically must follow a belief in total depravity. Calvinists declare that people accept Christ willingly despite their having no desire for God. Even though God's reprogramming of one's desires cannot be refused by the non-Christian due to irresistible grace, Calvinists claim the person is still choosing Christ willingly.

Imagine a man who is in love with a woman who does not love him. Because he is unable to woo her, he hypnotizes her into loving him. Left on her own, she wouldn't even want to be near the man, but now she loves him due to her altered state. How can anyone claim such a love relationship is genuine? Wouldn't it be more genuine for the man to find a woman who willing responded to his love and desired to have a relationship with him without first having to be hypnotized?

Calvinists will say, "There are no women (or men) who naturally desire to be in a relationship with God. So, God must alter the wills of His chosen ones, so they will want to be in relationship with Him." And why do Calvinists say that? They say it because of their belief in total depravity.

Do Calvinists really believe this is how God goes about establishing relationships with humans? If a person has absolutely no desire to become a Christian, but ends up one anyway, is it not against (at the very least) his/her original will? If it is not the person's will to have his will changed, isn't changing it going against the person's will?

If an outside force makes a person go against his natural desires without the person's consent, is it really because the person has willed it? No matter how the question is phrased, the answer is obviously the same. Yet, Calvinists declare that people accept Christ willingly despite having no desire for God. Even though God's reprogramming of one's desires cannot be refused by the non-Christian due to irresistible grace, Calvinists claim the person is still choosing Christ willingly. There is only one way anyone could honestly accept that as true. One would have to have a very convoluted definition of free will. That is, of course, exactly what Calvinists have.

Free Will?

Calvinists will say they believe in free will, but after the Fall, man's free will became limited to wanting only to sin. People are free to do whatever they want, but they only want to sin. The logic (there's that word again) is that people only do what they most want to do. They will never choose to do something that they have a lesser desire to do (e.g., seek or trust God) because that is not their nature.

If one accepts such reasoning (logic?), a person will never choose to whistle if he desires to sing more than whistle. The person is "free" to whistle but never will because his preference is to sing more than to whistle. If this seems baffling, it is because the term "free will" is being used so counter-intuitively.

By contrast, everyone except Calvinists know that free will must include the power of contrary choice (*libertarianism*). This means you are only free if you have the ability to choose between two different things even if you may prefer one over the other. You must be able to act on various inclinations and not just your strongest. You are free to whistle even if your normal preference is to sing. To claim that you are free to choose but you can only choose one thing (only that which is your strongest desire) is to redefine free will. Indeed, to say you have free will because you have another choice that you will never choose is not free will at all.

Calvinists hold to two competing beliefs. They believe in irresistible grace and, at the same time, they believe a person does not accept Christ against their will. The two conflicting ideas cannot be reconciled without redefining free will.

Key Questions

But the real problem with a belief in irresistible grace isn't that it requires a new definition of free will. The real problem is that Scripture disputes such a concept. If irresistible grace means people cannot resist God's offer of grace, we should not find any place in the Bible where someone was able to resist it. Yet, there are numerous cases in Scripture where people did exactly that.

God reminds Israel in Amos 4 of all the things He had done to try to get them to return to Him, but they did not. They resisted His grace. In verse 10 He says, "I sent plagues among you as I did to Egypt. I killed your young men with the sword, along with your captured horses. I filled your nostrils with the stench of your camps, yet you have not returned to me."

The first question to be asked is, If God determines who returns to Him and who does not, why give people the false impression they had a choice? God tells the Israelites that they should have returned to Him due to all of His efforts in trying to get them to return. If they really had no choice in the matter, God was being dishonest. Secondly, if God's grace is irresistible, why did His efforts fail? And thirdly, why did God even need to send plagues and destruction? If God's grace is irresistible there was no need to torture anyone. God could just cause them to return. Yet He tortures them for resisting His grace, which is supposedly impossible to do. If God's grace cannot be resisted these acts of torture by God make Him an evil, malevolent God.

Matthew 11:20 tells us, "Jesus began to denounce the towns in which most of his miracles had been performed, because they did not repent." Why chastise people for being unrepentant if only you can cause them to repent? And why mention the volume of mighty works performed if they have nothing to do with whom you chose to re-birth? It appears the number of miracles performed should have made a difference. The miracles (not God alone) should have caused the people to repent. This is shown in the following verse where Jesus goes on to say, "Woe to you, Chorasin! Woe to you, Bethsaida! For if the miracles that were performed in you had been performed in Tyre and Sidon, they would have repented long ago in sackcloth and ashes" (verse 21). If Tyre and Sidon had seen the miracles performed that Chorasin and Bethsaida had seen, they would have repented. How is that pos-sible if God and not mighty works determines who re-pents? Why would seeing miracles result in some cities repenting and not others if God alone decides who re-pents regardless of the number of miracles performed? According to Calvinism, God's decisions are not condi-tioned upon anything. So, why should the amount of mighty works make any difference? The wording of the passage makes it clear that such miracles were designed to influence the people's decision and not God's. But the mighty works failed because God's grace was success-fully resisted.

If you go back to the Old Testament you find God asking Moses, "How long will these people treat me with contempt? How long will they refuse to believe in me, in spite of all the signs I have performed among them?" (Numbers 14:11) It seems obvious from this question God was waiting for the Israelites to believe based on all the signs He had shown them. Otherwise, there would be no question as to when they would believe. They would believe when God decided they would believe. The question to Moses is ridiculous, unless the people are the ones who decide when they will believe. The fact they do not believe shows, once again, the ability of man to resist God's grace.

More Examples

In Matthew 23:37, Jesus said, "Jerusalem, Jerusalem, you who kill the prophets and stone those sent to you, how often I have longed to gather your children together, as a hen gathers her chicks under her wings, and you were not willing." Jesus wanted to save them, but they "were not willing." Instead, they resisted His offer of saving grace. Contrary to what Reformed Theology teaches, God's grace is not irresistible.

If God's grace is irresistible, why did Jesus say, "How hard it is for the rich to enter the kingdom of God! Indeed, it is easier for a camel to go through the eye of a needle than for someone who is rich to enter the kingdom of God" (Luke 18:24-25)? If no one can resist God's saving grace, why would it be more difficult for God to save a rich man than a poor one? Christ's statement only makes sense if the rich have a harder time making the right choice in the matter. It is because the rich are more likely to trust in their wealth than in Christ that makes it so difficult for them to enter the kingdom of God. The rich are more likely to resist God's grace.

In Acts 7:51, Stephen said to the high priest and Jewish leaders in Jerusalem, "You stiff-necked people! Your hearts and ears are still uncircumcised. You are just like your ancestors: You always resist the Holy Spirit!" Stephen could not have stated it any clearer. The Holy Ghost can be resisted. He was resisted by the Jewish leaders as well as by their ancestors.

As was stated earlier, the biggest problem with the assumption that God's grace cannot be resisted is that the Bible tells us it can be resisted and often is. So, do we abandon the Scriptures in favor of logic or do we trust the Bible?

Paul said he was speaking on Christ's behalf when he begged the Corinthians to be reconciled to God (2 Corinthians 5:20). If the elect can only be reconciled to God through His irresistible grace, why would Paul plead with the Corinthians to do something only God can do? Paul's injunction makes no sense if grace is irresistible.

Hebrews 12:15 would also be senseless if God's grace is irresistible. It reads, "See to it that no one falls short of the grace of God." If God's grace is irresistible then no elect person is going to fall short of it. God will make sure of that. So, there is no need to warn them. And there is no need to warn the non-elect about falling short of God's grace because there is nothing they can do about it anyway. They're going to fall short regardless, because God ordained them to. At least, that is what Reformed Theology teaches. What, then, is the purpose of warning people not to fall short of God's grace if it is useless information for both the elect and non-elect? Verses like Hebrews 12:15 would not be in the Bible if grace were irresistible.

Not only is the Bible filled with examples of people resisting God's saving grace, I myself have resisted His grace.

My Own Example

I was raised in a Christian home, so I never doubted there was a God. My parents told me He existed and I just assumed they were right. I never had any personal relationship with Him, however, even though I attended church on a regular basis with my family.

During my sophomore year in high school, I began to resent having to follow all the rules my parents required of me. Nothing unusual about teenage rebellion except my resentment spilled over into my attitude toward God. I blamed Him for all the rules as most were rules my parents claimed were commandments God wanted me to follow.

One day I became so angry that I went outside into the hayfield behind our house, climbed onto a tractor, shook my fist at God, and said, "God, I no longer want to have anything to do with you. I no longer wish to go to church or obey any of your ridiculous rules. You do your thing and I will do mine. You leave me alone and I will leave you alone." After that I seldom went to church and proceeded to do my own thing for about a year.

In December of my junior year of high school, the church where my father attended was having special revival services. Much to my father's surprise, I decided to go with him one night. I think my attitude was "I'll throw the old man a bone and go to church with him to show him I'm not such a bad guy." As soon as I sat down in the pew, however, the Holy Spirit started convicting me of my sin. Instead of thinking I really wasn't such a bad guy, I could only think that I was garbage. I never heard what the minister said or what Scriptures were read. I couldn't even tell you if any Scriptures were read because I spent the entire time wrestling with God.

Wrestling with God

I knew God wanted me to repent of my sin and accept His forgiveness through Christ. I also knew that at the end of the service there would be an altar call inviting anyone who wanted to become a Christian to go forward and kneel at the altar to do so. In my mind, I told God I would be willing to get down on my knees but not in front of everyone here at the church. I would do it after I got home beside my bed. I wasn't going to make a fool of myself in front of all these people. God responded by telling me that if I was too ashamed of Him to stand up in front of these people and confess Christ as my Savior, I wasn't serious about my desire to commit my life to Him. I countered by guaranteeing God that I would be very serious in my commitment later when I got home. Back and forth we went throughout the service.

Suddenly, I realized the minister was asking everyone to stand and sing the song, "Just as I Am." I stood and continued to struggle with God because I knew He wanted me to go forward. I argued with God through what seemed like a dozen verses of "Just as I Am." No one went forward, so the minister finally pronounced the benediction ending the service.

Then as clearly as if someone standing next to me had said it, I heard God say, "My Spirit will not always strive with man." I knew He was telling me this was my last chance. After tonight, He would agree to my earlier request to leave me alone and just do His thing while I continued to do mine. I panicked. I jumped out into the aisle and tried to run to the altar. By this time, however, the service had been dismissed and everyone was walking to the back of the church. Now, instead of being embarrassed by simply going forward, I added to the situation by almost knocking people over as I pushed and shoved my way through the departing crowd to the front of the church.

Needless to say, it was a very emotional experience for me. I wept and sobbed in great remorse for the way I had been living my life. My mother knelt down beside me and cried as well. My father had to find handkerchiefs for both of us. At the end, I got up from there feeling as if a pile of bricks had just been taken off my back. It's hard to describe, but I knew my sin was gone. I received what I had needed my entire life – forgiveness.

Decide

Reflecting back on that occasion, I realize God was calling me to repent and I had a choice to make. He wasn't forcing me, but I believe it was His last call to me and my last chance to repent and accept Christ as my Savior. I know I could have just as easily said, "No." I almost did. I am so very glad now that I said, "Yes." God could have passed me by and let me remain in my sinful condition, but He didn't. He reached out to me that night and said, "It's up to you. What will you decide?" I'm convinced He was also saying, "I will not pursue you forever. Seek me now while I can be found."

There is no question in my mind that up until then I had been successfully resisting the Holy Spirit. Had I continued to do so that evening in December, I believe I would have been bound for an eternity in hell. I have no doubt about the fact God was asking me to make a decision. God Himself spoke to me and told me He was giving me one last chance that night. It was as clear to me then as it is to me today that God's grace can be resisted. I did it for years.

We are offered forgiveness and new life only because of God's grace. But God does not force us to accept His grace. We must choose it or refuse it. We can refuse it because God's grace is not irresistible.

Assumption #6
Once We are Saved, We are Always Saved

IF YOU BELIEVE IN TOTAL DEPRAVITY and irresistible
grace, it's only logical that eternal security is true.
What possible reason would God have for saving a
person by His irresistible grace and then later
"unsaving" the person? Like all the previous assumptions, this assumption is based on the belief
that we have no say in whether or not we are saved.
Not only does God save us, even though we have
no interest in being saved, He will also prevent us
from rejecting Him after we are saved and we have
no say in that matter, either. Belief in the perseverance of the saints reasonably follows a belief that
we are saved by God's irresistible grace.

The question of whether or not once saved means always saved has always been hotly contested. Christians
on both sides of the issue quote numerous Bible verses to
"prove" their position to be the correct one. So, how do
we know which verses to accept? If we accept one set of
verses doesn't that mean the other set is false and should
be rejected? How can the Bible contain passages that contradict each other? Can both sets of verses be true?

If the Bible is the Word of God, then it is coherent and consistent with itself. God is not the author of confusion. He does not contradict Himself. We can never, therefore, set one part of Scripture against another. How then can we reconcile those verses that seem to teach eternal security with those that seem to teach otherwise?

The answer is simple. The two sets of verses are not talking about the same thing. Those verses that ensure eternal life are referring to God's side of the salvation covenant. He guarantees to keep us secure. He will not allow anything or anyone to take our salvation away from us. These assurances deal with the inability of any external factors to cause us to lose or be robbed of eternal life. God Himself will not permit it to happen.

A covenant involves two parties.

By contrast, those verses that say we can be lost, even after becoming Christians, are referring to internal factors within the believer himself/herself. These verses indicate that we can choose not to keep *our* end of the salvation covenant. A covenant involves *two* parties. While God promises to keep His end of the covenant, He does not promise to force Christians to keep their end. In fact, He warns us about the consequences of failing to keep our end. Thus, we can decide to reject the Lord even following our conversion. As a result, we forfeit God's promise of eternal life.

Non-Calvinists are able to explain the difference in the two sets of verses by demonstrating that they are talking about two different sides of the salvation covenant. How do Calvinists explain the difference in the two sets of verses? Calvinists offer three possible explanations for the verses that contradict their belief in eternal security. Glen Shellrude writes the following about the desperate attempts Calvinists make to avoid the obvious interpretation of these verses:

The New Testament contains numerous warnings against believers falling away and losing their salvation. These texts are a problem for Calvinists since they affirm that apostasy is impossible for the elect. However, if this were true then why warn against it? Once again theological determinists must resort to counterintuitive and contextually unsupported interpretations which do not take account of the historical context in which the warnings were given. The three main approaches to the warning texts used by Calvinist interpreters are: 1. the warnings have to do with the loss of rewards, not salvation; 2. the warnings have in view those who are not genuine believers; 3. the warnings are the means God uses to ensure that the elect do not commit apostasy.

The first approach fails to take account of the contexts and language of the warnings. The problem with the second approach is that if the real problem is that some are deluded about being genuine believers, why not speak to that issue directly rather than address them as believers and warn them about the possibility of apostasy? The warnings should be about the danger of being self-deluded that one is a believer rather than about the danger of apostasy. The problem with the third approach is that it requires the logically and ethically challenged assumption that God warns about something that could not happen as a means of ensuring that it doesn't happen. It calls in question the moral integrity of God that he would warn about something as though it were a real possibility when in fact this was not the case.[53]

Eternal Security Refuted

Because the Bible is replete with passages that tell us Christians can fall away and be lost, Calvinists must come up with alternative explanations of the verses in order to maintain their theology of eternal security. Their attempts, as Shellrude points out, fail. Consider the following:

When the disciples (followers of Jesus) asked Jesus to tell them what the signs would be for His coming and the end of the world, He said, "The love of many shall wax cold. But he that shall endure unto the end, the same shall be saved" (Matthew 24:12-13 KJV). The obvious implication is some shall not endure unto the end and thus shall be lost. It is not up to God to endure to the end in order to be saved. It is up to the followers of Jesus, His disciples, to endure.

Paul wrote similar words in 2 Thessalonians 2:3, "Let no man deceive you by any means: for that day shall not come, except there come a falling away first" (KJV). Who are the "you" that might be deceived? Paul is writing to the Christians at Thessalonica (see the first three verses of chapter 1). He calls them *brethren*. Only Christians can fall away. If Paul is talking about non-Christians (who are already fallen) what do they fall away from?

Writing to Timothy, Paul says, "Here is a trustworthy saying: If we died with him, we will also live with him; if we endure, we will also reign with him. If we disown him, he will also disown us" (1 Timothy 2:11-12). Paul is here telling Timothy, a follower of Christ, that we must endure in order to reign with Christ. Paul then tells Timothy that if we disown Christ, He will disown us. Both Paul and Timothy are Christians; yet, Paul says that if we do not endure or if we disown Christ, we will be lost. The language makes it clear that eternal security is conditional.

Paul goes on to remind Timothy about, "Hymenæus and Philetus, who have departed from the truth. They say that the resurrection has already taken place, and they destroy the faith of some" (1 Tim. 2:17-18). Even if you contend that one can depart from the truth without first being a believer in the truth (e.g., a Christian), how can anyone's faith be destroyed if they never had the faith in the first place?

Later, Paul tells Timothy that it is the *faith,* specifically, that some will fall away from. Paul writes, "The Spirit clearly says that in later times some will abandon the faith" (1 Timothy 4:1). Only Christians have "the faith" to abandon.

After telling Timothy *some will abandon the faith,* Paul then warns Timothy not to be one who abandons the faith. In the same chapter 4, Paul writes, "take heed unto thyself, and unto the doctrine; continue in them: for in doing this thou shalt... save thyself" (1 Timothy 4:16 KJV). Timothy must *continue* in the doctrine in order to be saved. The reverse implication is that if Timothy does not continue in the doctrine, he will not be saved. He will be like those who abandon the faith. Paul is not telling Timothy he is eternally secure. Paul is telling Timothy just the opposite.

In the next chapter, Paul tells Timothy about those "Having damnation, because they have cast off their first faith" (1 Timothy 5:12). Then just three verses later, Paul says, "For some are already turned aside after Satan" (1 Timothy 5:15). Only Christians can turn aside after Satan, because non-Christians are already on Satan's side.

In Mark 13:13, where Jesus is talking directly to His disciples again about the last days, He says, "Everyone will hate you because of me, but the one who stands firm to the end will be saved." When Christ uses the word "you," He is not talking about non-believers but His followers, His disciples. Non-believers are not hated because of Christ. The reason the disciples will be hated by everyone is because they are followers of Christ. To these same followers, Christ says they must stand "firm to the end" in order to be saved. The King James Version says followers of Christ must "endure" in their faith (which has nothing to do with works) in order to be saved. Conversely, those who do not "endure unto the end" will be lost. Jesus did not say, "God will endure for you" or even that "God will enable you to endure unto the end." He says the disciples themselves must endure.

The Vine and the Branches

In John 15:5-6, Jesus says, "I am the vine; you are the branches. If you remain in me and I in you, you will bear much fruit; apart from me you can do nothing. If you do not remain in me, you are like a branch that is thrown away and withers; such branches are picked up, thrown into the fire and burned."

Jesus is once again talking only to His disciples (after Judas had left) and not the crowds. It is while He is alone with them for the Last Supper that He tells them they are the branches *clean because of the word* (verse 3). They are already His disciples, already branches in Him. Yet, he tells them (His very own chosen disciples) that if a person does not *remain* in Him, he will be cast into the fire. You cannot be cast away from the vine if you were never part of it in the first place.

We again find Paul echoing similar words as those of Christ's in his letter to the Church at Rome. He states in Romans 11:19-23:

You will say then, "Branches were broken off so that I could be grafted in." Granted. But they were broken off because of unbelief, and you stand by faith. Do not be arrogant, but tremble. For if God did not spare the natural branches, he will not spare you either. Consider therefore the kindness and sternness of God: sternness to those who fell, but kindness to you, provided that you continue in his kindness. Otherwise, you also will be cut off. And if they do not persist in unbelief, they will be grafted in, for God is able to graft them in again.

It becomes repetitious, but it must be said that here, too, Paul is speaking to Christians. In the very first chapter, Paul says he is writing to "all in Rome who are loved by God and called to be his holy people" (verse 7). In this passage, Paul is warning Gentile Christians not to be "high-minded" just because they were able to become Christians (grafted in) after the Jews (the natural branches) rejected Christ and were broken off. The reason they should avoid pride is because God will cut off Gentile Christians who do not "continue in his kindness" just like He cut off the unbelieving Jews. Furthermore, He will graft the Jews back in if they do not persist in unbelief. *Continue* and *endure* (the word used in Matthew) convey the same meaning as does the idea of *remaining in Christ*. Christians who do not continue in their faith, endure, or remain in Christ will be lost.

It should be pointed out that the Jews who were broken off were not Christians. All Jews were originally part of the olive tree before any grafting ever took place. They were there naturally because they were God's chosen people. Many were broken off due to their lack of faith in God (Jeremiah 11:16). Those who were not broken off were those who had faith in God. They were people like Noah, Abraham, Moses, Joshua, and Daniel. All these are said to have trusted God. Conversely, Jews lacking such faith were broken off (compare with Hebrews 3:7-12). After Christ's death and resurrection, such unbelieving Jews can be grafted back into the vine by trusting in Christ to be their Savior. Christians, on the other hand, cannot be grafted in again once they are broken off. Such branches are *thrown into the fire and burned* (John 15:6). Obviously, a branch that is burned up cannot be grafted back into anything. Thus, a branch that was once "saved" by being grafted in has now become eternally lost.

Paul says he is writing the book of Colossians to "God's holy people in Colossæ, the faithful brothers and sisters in Christ" (Colossians 1:2). And if that isn't clear enough, he goes on to say he prays for them and gives thanks for them because he heard of their faith in Christ Jesus and of the love they have for all God's people (verses 3-4).

Later, in that same first chapter, he says this to them:

> Once you were alienated from God and were en-
> emies in your minds because of your evil behav-
> ior. But now he has reconciled you by Christ's
> physical body through death to present you holy
> in his sight, without blemish and free from accu-
> sation— if you continue in your faith, established
> and firm, and do not move from the hope held
> out in the gospel (verses 21-23).

They are reconciled, holy, without blemish, free from accusation *if* they continue in the faith and are not moved "from the hope held out in the gospel." The word *if* means all these things are conditional. Clearly, Paul believed a Christian could move from the hope of the gospel by not continuing in the faith.

How can this be?

The obvious question for those believing in eternal security is this: Why do faithful, reconciled brethren in Christ have to continue in the faith if they are already guaranteed eternal life by virtue of the fact they are Christians? These verses indicate that eternal security is not guaranteed to Christians unless they "continue in the faith." Whether it is *endure, remain,* or *continue in the faith*, there is something required of Christians in order for them to be saved and remain saved. The verses do not say God does this for Christians. All these verses cannot be ignored simply because they do not fit into one's personal theology.

Even the most often quoted verse in the Bible disputes eternal security. Regarding John 3:16, Paul Butler writes, "We must note that the promise of eternal life is to whosoever *continues* to believe in the Son. The word 'believe' is in the Greek present tense and indicates continued action."[54]

Interestingly, Calvinist Alan P. Stanley agrees with Butler:

> The most well-known verse in the entire Bible is un-doubtedly John 3:16... Yet, while it is well-known, it may well be the least understood. Most probably think this verse is expressing the need for a simple confes-sion of faith in Jesus to receive eternal life, that thus we believe *once* and have eternal life. Virtually all com-mentators on John's Gospel, though, would agree that in keeping with the Greek present tense and John's theology, John 3:16 in fact means, "For God so loved the world that he gave his one and only Son, that whoever *continues to believe* in him shall not perish but have eternal life.[55]

This same theme of continued faith rather than one-time faith is consistent with other verses in the Bible that address the issue of belief. John 6:40 should literally be translated, "For this is the will of My Father, that every-one continuing to behold the Son and continuing to be-lieve on Him is continuing to have eternal life and I my-self shall raise him in the last day."[56]

John 5:24 is another example. Dr. Robert Shank wrote this regarding the verse:

> Perhaps no verse has been more cited in evidence by advocates of unconditional security than has John 5:24, "Verily, verily, I say unto you, He that heareth my word and believeth on him that sent me hath everlasting life, and shall not come into condemna-tion, but is passed from death unto life." Please un-derscore the words 'hath everlasting life,' say the ad-vocates of unconditional security. Indeed! But please underscore also the words 'he that heareth... and believeth,' for they denote the condition governing the promise of everlasting life and deliverance from

condemnation and death. And the hearing and be-lieving of which Jesus spoke are not the act of a mo-ment... [One must take] into account the durative [continuous] quality of the present participles *akouôn* ["hearing"] and *pisteuôn* ["believing"]... [57]

In other words, the verse should read, "Truly, truly I am saying to you, that the one who continues hear-ing my word and continues believing on the One who sent Me continues having eternal life and into judg-ment is not going to come, but has passed over out of death into life."[586]

Paul wrote, "I endure everything for the sake of the elect, that they too may obtain the salvation that is in Christ Jesus" (2 Timothy 2:10). Haven't the elect already obtained salvation whether or not Paul (or anyone else) endures all things? By using the word "may" Paul is say-ing there is no guarantee the elect will be saved eternally. Rather than teaching eternal security, Paul is teaching just the opposite by implying that the elect *may not* ob-tain salvation.

Toward the end of his life, Paul said, "I have kept the faith" (2 Timothy 4:7). The implication is that Paul might not have kept the faith, but he did. More importantly, he didn't say God kept the faith for him. Paul said he did it.

The writer of Hebrews tells his "holy brethren" (He-brews 3:1) to "Hold fast the profession of *our* faith with-out wavering." According to Reformed Theology, Chris-tians don't need to be told to hold onto their faith be-cause they will never let go of it. They are eternally se-cure, so losing their faith is not a possibility.

Hebrews 3:12 reads, "See to it, brothers and sisters, that none of you has a sinful, unbelieving heart that turns away from the living God." How can you depart from the living God if you were never close to Him to start with? The author is not warning the unregenerate here.

He is writing to his "brothers and sisters" or fellow Christians and warns *them* about having an unbelieving heart and turning away from God. The author is definitely not promising Christians eternal security.

The passage continues with the words, "But encourage one another daily, as long as it is called 'Today,' so that none of you may be hardened by sin's deceitfulness. We have come to share in Christ, if indeed we hold our original conviction firmly to the very end" (verses 13-14). It is the brothers and sisters in Christ who must hold their faith ("conviction") firmly unto the end. It is not God who must hold steadfast to the very end or God who must hold them steadfast.

If eternal security is true then all these verses are false, making the Bible contradict itself. The other possibility is that all these verses are true, and it is eternal security that is false.

No one doubts Paul was a Christian following his Damascus Road experience. Yet, he tells the Church at Corinth that even he could be lost when he writes, "lest that by any means, when I have preached to others, I myself should be a castaway" (1 Corinthians 9:27 KJV). If Paul believed in eternal security why would he think it possible that he could become a castaway?

Later in chapter 15, in the same letter to the Corinthians, he writes, "Now, brothers and sisters, I want to remind you of the gospel I preached to you, which you received and on which you have taken your stand. By this gospel you are saved, if you hold firmly to the word I preached to you. Otherwise, you have believed in vain" (1 Corinthians 15:1-2). The salvation of the Corinthian Christians (Paul's "brothers and sisters" in Christ) was conditioned upon their holding firm to the gospel preached to them. Otherwise, they believed in vain. Rather than telling them (*those who received the gospel and took their stand on it*) that they are eternally secure,

Paul tells them just the reverse. In order to be saved eternally, he tells them they must continue to hold firmly to the Gospel even after they had become believers.

In the parable of the sower, some seed did not take root and some did. In one case, seeds took root and grew into living plants. Those *live* plants were later choked by thorns (Matthew 13:7). If the seeds became living (reborn) plants but subsequently died, how can eternal security be true?

Throughout the Bible right up to the very end, God tells His people (Christians) it is "to him who overcomes I will give to eat from the tree of life" (Revelation 2:7 NKJV). It was to the *churches* that these words were directed. They (not God) had to overcome in order to guarantee their salvation. They had to avoid abandoning their faith in Christ in order to obtain eternal life.

Further Clarity

If the previous passages aren't clear enough, further evidence for the nonexistence of eternal security is found in the verses that declare what happens to those who *do* turn from the faith.

Consider the words of the author of Hebrews, chapter 6, verses 4-6:

> It is impossible for those who have once been enlightened, who have tasted the heavenly gift, who have shared in the Holy Spirit,who have tasted the goodness of the word of God and the powers of the coming age and who have fallen away, to be brought back to repentance. To their loss they are crucifying the Son of God all over again and subjecting him to public disgrace.

Christ cannot be crucified twice. Christ "died to sin once for all" (Romans 6:10). So, you cannot be saved again after falling away. Notice the writer is talking about those who "have shared in the Holy Spirit" (Christians) falling away and being unable to repent again. Non-Christians have not shared in the Holy Spirit. God saves non-Christians who repent of their sins but not Christians who fall away after being saved.

Sproul challenges this by arguing that Christians are being warned against doing something that will never happen. Huh? Sproul writes, "I believe the author of Hebrews is stating what could happen, but it never does because no true believer commits the sin the author is talking about. In verse nine, he writes, 'But, beloved, we are confident of better things concerning you, yes, things that accompany salvation.' The author expresses confidence that the people he addresses will not do the things he has warned against but that they will do that which accompanies salvation."[59]

If that is true, why warn them about something they do not have to be warned about? Even if the author is confident those he addresses will not do these things, it does not follow that he is equally confident that all Christians will not do these things. If no believer ever does what the author warns against, why bother with such a warning?

Hebrews 10:26-29 warns,

> If we deliberately keep on sinning after we have received the knowledge of the truth, no sacrifice for sins is left, but only a fearful expectation of judgment and of raging fire that will consume the enemies of God. Anyone who rejected the law of Moses died without mercy on the testimony of two or three witnesses. How much more severely do you think someone deserves to be punished who has trampled the Son of God underfoot, who has treated as an unholy thing the blood of the covenant that sanctified them, and who has insulted the Spirit of grace?

The writer uses the word "we" to describe those he is referring to. If he were talking about non-Christians, he should have said, "If *they* deliberately keep on sinning after *they* have received the knowledge of the truth." And how can a non-Christian be "sanctified by the blood of the covenant" (verse 29)? The author leaves no room for doubt that he is talking about Christians who have no sacrifice for sins left.

What then does the author mean by the phrase "no sacrifice for sins is left"? He answered that question previously in chapter 6. Read that passage again.

> It is impossible for those who have once been enlightened, who have tasted the heavenly gift, who have shared in the Holy Spirit, who have tasted the goodness of the word of God and the powers of the coming age and who have fallen away, to be brought back to repentance. To their loss they are crucifying the Son of God all over again and subjecting him to public disgrace (Hebrews 6:4-6).

For whom is it impossible to be brought back to repentance? The passage says it is those who "have once been enlightened," those who "have tasted the heavenly gift," those who "have shared in the Holy Spirit," those who "have tasted the goodness of the word of God," those who have tasted "the powers of the coming age." What other terms could the author have used to better explain that he is talking about Christians? It is "those who have shared in the Holy Spirit" (Christians) who have fallen away who cannot repent again. It is Christians who are then lost. Rather than guaranteeing eternal security, these verses warn us that there is no such guarantee.

In Hebrews 10:38 God is talking about those who "live by faith" and tells them, "I take no pleasure in the one who shrinks back." God takes no pleasure in those who shrink back from the faith. Does it make sense that God would want those He takes no pleasure in to be with Him for all eternity?

What does Peter say?

1 Peter 5:8 tells Christians to *be alert* because "your enemy the devil prowls around like a roaring lion looking for someone to devour." The reprobate are already devoured, so Peter must be talking to Christians. In chapter 1, verse 2, he says he is writing to the "elect." But, if eternal security is guaranteed, it would be impossible for Satan to devour a Christian. Satan could harm a Christian, but never completely devour him. So, why does Peter warn Christians about the possibility of Satan doing something to them that he can never do? Belief in eternal security means Peter is warning Christians about the danger of something that could never happen.

Peter is even clearer in his explanation of the truth that Christians can be lost in his second epistle. Again, he is writing to Christians, those "who through the righteousness of our God and Savior Jesus Christ have received a faith as precious as ours" (2 Peter 1:1). In verse 10, he writes, "Give diligence to make your calling and election sure." Isn't our election already sure? If not, there is nothing we can do about it because we have no say in the matter (if Reformed Theology is correct). This sentence is asking us to do something we cannot do. And if those words weren't confusing enough for believers in eternal security, Peter goes on to say, "For if you do these things, you will never fall." The implication here is that the reverse is also true. If you don't do these things, you will fall.

Then Peter writes these words in chapter 2, verses 20 through 22:

> For if after they have escaped the pollutions of the world through the knowledge of the Lord and Savior

Jesus Christ, they are again entangled therein, and overcome, the latter end is worse with them than the beginning. For it had been better for them not to have known the way of righteousness, than, after they have known it, to turn from the holy commandment delivered unto them. But it happened unto them according to the true proverb, The dog is turned to his own vomit again; and the sow that was washed to her wallowing in the mire (KJV).

Notice how Peter describes those he is talking about. He says they are people who "have escaped the pollutions of the world through the knowledge of the Lord and Savior Jesus Christ." Peter doesn't say they simply had knowledge about Jesus, but that they knew Him as "Lord and Savior." The word translated as "knowledge" in this passage is *epignosis* in Greek, from the root *gnosis*, which also means knowledge. *Gnosis* by itself refers to general knowledge and is found in verses like 1 Corinthians 8:1, "Knowledge puffs up while love builds up" and 1 Corinthians 13:8, "Love never fails. But where there… is knowledge, it will pass away."

Epignosis, on the other hand, has a deeper meaning. It is not knowledge that puffs up or will pass away. It suggests knowledge of the truth – *saving* truth – rather than general knowledge or information. It is found in verses such as Ephesians 1:17: "The God of our Lord Jesus Christ, the Father of glory, may give unto you the spirit of wisdom and revelation in the knowledge of him" (KJV). Ephesians 4:13: "Until we all reach unity in the faith and in the knowledge of the Son of God." 1 Timothy 2:4: "Who will have all men to be saved, and to come into the knowledge of the truth" (KJV). Again, the word used in 2 Peter 2:20 is *epignosis*, the knowledge of saving truth, and not *gnosis*, general knowledge. Thus, when Peter says, "They have escaped the pollutions of the world through the knowledge of the Lord and Savior Jesus Christ," he is talking about saved individuals, those with the *knowledge* that gives "all things that pertain unto life" (2 Peter 1:3 KJV).

If Peter is talking about non-Christians in this passage, why does Peter describe them in the way he does? Peter could have chosen words that would make it much easier to understand that he was talking about the unregenerate. In fact, he could have said these people were unregenerate in order to avoid any misunderstanding about them, but he doesn't. Instead, he says, "they have escaped the pollutions of the world through the knowledge (*epignosis*) of the Lord and Savior Jesus Christ." If that is a description of non-Christians, Peter wrote in a terribly misleading way. And if that wasn't misleading enough, Peter made matters even worse by the words he used earlier in his letter. In the very beginning of his letter, Peter uses the same phrases to describe the Christians he is writing to as he does to describe the dog and the pig. Compare the descriptions:

Peter's description of the Christians he is writing to	Peter's description of the pig and dog who return to mud and vomit
Peter describes the Christians ("those of like precious Faith") as those who have been given all things that pertain unto life and godliness *through the knowledge of him* (Jesus). (2 Peter 1:3 KJV)	In the same letter, he describes the dog and the pig as those who have escaped the pollutions of the world *through the knowledge of the Lord and Savior Jesus.* (2 Peter 2:20 KJV)
Peter describes the Christians he is writing to as those who have *escaped the corruption that is in the world* (2 Peter 1:4 KJV)	He uses the same wording to describe the dog and the pig. He says they have *escaped the pollutions of the world.* (2 Peter 2:20 KJV)

If the dog and pig are not really analogous to Christians, why does Peter describe them in chapter 2 using the same terms he uses to describe the Christians he is writing to in chapter 1? Using the same words to describe non-Christians as he does to describe Christians in the same letter does nothing but confuse readers. I don't think Peter (and more significantly, God) would make the mistake of creating confusion in this way. Peter used the same words in chapter 1 as he did in chapter 2 in order to make it clear the dog and pig were the same as those he was writing to (those of like precious faith). They were Christians who returned to the way they were before they were saved (cleansed). They escaped the pollutions of the world, but they return to the pollutions of the world (mud and vomit) and as a result they are lost forever.

Calvinists have offered any number of explanations in their attempt to avoid the obvious meaning of Peter's words. Not one of their explanations, however, succeeds in accomplishing their goal. One of their contentions is that the illustration is talking about those who look clean, but the cleaning is superficial. Like the Pharisees, the pig looks good on the outside but inside the pig is still full of sin. The pig was never truly converted.

Cats and Dogs

One might be able to make that argument if cats and dogs had been used in the illustration. Cats lick themselves clean. Dogs shake off dirt. Pigs, on the other hand, do nothing to try to clean themselves. Ask a pig farmer what pigs do to clean themselves and he will tell you, "Pigs do *nothing* to clean themselves." Even if they had the ability, which they do not, they have no inclination to clean themselves. Hose down a pig and the pig will immediately go back to wallowing in the mud. Whether it is because the mud protects them from the sun or from insect bites or they just enjoy being dirty, pigs do not clean themselves. Unlike the Pharisees, a pig does not attempt to look good through his own efforts.

Given this fact, one must then ask the question, Who washed the pig? If a pig has neither the ability nor the inclination to be clean, and thus never even makes an effort, how did the pig in the parable become clean? Someone else (i.e., God) had to clean the pig.

The mud in the parable represents sin. You cannot wash away sin on your own, just as a pig cannot wash away mud on its own. Only God can do that. Furthermore, I don't believe it was by accident that Peter tells not only of the pig, but also of the dog. Peter, being led by the Holy Spirit, was wise enough to realize that some people might conclude the pig's cleaning was only on the outside (superficial). The dog, however, is purged of the sin inside of him. Thus, the mud and the vomit represent sin both outside and inside.

The dog and pig are not Pharisees. Jesus called the Pharisees hypocrites because they were only concerned with their external appearance, while they ignored the sins on the inside. That's not the lesson Peter is teaching here. Unlike the Pharisees, the dog and pig are not concerned about how they look on the outside, nor are they cleaned up through their own efforts. They were cleaned "through the knowledge of the Lord and Savior."

Another Attempt to Explain it Differently

Calvinists have pointed out that in the illustration, the pig remains a pig and the dog is still a dog even after they are washed, so they couldn't have been truly converted.

That response is meaningless. A human is still a human even after becoming a Christian. By their argument, Calvinists are attempting to apply 2 Corinthians 5:17 to this passage, but it doesn't work. A Christian becomes "a new creature" only in a spiritual sense, not a literal one.

Becoming a Christian doesn't cause one to become a different animal; he/she remains a *human*. If the pig were really converted, would it become a donkey, a camel, or a sheep? Would the dog become a cat, lizard, or gorilla? Trying to overlap the meaning of the Corinthians verse with this passage is simply poor exegesis.

A Third Attempt to Avoid the Obvious

Calvinists have also proffered this argument: "Whenever a pig is used as an illustration in the Bible, it always refers to a depraved state."

There are at least two problems with this exegesis. For one, Peter also uses a dog in his illustration. Does the Bible always refer to a dog in the same way it does a pig? Secondly, even if you could show that both a pig and a dog always represent a depraved state, both are cleansed of their sins. Thus, they do not remain in their depravity. A person who is cleansed of his sins is no longer in a depraved state. So, arguing that the pig always represents a state of depravity fails to take into account the whole story. To dismiss the difference between the filthy pig and the clean pig is to miss the central meaning of the illustration.

Yet Another Attempt to Explain it Away

In order to hold to their belief in eternal security, Calvinists cannot allow this passage to say what it says. They must explain it away. Another attempt they make to avoid the passage's obvious meaning is to argue that those being compared to a pig are not called born again Christians but *false teachers* (2 Peter 2:1).

In making such an argument, Calvinists assume that Christians cannot teach false doctrine. But Christians are constantly teaching false doctrines (eternal security being one of them). In context, those being talked about are those who became false teachers after they had become Christians. The reason they became false teachers was because of their desire for carnality. Look at verse 15. It says they "have forsaken the right way and are gone astray" (KJV). You must possess something before you can forsake it. You cannot stray from a place you were never at in the first place. These people were walking in the right way and then forsook it and went astray.

The passage does not say the false teachers claimed to be Christians but were not. Nor does the passage say the false teachers thought they were Christians but were mistaken. The passage does not say they tried to become Christians but failed. The passage says they were those who "escaped the pollutions of the world through the knowledge of the Lord and Savior Jesus Christ." Furthermore, verse 1 of chapter 2 states that these false teachers end up "denying the Lord that bought them." Calvinists, of all people, have to say the false teachers were Christians because Calvinists believe in limited atonement. If Christ "bought them" then they had to be of the elect unless limited atonement isn't true.

More Assumptions

Still, Calvinists maintain that the false teachers were never truly believers. They appeal to the verse found in 1 John 2:19 which speaks of false teachers who went out from the church as never having truly been part of the church.

Here Calvinists are generalizing from one situation and making it apply to all situations. They assume what is true for some people has to be true for everyone. Furthermore, unlike Peter, John never claims the particular false teachers he was talking about were ever truly believers in the first place. If we must conclude all who turn from Christ were never believers to begin with, we would also have to conclude that when a "righteous person turns from his righteousness" (Ezekiel 18:24), he was never righteous to begin with. When Jesus tells His disciples to remain in Him or be like branches cut off, "thrown into the fire and burned" (John 15:6), He meant the branches were never really in the vine in the first place. And when Peter gives the warning to "beware lest you fall from your secure position" (2 Peter 3:17), those he was warning were never in a secure position from the start. Assuming people are not what the Bible says they are makes it impossible to trust anything the Scriptures claim.

If Peter (under the guidance of the Holy Spirit) wanted readers to understand these false teachers were not Christians, he failed miserably. He not only neglected to say anything of the sort, but he worded his letter in such a way as to make it clear he was talking about Christians.

Finally, Peter's whole point in bringing up the false teachers is to warn Christians that they could become just like the false teachers. If eternal security is true, then there is no need to warn Christians about becoming like the false teachers. It's something that will never happen. But Peter believes it can happen. Read Peter's words at the end of the chapter where he warns the Christians he is writing to with these words, "Therefore, dear friends, since you have been forewarned, be on your guard so that you may not be carried away by the error of the lawless and fall from your secure position" (2 Peter 3:17). The King James Version says, "Beware lest ye also… fall." The word "also" means there have been others who have fallen. Who has Peter been talking about? The false teachers. The false teachers fell and so could they, even though they were Christians. Peter is warning his Christian brothers and sisters that they too could be led away just like the Christians who became false teachers were. Christians can return to the mud and vomit. Peter is holding up the false teachers as examples of that happening.

If the false teachers were never saved then they would still be dirty, but they are washed and only God can make the foulest clean. David understood this. That is why, after Nathan the prophet pointed out his sin, David asked God to "wash me, and I will be whiter than snow" (Psalms 51:7). Revelation 1:5 tells us it is Jesus Christ who has "washed us from our sins in his own blood" (KJV). The only one who could have washed the false prophets of their sins would have been Jesus by His blood which was shed on the cross at Calvary. In other words, they could not have been washed clean of their sins unless they had become Christians. There is no way to legitimately explain the language used in this passage in any other way.

Why are they worse off?

But the most difficult question of all to answer is, Why does the passage say, "the latter end is worse with them than the beginning" (2 Peter 2:20)? If the dog and pig were never converted, then they were, are now, and continue to be lost. And if you are lost, you are lost. What makes the situation worse? The answer is found in the previous passages mentioned (Hebrews 6:4-6 and Hebrews 10:26-29). The converted dog and pig can only be in a worse situation because they have turned away from their salvation and now have no hope of retrieving it.

This concept is found in many other places in the Bible, as was previously pointed out. Hebrews 10:38, for example, says, "the just shall live by faith: but if any man draw back, my soul shall have no pleasure in him" (KJV). Who is it who draws back? The just.

Jesus said, "No man, having put his hand to the plough, and looking back, is fit for the kingdom of God" (Luke 9:62 KJV). Who is not fit for the kingdom of God? It's not the person who refuses to plow, but the one who has already put his hand to the plow and looks back.

Objection

A Calvinist once wrote to me, "So, we get one chance to get it right. If we blow that one chance, then too bad. That interpretation is harsher than anything Calvinism teaches."

In his view, not offering anyone a second chance to be saved was harsher than not offering the majority of mankind even one chance. He assumed that what I was saying was that God refuses to give anyone a second chance despite their desire to have one. But that was a false assumption because such people do not desire to have a second chance. I wrote back to him, "Not at all. A second chance for the Christian who rejects Christ is not an option because the individual himself will not seek it. If you *taste and see that the Lord is good* (Psalm 34:8 and 1 Peter 2:3) and then turn from the Lord, why would you turn back to Him a second time? You have already known Him to be good, but you decided you were not interested in continuing the relationship anyway. The Lord will not change. He will always be good. So why would you desire something a second time that you already know you don't want from the first encounter? And if you decide to reject Christ after knowing Him to be good, you have rejected the only way to eternal life because there is no other way. 'No sacrifice for sins is left' (Hebrews 10:26). Even if someone should want to be reborn a second time after trampling the Son of God underfoot and treating as an unholy thing the blood of the covenant that sanctified them and insulting the Spirit of grace (Hebrews 10:29), God would be justified in rejecting such a request."

An analogy that might be helpful in understanding this one-chance-only concept would be that of a soldier serving in an army. You are not a soldier until you enlist (Calvinists would say you are drafted). If sometime after becoming a soldier you become a traitor, you are executed or, at the very least, dishonorably discharged. In either case, the act of treason permanently disqualifies you from a second opportunity to serve. No one thinks it unreasonable to deny a turncoat traitor another chance to be a loyal soldier.

The awkward attempts by Calvinists to debunk passages like 2 Peter 2:20-22 are many. One prevalent attempt involves the use of false assumptions. Rather than accept the obvious meanings stated in verses, Calvinists turn to baseless assumptions to make the verses mean what they want them to mean. Dubious assumptions play a major role in much of Reformed Theology. For example, to support their belief in eternal security, Calvinists contend that once someone discovers how awesome God is, they will remain eternally faithful to Him. That assumption is both unbiblical and completely false. Knowing how awesome God is has never guaranteed faithful obedience. The Israelites saw firsthand how awesome God is but that didn't stop them from turning away from Him. Judas lived with Jesus (God Himself) for years and saw how awesome He was. Angels (including Satan) knew how great, loving, and wonderful God was, yet they chose to reject the relationship they had with Him. Why would Christians (who know even less than the angels or even Judas about how awesome God is) be immune from turning away from Him? Even being chosen by God does not automatically result in love toward Him. The history of Israel demonstrates that being chosen by God results more often in turning away from God than it does in loving Him. There is not a single verse in the entire Bible that states a Christian will never abandon his/her faith. On the contrary, as has already been demonstrated, the Bible is full of verses that make it clear we can, indeed, abandon our faith and be lost forever.

Does God have a pencil without an eraser?

Calvinists will say that God's pencil does not need an eraser, because He never makes a mistake. Once He writes a person's name in the Book of Life, He will never erase it. They quote Revelation 3:5 as evidence for their contention: "He that overcometh, the same shall be clothed in white raiment; and I will not blot out his name out of the book of life" (KJV).

Assuming blotting out is the same as erasing, the critical words to understand in this passage are "he that overcometh." The verse doesn't say God will overcome or that His grace will enable the saved to overcome. No, the verse says the saved person must overcome to ensure salvation. The obvious implication is there will be those who do not overcome, and they *will be* blotted out of the book of life.

Exodus 32:33 reads: "The LORD replied to Moses, 'Whoever has sinned against me I will blot out of my book.'" God does, indeed, have an eraser. If believers are eternally secure, then those who are blotted out of God's book of life must be nonbelievers. The obvious question then is, Why were their names (as nonbelievers) listed in God's Book of Life in the first place?

There are simply far too many verses in the Bible that refute the Reformed concept of eternal security to believe it to be true.

It's not found in Scripture.

Furthermore, the glaring omission of even one verse in the Bible that states that a Christian will never leave God, or a believer will never stop believing, or any words to that effect makes for the argument that a believer can. If a believer cannot do any of these things, why doesn't the Bible say that?

But what about the verses Calvinists claim support a

belief in eternal security? A careful examination of the verses reveals that they do not teach what Calvinists claim. Consider the following examples of verses commonly quoted by believers in eternal security.

Examine the verses.

John 6:37-39 reads, "Whoever comes to me I will never drive away. For I have come down from heaven not to do my will but to do the will of him who sent me. And this is the will of him who sent me, that I shall lose none of all those he has given me, but raise them up at the last day."

Yes, Jesus said He will neither drive believers away nor lose them. What Christ did not say, however, is no believer will ever walk away from Him. Nowhere in Scripture does Christ say He will force believers to stay with Him or that he will not let believers leave Him. Thus, this passage is only assurance of Christ's part and not the believer's part. We can be sure Christ will never be the cause of us losing our salvation, but there is no guarantee given here that we are incapable of being the cause.

Grammatically, Christ is the subject in this passage, not the object. In other words, He will not lose or drive away the object (the believer). But when someone leaves, they (the believers) are the subject of the action and not the object. Thus, the statement can be (and is) true as to what Christ will and will not do regarding believers, but it does not even imply what believers may or may not do. Therefore, this passage cannot be used as a text to support eternal security.

John 10:27-28 reads, "My sheep listen to my voice; I know them, and they follow me. I give them eternal life, and they shall never perish; no one will snatch them out of my hand."

Here again, Christ is promising to protect believers (His sheep). He promises them eternal life and guarantees no one will ever snatch them out of His hand. What He doesn't promise, as in the previous passage, is that no one will ever *leave* His hand. Sheep are known to leave the fold and be lost.

Calvinists are quick to point out the words "no one will snatch them out," which they claim would include the believer himself.

That, however, is not true. The believer cannot snatch himself. You cannot lift yourself up and out. Snatching a person requires someone or something from the outside reaching down to lift a person away. So, the statement as worded remains true, even if the believer leaves on his own. Jumping out is not the same as being snatched out. Christ promises believers He will protect them from all outside (external) influences. He does not promise us protection from ourselves. He leaves out any mention here of the consequences of our own choices.

We are eternally secure as long as we choose to be.

In Romans 8:38-39, Paul says, "For I am convinced that neither death nor life, neither angels nor demons, neither the present nor the future, nor any powers, neither height nor depth, nor anything else in all creation, will be able to separate us from the love of God that is in Christ Jesus our Lord."

It could be said that this passage does not even refer to salvation, but rather to God's love from which nothing can separate us. More probable, however, is that the love "that is in Christ Jesus our Lord" refers to salvation from which nothing can separate us. If it is salvation and not just God's love, is Paul teaching eternal security here?

Paul, in these verses, specifically lists various persons and things that are unable to separate a believer from God's love. Notice that Paul is talking about everything outside of "us" not being able to separate "us" from God's love. That is not the same as saying we will never leave His love. In the King James Version, it says *nor any other creature*. Calvinists insist that because a believer is one of God's creatures, then the believer must be included in the list of things that cannot separate us from God's love. One cannot deny that a believer is one of God's creatures, but that does not make the statement say what Calvinists claim. We are not guaranteed eternal security by these verses. Once again, to separate two objects or persons requires an outside (third) party. To separate means to pull two things apart. You cannot pull two things apart if you are one of those two things. As before, the assurance is that no external forces (outside persons or things) are ever going to be able to come in and separate the believer from God's love. It does not say the believer cannot choose to move away from God's love on his/her own. Why else would Jesus tell his disciples to remain in His love (John 15:9) if they have no choice but to do so? His command makes no sense unless it is possible for them to leave His love. Jude wrote to "them that are sanctified by God" (i.e., Christians) and told them, "Keep yourselves in the love of God" (Jude 21). Why would Jude tell them to *keep yourselves in the love of God* if nothing can keep them from the love of God?

In Christ's high priestly prayer, Jesus says, "Those whom You gave Me I have kept; and none of them is lost" (John 17:12). Calvinists argue that those God gives Jesus are the elect and Jesus says *"none of them"* is lost.

The problem with quoting this verse as evidence for eternal security is that Jesus isn't talking here about all of the elect. He is talking only about His disciples and even one of them is lost. If you quote the complete sentence you find Jesus actually says, "none of them is lost except the son of perdition." Not only is the group limited to just the twelve disciples rather than all the elect, but even one of them (Judas) was lost. If anything, the verse disputes eternal security rather than supporting it.

Hebrews 6:19 compares our hope of eternal life to an anchor for the soul. Calvinists take that to mean our salvation is secure.

But *hope* of eternal life is not the same as a guarantee of it. The anchor metaphor also fails to prove eternal security when one considers how an anchor is secured. An anchor secures a boat only as long as the person in the boat doesn't choose to pull up or unhook the anchor and leave. Christ is our secure anchor as long as we remain connected to Him.

Hebrews 7:25 says Christ is "able to save completely those who come to God through him."

This passage tells us what Christ is able to do. This is very reassuring for anyone who might wonder if Christ will hold up His end of the new covenant. But being *able* to do something and actually *doing* it are two different things. There is no guarantee here that, because Christ is able to save completely, He is required to do so in every situation. Being able to do something and being under some kind of mandate to do it are not the same. It's wonderful to know that Christ is able to save "completely," but He won't do so if the believer doesn't want to be or refuses to be saved "completely." Christ promises to keep us secure and to keep His end of the new covenant, but He doesn't force us to keep our end.

We must continue trusting in Christ in order to fulfill our end of the new covenant agreement. This need for continued faith is explained in many verses found in the Bible, some of which were referenced earlier, including John 3:16. 1 Peter 1:3-5 is yet another one. Interestingly, this verse is sometimes quoted as evidence for eternal security. The verse reads,

> Praise be to the God and Father of our Lord Jesus Christ! In his great mercy he has given us new birth into a living hope through the resurrection of Jesus

Christ from the dead, and into an inheritance that can never perish, spoil or fade. This inheritance is kept in heaven for you, who through faith are shielded by God's power until the coming of the salvation that is ready to be revealed in the last time.

The operative words here are "through faith." We are shielded by the power of God "through faith." Our faith is required for us to receive eternal salvation.

The Bible doesn't contradict itself.

Most of the exegesis used by Calvinists to interpret verses that deal with eternal security is speculative and full of assumptions. In the case of the second set of verses that seem to support eternal security, Calvinists often try to make the verses say more than they actually do. By contrast, the exegesis used by non-Calvinists enables one to accept the actual wording of both sets of verses without contradiction. That's because non-Calvinists understand that the two sets of verses are not contradicting each other but complementing each other.

The passages that seem to support eternal security are dealing with the promises of God. These verses give Christians the assurance that God will not allow anything or anyone, including Himself, to take away our eternal life as long as we continue to believe. The other set of verses teaches us that we can choose to stop believing and, as a result, lose our salvation. All passages of the Bible must be consistent with each other. If Christians incorrectly interpret a few cherry-picked passages and press them into saying we cannot lose our salvation, then the Bible contradicts itself. Both sets of verses are found in the Bible and they cannot be reconciled if one believes in eternal security. The only way the two sets can be reconciled is to understand that they are talking about two different things. One set tells us God promises to keep His side of the new covenant agreement. The other set warns us that we must keep our side. God will not allow anything to keep us from heaven except ourselves. We are eternally secure as long as we want to be.

Why worry?

Christians want to believe in eternal security because the alternative is frightening. One could lose a great deal of sleep wondering if one has lost his salvation. That needn't happen, however, because as long as an individual has faith in Christ and His atonement, that individual has not lost his salvation. Furthermore, if one is concerned about his relationship with God that is a sign the person has not turned his back on God. God, of course, will never turn His back on a believer. So, there is no reason to worry.

Calvinists, on the other hand, do have a legitimate reason to worry. If eternal security is not true and Christians can fall from God's grace, then Reformed Theology is not true. So, Calvinists must force incredulous interpretations on all the passages that state that Christians can be lost. Their theological bias requires them to come up with meanings for verses that ignore good exegesis. Despite their efforts, however, the verses remain in the Bible for any literate Christian to read and be warned by.

Assumption # 7
Human Faith Leads to Pride

CALVINISTS ASSUME THAT if a person chooses of his own accord to trust Christ, he cannot escape being proud of himself for doing so. In other words, human faith inevitably leads to pride. Quoting Calvinist G. C. Berkouwer:

> In no form... is it possible to escape the conclusion that man owes his salvation not solely to God but also to himself. Still more accurately, he may thank himself – by virtue of his decision to believe – that salvation actually and effectively becomes his in time and eternity... This conclusion cannot in the long run be avoided and it is clear... it results in a certain amount of human self-conceit.[60]

Where does Berkouwer find evidence for his claim that "it is clear" faith "results in a certain amount of human self-conceit"? I have never met a Christian who was proud of himself for accepting God's gift of salvation. Christians are only grateful they did. More importantly, the Bible does not teach that pride must follow a "decision to believe." Romans 3:28 says, "We maintain that a person is justified by faith." The previous verse (verse 27) reads, "Where, then, is boasting? It is excluded. Because of what law? The law that requires works? No, because of the law that requires faith." The law that requires faith (trusting Christ to save us) excludes boasting, but it does not exclude faith. In fact, the verse says faith is *required*. Calvinists view faith as a meritorious work, even though the Bible does not.

As a result of their faith, Joshua and Caleb were saved by God from the giants and they alone entered the Promised Land. Shadrach, Meshach, and Abednego were willing to trust God and face the fiery furnace rather than bow down to an idol. God saved them from the flames. Daniel faced the lions' den rather than disobey God. As a result of his faith, God saved him from the lions. Did even one of these men "thank himself – by virtue of his decision to believe – for God's salvation?" Berkouwer says they all did because pride is an inevitable result of faith. He says, "This conclusion cannot in the long run be avoided and it is clear… it results in a certain amount of human self-conceit."

Rather than being criticized for "self- conceit," however, the Bible says these men "were all commended for their faith" (Hebrews 11:39) because they had the kind of faith that pleases God (Hebrews 11:6). Yet, according to Calvinists like Berkouwer, it is impossible for these men to have remained humble servants of God because they chose to put faith in God to save them.

How is it prideful to believe from our heart that we are foolishly sinful, to realize only Jesus can save us from our sins, to recognize our need to humbly kneel before the cross in great sorrow and remorse, to repent of our sin and ask Jesus for forgiveness, and to accept it when He gives it? I am unable to fathom how any of these things can be done with a sense of pride.

If a beggar is given a million dollars, does the beggar

become proud of himself for trusting the giver and accepting the gift? If he did nothing to deserve it, is it inevitable that he will be filled with self-conceit? What warrants the self-conceit? The beggar responds with gratitude, not pride. The idea that the beggar becomes proud of himself for willingly receiving the gift is absurd.

Lost and Found

Suppose someone is told not to wander into the forest because he will become lost and he does so anyway. His resulting lost condition is obviously his own fault. It may take some time before the person fully realizes he is unable to find his way back, but eventually he will come to that conclusion. Try as he might, he is hopelessly lost.

Now suppose a rescue party arrives to take the lost individual home. The lost person now has a choice to make. He can decide not to trust the rescuers and so decline their offer due to a lack of faith in their ability to save him from his situation. He may even deny his lost condition and so refuse to go with the rescuers. He might be too proud to admit he is lost and decide to continue to find his own way out. He might be unwilling to face anyone and the humiliation of having to admit his foolishness in going into the woods in the first place and so decline the offer to leave. He may even decide that after all this time he actually enjoys being lost or living alone in the forest. The wise person will, of course, decide to trust the rescuers, accept their offer for rescue, and return home safely.

After the lost man is home and the facts are known, does anyone report that the lost man assisted in his rescue? Certainly not, because he didn't assist in any way. In fact, the only part the lost man played in the whole situation was in creating a need for his rescue by becoming lost in the first place. To praise him for that act would be ridiculous. Nor would the man be filled with self-conceit for accepting the offer to be rescued. He would far more likely feel shame for being so foolish as to make his rescue necessary. His greatest feeling, however, would be a sense of gratitude that he was saved and no longer lost. There would be no sense of pride. Yet, that is the assumption of Calvinists when it comes to an individual's eternal rescue. Somehow the lost person who decides to accept God's offer to be rescued deserves some credit for his rescue. So, he will become proud of himself for doing his part. How can that be true? God cares enough about our lost condition to come to our rescue, He provides the means for our rescue, and He rescues us. He does it all, so man is due no praise.

Sproul wrote the following:

> The real question, however, is why does God save any person? I know of no more difficult a theological question to deal with than this one. I've been studying theology for many years, and I still can't come up with any exhaustive reason to explain why God would save me, or anyone else for that matter.
>
> Some people give a very simple answer to this question. They say that God saved you because you put your trust and faith in Christ when you answered the summons of the gospel. On the surface that's certainly a legitimate answer because we are justified through faith and we are called to make that response.
>
> But the deeper question is, Why did you respond to the gospel when you heard it, but someone else who heard it — even the very same presentation at the same moment — did not respond to it? What was there in you that caused you to respond positively while others are caused to reject it? I ask that about my own life. I could say the reason I responded was that I was more righteous than the other fellow. God forbid that I ever say that on the Judgment Day. I might think I'm more intelligent than somebody else,

but I wouldn't want to say that either. Some might say that I recognized my need more than somebody else recognized his need, but even that recognition is a mixture of at least some measure of intelligence and some measure of humility, most of which would find its ultimate roots in the grace of God. I have to say with the ancient man, there but for the grace of God go I. I can't give any reason other than God's grace for why I am saved.[61]

It's hard to understand how an intellect like Dr. Sproul who studied theology for many years was unable to come up with the answer as to why one person is saved and another is not. The answer is clearly given in the Scriptures. So, either Sproul deliberately ignored it or, more likely, he somehow missed it due to his theological bias. The Bible gives the answer. The one who trusts in Christ is wiser than the one who doesn't. Jesus Himself said, "The wise man builds his house upon the rock" (and that Rock is Jesus) and the foolish man does not (Matthew 7:24). The reason a person is saved is because he is wise enough to put his faith in Jesus. Psalm 14:1 tells us, "The fool says in his heart, 'There is no God.'" Thus, deists are wiser than atheists. In the same way, Christians are wiser than non-Christians. Paul tells Timothy, "You have known the Holy Scriptures, which are able to make you wise for salvation through faith in Christ Jesus" (2 Timothy 3:15). The foolish ignore the Word of God. I find it astounding that Sproul missed this truth after all his years of studying the Word. Jesus tells the story of the ten virgins, calling five of them wise and five of them foolish. The wise virgins prepared for the coming of the bridegroom (Jesus) and the foolish virgins did not. Trusting in Christ is the wise thing to do.

Calvinists howl at such an idea. They immediately respond by asking, "How can a person be so wise and not be proud of himself?"

Pride doesn't inevitably follow wisdom.

The answer is simple. If I am truly wise, I will remain humble. Calvinists, as they so often do, make an incorrect assumption. In this case, they assume pride inevitably follows wisdom. On the contrary, the truly wise are humble. Just because a drowning man is wise enough to grab hold of a life preserver that is thrown to him doesn't mean he will inevitably be full of self-conceit for doing so. Instead, he will be grateful that someone had a life preserver and was compassionate enough to throw it to him/her. Pride never enters the saved person's heart or mind because the person is too full of gratitude.

Do you think the prodigal son was proud of himself for returning to the father? The Bible says when he wised-up and *came to his senses,* he returned [on his own] to the father. Is it possible to conclude from the story that he failed to come in great humility, realizing what a fool he had been? By asking the father to be a lowly servant, is the son evidencing pride? Do you really think after the father welcomed him back, not just as a servant but as a son, he became full of self-conceit rather than sheer gratitude?

John 5:5-8 tells the story of the man at the pool of Bethesda who had an infirmity for 38 years and who, by his own admission, could do nothing to heal himself (verse 7). Christ asks him, "Do you want to get well?" There's little doubt the man said, *"Yes."* Is he therefore due some credit for his healing? That's a rhetorical question. The answer is obviously, No! Does the man evidence self-conceit for accepting the offer to be healed? No, because Jesus did it all, including making the offer in the first place.

Even though the man chose to accept Christ's offer for healing, no one (including the man himself) would say the man partially healed himself. Pride, therefore, is not even an issue. How is it that a man who requests healing for his body is undeserving of any credit for his healing, but a man who requests salvation for his soul does? Why would anyone "thank himself" for being wise enough to accept a desperately needed gift (physical healing, spiritual healing, or any other gift) if the person had done absolutely nothing to earn it?

In Luke 18:10-14, Jesus tells of two men who went up into the temple to pray, one a Pharisee and the other a tax collector. Jesus said, "The Pharisee stood and was praying this to himself: 'God, I thank You that I am not like other people: swindlers, unjust, adulterers, or even like this tax collector. I fast twice a week; I pay tithes of all that I get.' But the tax collector, standing some distance away, was even unwilling to lift up his eyes to heaven, but was beating his breast, saying, 'God, be merciful to me, the sinner!' I tell you, this man went to his house justified rather than the other; for everyone who exalts himself will be humbled, but he who humbles himself will be exalted."

What if Jesus had told the tax collector that he had been justified? According to Calvinists, the tax collector would have immediately become full of self-conceit. Calvinists claim he would instantaneously go from his humble admission of guilt to a sense of pride. Why? Because, according to Calvinists, the tax collector would believe he was justified by his admission of sin and his desire to be forgiven. But that's not how he received justification. He obtained justification because God chose to give it to him. Furthermore, there is no basis for assuming the tax collector would think he was justified by anything other than the mercy of God. On the contrary, it is safe to assume that the tax collector would be overwhelmed with gratitude rather than pride, knowing he did not deserve to be justified. He would go home knowing he was justified because of God's grace and God's grace alone. The fact that people have libertarian free will to choose and are responsible to repent and believe does not negate the truth that salvation is completely and totally of God alone.

In summary, the idea that pride is inevitable if one chooses to trust in Jesus is a total myth. It is a myth (an assumption) that has been perpetrated by Calvinists with absolutely no experiential or biblical evidence. The idea exists only in the minds of Calvinists (placed there by other Calvinists).

Assumption #8
We are not Christians by Choice

CALVINISTS DO NOT BELIEVE we choose to accept Christ of our own free will. They assume we are altogether passive as God chooses for us. The sole reason anyone believes in Jesus is because God causes them to believe. He makes believers out of the few He wants to save and sends the rest (the majority) to hell. If you examine those in the Bible who became believers in Christ, however, not one is said to have become a believer because God caused them to believe. Nor does anyone say they became followers of Christ because they had no choice. Despite the absence of any such statements, Calvinists still assume that God creates Christians against their natural desires based on other Scriptures that Calvinists believe teach individual predestination.

There are several verses Calvinists appeal to as evidence for their belief in individual predestination. The passage of Scripture most often referenced by Calvinists is the story of Jacob and Esau found in Genesis 25. Not only is this story taken from an Old Testament historical book, but the story is not even dealing with the subject of individual salvation. In Malachi 1:2-3, it states that God loved Jacob and hated Esau. Romans 9:11-13 reads, "Before the twins were born or had done anything good or bad—in order that God's purpose in election might stand: not by works but by him who calls—she was told, 'The older will serve the younger.' Just as it is written: 'Jacob I loved, but Esau I hated.'" Calvinists emphasize the fact that Paul states the grounds of God's election of Jacob over Esau did not lie in the actions of either brother. Furthermore, God not only selected Jacob over Esau, but Paul says God actually hated Esau.

Here we must apply the principle of biblical interpretation (hermeneutics) which says a theological conclusion drawn from an historical passage cannot differ from the teachings of the didactic passages. If there is a contradiction, then the conclusion drawn from the historical passage must be abandoned. For example, Paul was struck blind on the Damascus road. That historical fact does not mean we should conclude that everyone must be struck blind in order to be saved. That event was unique to Paul for a special purpose. The correct theology of how one is saved is taught in other instructional passages, and they make it clear that blindness is not a required element. In the same way, we should not conclude God does not love the lost based on the historical record of Jacob and Esau. The Bible has too many didactic passages that teach otherwise. Matthew 5:44, for example, tells us to love our enemies. The Bible also tells us to love our neighbors (everyone) as ourselves (Matthew 19:19). So, how do we explain the fact that God said He hated Esau?

There are a number of different English translations for the Hebrew word *sawnay*. "Hate" is one of those. It is also used in the sense of "reject" or "prefer less." In this context, it is similar to our being told by Christ that we should *hate* our fathers and mothers to be His disciple

(Luke 14:26). Obviously, Christ was not asking us to despise our parents, as we are told in other places in the Bible to love and honor our parents (e.g., Matthew 19:19). The idea here is that if our parents come between us and God, we must choose God over them. It is not required, however, that we must hate our parents in order to love God. One can love both. Only if the decision requires that we must choose one over the other are we to reject one. In the Genesis situation, God had to choose one brother over the other because He could not choose both to fulfill His plans for the Jews. God chose Jacob over Esau. The word "hated" then in this passage means God "rejected" Esau because the situation required a choice to be made. It is also clear that God was not saying He would save Jacob and/or send Esau to hell.

Because of his faith, Abraham was chosen by God to be the father of the nation of Israel. For each new generation of Abraham's lineage, a son had to be selected to be the one through whom the nation would continue. Thus, the line went from Abraham to Isaac to Jacob. Why God chose Jacob over Esau we do not know for certain. It would be reasonable to assume it was because God knew Jacob would make a better leader. We *do* know it had nothing to do with the amount of righteousness in either brother. We know this because God made the decision before they were even born before they "had done anything good or bad" (Romans 9:11). So, we cannot conclude Jacob was more righteous than Esau.

While we don't know why God chose Jacob, we do know what he was chosen for. He was chosen to become a leader of the Jews. He was selected for a special service. What he was not selected for was individual soul salvation. Again, God did not predestine Jacob to heaven nor Esau to hell. When examining predestination, Calvinists fail to distinguish between service and salvation. They are two separate things. Thus, we cannot conclude that the story of Jacob being chosen for service represents the way God deals with human salvation (choosing some over others). Nor can we conclude that Jacob was chosen for salvation in addition to service. There is no mention of his eternal destiny when he is chosen for service. Jacob was not selected for eternal life, but for the honor of being the one through whom God would work to create the nation of Israel. The Bible does not say Jacob or his descendants received eternal life, even though Jacob was chosen to perform a particular service. In fact, many of Jacob's descendants were condemned by God because of their wickedness. Conversely, Esau and his family were not condemned to hell, even though God did not choose Esau to lead Israel. Esau received many of God's blessings (Genesis 33:8-16). All this to say, the story of Jacob and Esau is not a demonstration of God's individual predestination to salvation.

Election to Service

We see the difference between being chosen for service and being chosen for salvation in several places in the Bible. We see it in both the Old and New Testaments. All the Jews, for example, were chosen by God for a special service, but they were not all saved. Hebrews 3:10-11 tells us that when God was speaking of the Israelites rescued out of Egypt, He said, "That is why I was angry with that generation; I said, 'Their hearts are always going astray, and they have not known my ways.' So, I declared on oath in my anger, 'They shall never enter my rest.'"

God's rest here is not talking about the Promised Land only, but His eternal rest (i.e., Heaven). This is made evident later in the book of Hebrews when the people of that day were warned not to make the same mistake the Jews did. Hebrews 4:1 states, "Therefore, since the promise of entering his rest still stands, let us be careful that none of you be found to have fallen short of it." Obviously, the Jews being addressed in Hebrews were already in the Promised Land, so not entering into God's rest meant they would not go to heaven. So again, even though the Old Testament Jews were God's *chosen* people, it did not mean they were all chosen for heaven. The Old Testament is full of examples of people being chosen for service, but not for salvation.

We see the same thing in the New Testament. Jesus told his disciples He had chosen them and they had not chosen Him. Did He mean they were personally saved through His irresistible grace? No. We know, for example, even though Judas was one of the chosen, he betrayed Christ. John 6:70 reads, "Jesus replied, 'Have I not chosen you, the Twelve? Yet one of you is a devil!'" The disciples were chosen for service in the same way Esau was chosen to serve Jacob. None of them were chosen for personal salvation. God chooses servants based on what the situation calls for. He chooses sons, however, on the basis of their receiving Him by faith. As John 1:12 tells us, "As many as received him, to them gave he power to become the sons of God, even to them that believe on his name" (KJV). Because God has to choose someone to do a particular job here on earth, it necessitates the rejection of everyone else for the job. Nobody, however, has to be chosen to go to heaven. Heaven is open to "as many as received him." So again, the way God may select the best candidate for service is not even a metaphor for the way an individual obtains eternal salvation.

Negative Service

Another Old Testament historical event Calvinists often quote in defense of their belief in individual predestination is the story of Pharaoh. The Bible says God "hardened Pharaoh's heart, and he would not let the Israelites go out of his country" (Exodus 11:10). The argument goes like this: It was God who hardened Pharaoh's heart and not Pharaoh himself. Pharaoh refused to let God's people go because God caused his heart to reject Moses's request. Because it was God who determined what Pharaoh would do, one must believe in individual predestination. There's no other explanation for what happened.

This is another example of trying to build a theology from a book of history rather than from the didactic books. As with the story of Jacob and Esau, the assumption is made that if one is chosen for a particular service, that also means the person is being chosen for salvation. The situation with Pharaoh has nothing to do with individual salvation. God hardened Pharaoh's heart, not against his eternal destiny, but against his letting the Israelites leave Egypt. Being chosen by God for a particular purpose can be negative as well as positive, as in this case.

Moreover, there are several ways to interpret this situation other than the one Calvinists insist upon. One way would be to understand it to be an exception to God's normal way of dealing with man, just as God made an exception to His natural laws when He stopped the sun for Joshua (Joshua 10:13) or when He brought it backwards for Hezekiah (2 Kings 20:11).

This interpretation is strengthened by the fact that Paul saw a need to explain why God would do what He did to Pharaoh. In Romans 9:17 Paul explains what happened to Pharaoh was done to show God's power and that His "name might be proclaimed in all the earth." And for those who think this is wrong (perhaps because they have not known God to operate this way), Paul points out God has the right to do whatever He desires. Paul says, "God has mercy on whom he wants to have mercy, and he hardens whom he wants to harden" (verse 18). It is interesting to note in this same chapter that Paul also refers to what might be considered the other exception – the story of Jacob and Esau.

If God should make an exception to a rule for His greater purpose, who are we to find fault with God? After all, God is the one who created us with our sense of right and wrong in the first place. How can we be justified in accusing God of wrongdoing when we would not even know right from wrong if He had not created us with such an ability? In verse 20, Paul asks this rhetorical question, "Shall what is formed say to the one who formed it, 'Why did you make me like this?'" While this might be one way to view these verses, such an interpretation is highly unlikely. The exception interpretation is weak, and it makes God inconsistent.

Another way to interpret Pharaoh's unusual situation is to realize Pharaoh made a decision to keep the Israelites in captivity long before Moses ever came on the scene to ask for their release. He made that choice when he first decided to enslave the Jews. All God did was take away any second chances he might have to change his mind. In other words, his choice from the beginning was made of his own free will and, once he had made up his mind, his fate was sealed. Pharaoh wasn't given a second chance. This interpretation is consistent with other passages that show that God only hardens men's hearts *after* (and because) they have first rejected His will. Isaiah 44:18 is an example. God shut the eyes of the Jews because of their previous idolatry. The passage is specifically talking about Jews who prayed to a wooden idol saying, "Save me! You are my god!" (verse 17). It was only after they had turned against God to worship idols that their eyes were shut, and their hearts could not understand. God's hardening is always a consequence of previous actions taken by sinners.

J. Vernon McGee explained the situation this way:

> If Pharaoh were a tenderhearted, sweet fellow who desired to turn to God and was happy to have Moses deliver the children of Israel because Pharaoh wanted

to do something for them, then it was mean of God to harden the heart of this wonderful Pharaoh. If that is the way you read it, friends, you are not reading it right. The hardening is a figurative word, which can mean twisting. It means God twisted the heart of Pharaoh. He was going to squeeze out what was in it. God's part in this was to bring to the surface that which was already there.[62]

Even Calvinists have to admit Pharaoh's heart was already hardened, if for no other reason than because of the Fall. God simply hardened securely what was already there. Pharaoh had hardened his heart against the Jews before God did. One cannot assume that God alone hardens hearts. People harden their own hearts. There are many didactic passages warning men not to "harden your hearts" (e.g., Hebrews 3:15).

The truth that a man can choose to harden his own heart is further bolstered by such Scriptures as Mark 3:5. In this passage, it tells us Christ looked around at the Pharisees and was "grieved for the hardness of their hearts." Why would Christ be grieved with something He or the Father did? The answer is He wouldn't, so neither He nor the Father hardened their hearts; the Pharisees did. God only securely hardens hearts that are already hardened.

We see this in the case of Pharaoh. He had a hardened heart even before God further hardened it. We also see that Pharaoh was chosen by God not in regard to his personal salvation, but for an act of *service* (albeit a negative one).

Another Verse Used to Support Individual Predestination

Jesus said in Matthew 25:34, "Then the King will say to those on his right, 'Come, you who are blessed by my Father; take your inheritance, the kingdom prepared for you since the creation of the world.'"

The verse says the kingdom was prepared since the creation of the world. It does not say God's blessing was given then. If you read the verse in context, you discover that the blessing was given as a reward for what the people did. It was given after the actions of the people. The people were blessed for feeding Jesus when He was hungry, giving Him drink when He was thirsty, and so on. The "sheep" entered into life eternal because they had acted differently toward Christ than the "goats." If anything, this verse refutes the idea of individual predestination in which man is altogether passive.

Vessels of Honor and Dishonor

In Romans 9:21, Paul said, "Does not the potter have the right to make out of the same lump of clay some pottery for special purposes and some for common use?" The King James Version uses the word "vessels" instead of "pottery." Calvinists contend that this verse means God (as the potter) has the right to save some individuals and not others. And He does so without consulting the pottery beforehand.

There are several problems with this interpretation. For one, the difference in the vessels (pottery) refers to the two kinds of *service* they are used for (*special* and *common use*) and not their eternal destinations. If the illustration was referring to saved versus unsaved, then the vessels would not be described in terms of ways they are used, but in terms of whether they are kept or destroyed.

Calvinists point out that the next verse (verse 22) refers to vessels *prepared for destruction*. But that verse is prefaced by the word "if." Not that this would actually happen, but what *if* it did. In addition, the vessels prepared for destruction are described in the Greek in the middle voice. The middle voice signifies that those being referred to prepared themselves for destruction, not that God predestined them for destruction. Thus, the vessels were deserving of destruction, but were not inescapably doomed to it. We find this to be the case when we go back and read Jeremiah 18, which is the passage Paul is quoting here.

The Nation of Israel

When we read Jeremiah 18:1-10, the first thing we discover is that the passage is not even talking about individual souls, but about the nation of Israel. Jeremiah watches a potter make a pot (vessel) that was *marred in his hands*, so he made it into *another pot, as seemed best to him* (verse 4). At that point, Jeremiah says, "Then the word of the Lord came to me. He said, 'Can I not do with you, Israel, as this potter does?' declares the LORD. 'Like clay in the hand of the potter, so are you in my hand, Israel'" (verse 6).

Not only is the passage talking about the nation of Israel, but it also informs us that the nation (or any nation) is not inevitably doomed to destruction but is going to receive God's mercy or His wrath based on what the nation does. Immediately following verse 6, we read, "If at any time I announce that a nation or kingdom is to be uprooted, torn down and destroyed, and if that nation I warned repents of its evil, then I will relent and not inflict on it the disaster I had planned. And if at another time I announce that a nation or kingdom is to be built up and planted, and if it does evil in my sight and does not obey me, then I will reconsider the good I had intended to do for it" (verses 7-10). God will change His mind about whom He will have mercy on and whom He will not, based on what is done by the vessels. The choice is up to the people.

Paul goes on to explain in the next chapter that regardless of which kind of vessel you are, you can be saved by calling on God. He writes, "For there is no difference between Jew and Gentile—the same Lord is

Lord of all and richly blesses all who call on him, for, 'Everyone who calls on the name of the Lord will be saved'" (Romans 10:12-13).

Finally, if the vessels were created by the potter for the specific purpose of destroying them, that would mean God creates some people simply for the purpose of sending them to hell, which makes Him monstrous.

We find this same vessel illustration used again by Paul in 2 Timothy 2:19 where he exhorts Christians to *depart from iniquity*. He then tells them, "There are not only vessels of gold and of silver, but also of wood and clay, some for honor and some for dishonor. Therefore, if anyone cleanses himself from the latter, he will be a vessel for honor" (2 Timothy 2:20-21 NKJV). Notice it says "if anyone cleanses *himself*, he will be a vessel for honor."

In every instance where the vessel illustration is found in Scripture (including Romans 9), the vessels of honor and vessels of dishonor have a choice as to which they will ultimately become. Thus, there is no support in any of them for a belief in individual predestination.

God's Mercy

Calvinists like to zero in on verse 15 where God says, "I will have mercy on whom I will have mercy." They assume that this verse means God decides who is saved and who is not. But that is not what the verse says. Calvinists do not ask themselves, Who is it that God has decided to have mercy on? The answer is not that He has mercy on those He has predestined to eternal life without giving any reason. In context, Paul is informing his readers that God has mercy on Gentiles as well as Jews.

The Jews could not accept the idea that God would have mercy on Gentiles. After all, the Jews were His chosen people. They were convinced God's mercy was only given to them. It was for that reason Paul reminds them what God said to Moses: "I will have mercy on whom I will have mercy" (Exodus 33:19). Yes, God decides on whom He will have mercy and He has decided to have mercy on both Gentiles and Jews. He will not have mercy on those who attempt to earn it by keeping the law (by their own efforts) even if they are chosen people. Paul's point is that no one is chosen for salvation through works, which is what the Jews were trying to do.

That is what the illustration of Jacob and Esau teaches and why Paul refers to it here. God chose Jacob over Esau without regard to their works (even before they were born and could have done anything good or bad). That's what doing "good or evil" is. It's trying to be righteous through our good behavior. The story makes it clear that God does not choose someone over someone else on the basis of their own righteousness. That does not necessarily lead to the conclusion that faith and repentance have nothing to do with it. Paul is simply explaining that the reason some are chosen over others (whether for service or salvation) has nothing to do with their works. God will have mercy on whomever He chooses, and He chooses to have mercy on those who repent of their sins and put their faith in Christ rather than on those who try to earn it by commandment keeping.

Using Romans 9 as evidence for individual predestination can only be done if the chapter is taken out of context. When read in context, rather than proving Calvinism, Romans 9 actually refutes it. The vessels we become depends on us, not by works but by faith.

Other Verses

After Paul and Barnabas had finished preaching, Acts 13:48 states that "As many as were ordained to eternal life believed" (KJV). It is worth noting that this verse is again an historical account and not a didactic verse. The writer is not teaching doctrine here but recording history. Even so, it is a favorite among Calvinists. Calvinists assume it was God who ordained these Gentiles to eternal life because only He can ordain (predestine) salvation.

But the verse doesn't say it was God who ordained anyone for eternal life. If Calvinists are correct, the verse would read "as many as God ordained for eternal life." But it doesn't. Even if you interpret this verse to mean God ordained these people for eternal life, one must ask, *Why* were they ordained? They may have been ordained because God foreknew they would respond positively to the Gospel. But that question need not be asked because God is not the one who ordained them for eternal life. If you read the beginning of the verse, you find that the people ordained themselves for eternal life by gladly embracing the message of eternal life.

Once again, like Romans 9:22, the verb in Greek is in the middle voice. The middle voice signifies that those being referred to prepared themselves for eternal life. This is further evidenced by the context. In context, the Gentiles' response to the gospel is being contrasted with that of the Jews. The Jews rejected the gospel and thus judged *themselves* to be unworthy of eternal life (verse 46), whereas the Gentiles received it gladly and embraced the message of eternal life (verse 48). In both cases the decision was a matter of free choice.

Calvinists ask, In what way did these Gentiles ordain themselves to eternal life before Paul and Barnabas preached to them? The answer is by being open to the Gospel, unlike the Jews who were not. That's why it took place *prior* to Paul's and Barnabas's preaching. If they had not been open to the preaching, then they would not have listened to it nor would they have been saved.

Later in Acts, Paul uses similar words. After reminding the Jews that they were unwilling to turn to God, Paul tells them that "God's salvation has been sent to the Gentiles, and they will listen" (Acts 28:28). The Gentiles were willing to do what the Jews were not willing to do. The

Gentiles chose to listen. Rather than saying the Jews were not of the elect but the Gentiles were, the verse tells us the difference in the two groups was in the response they chose. God's salvation was offered to the Gentiles; not because God predestined to save them and not the Jews, but because of their openness to God and His truth.

An excellent exegesis of this verse by Greek scholar Prof. Jack Cottrell can be found in Appendix B.

Robert Shank also explains how the Greek mitigates against the Reformed understanding of this verse. He points out that the Greek word for "ordained" is *tassô*. *Tassô* means "dispose" or "determine." It does not mean "predisposed" or "pre-determined." Being ordained is not the same as being preordained from eternity's past. Notice that the word used by the author is not "ðñïåôïìéÜæù " which means "to prepare before, to make ready beforehand" (Thayer). Nor is the word "ðñïïñíñíáù " used, which means "(1) to predetermine, decide beforehand; (2) in the NT of God decreeing from eternity; (3) to foreordain, appoint beforehand" (Thayer). These were the words New Testament authors used when speaking of that which was predetermined or foreordained, but these are not the words used in Acts 13:48. The word used is "ôåôáãìåíïé," which includes no idea of predestination or foreordination. If the author wanted to communicate predestination to eternal life, he had Koine Greek words available to him to do so, but these he didn't use. Nor does anything in the passage suggest that the author was touching upon a free-will controversy. Instead, he is making a general reference to the fact that it was a fruitful conversion of the Gentiles, in contrast to the unbelieving Jews. Shank writes: "The fact that human agency is explicitly asserted in verse 46 strongly militates against any assumption of divine agency in verse 48."[63] Acts 11:21 says that "a large number who believed turned to the Lord." Notice that they believed first before turning to the Lord. Elsewhere in Acts, *tetagmenoi* is clearly referring to the actions, attitudes, and decisions of people, rather than to something divinely ordained (e.g., Acts 15:2; 28:23). Nowhere else in the entire Bible is *tetagmenoi* used of election. Acts 14:23 reads, "When they had ordained [*tetagmenoi*] them elders in every church."

Do Calvinists infer from this verse that the elders were foreordained to be elders? If not, why do Calvinists read a foreordination into Acts 13:48?

Dr. Brian Abasciano, a notable Greek and New Testament scholar, writes,

> The best understanding of 'tasso' [appointed] in Acts 13:48 is that it refers to Gentiles who were 'in position for eternal life' — 'ready for eternal life' — or even 'intent on obtaining eternal life' (particularly in contrast to the Jews of the same episode who opposed Paul and rejected the gospel, and so who judged themselves unworthy of eternal life [Acts 13:46]), and that the most accurate translation of the phrase in question would be something like: 'as many as were disposed to eternal life believed' or 'as many as were aligned for eternal life believed' or 'as many as were positioned for eternal life believed.'[64]

Dr Abasciano also quotes retired professor Carl Conrad, who is an incredibly knowledgeable Greek scholar and an expert on Greek voice in particular. Conrad said this regarding Acts 13:48:

> The author clearly is not concerned to make a statement about how it happened that these particular Gentiles were "ordained to eternal life" or about WHO ordained them to eternal life–he wants to say only that they were in this state of being "in line" and so believed.
>
> I really don't think anything more is meant by this

phrase than we mean by saying "All those who were prepared for the test passed it with flying colors." Nothing is said about who prepared the persons in question, whether they had hit the midnight oil for several nights in a row or someone had given them half a dozen help sessions to make sure that they understood all the problems on which they would be examined. What the phrasing says is nothing more than "those who were ready for the test passed it" and of course it's also implied that "those who weren't ready didn't pass it."

Matters regarding this verse are that simple and there's no need to make this verse the buttress for more than it actually says.[65]

Does this passage support individual predestination?

Calvinists claim that Ephesians 1:4-5 is evidence for individual predestination, but their particular interpretation is based upon their presuppositions and theological bias. For example, when they quote Ephesians 1:4, "He chose us in Him before the creation of the world," they often leave off the rest of the verse which says, "to be holy and blameless in his sight." Paul is not saying that God chooses certain people for salvation. Paul is writing to Christians and is telling them that we (Christians) are chosen *to be holy and blameless* just as we are *to be conformed to the image of His Son* (Romans 8:29). The verse is telling us *what* God has chosen Christians to be. Even if you leave off the words, "to be holy and blameless," the verse says, "He chose us in Him" not "He chose us *to be* in Him." In other words, even if one extracts just part of the verse, it would be saying that Christians (those Paul is writing to) were chosen because they are *in Christ* (already in Him). Thus, even without the complete wording of the verse, it would not be saying that God chose who would become Christians for reasons known only to Him. The verse tells us the reason we are chosen is because we are in Christ. And we have a choice as to whether we are in Christ or not.

The next verse, Ephesians 1:5, informs us that "He predestined us for adoption to sonship through Jesus Christ." Calvinists claim the words speak for themselves. God *predestined us for adoption*. Once again, there is a failure to complete (or at least, emphasize) the entirety of what Paul is saying. Paul ends his sentence with the words *through Jesus Christ*. What is predestined here is the *how* of salvation (*through Jesus Christ*) not anyone's individual salvation. God predestined that it would be through Jesus Christ that people would be adopted into His family. Even if you pull out just the words "predestined us for adoption," nothing is said about *why* God predestined anyone for adoption. The previous verse (verse 4) tells us why a person is chosen. It is because God foresaw that they would be in Christ. And we are in Christ by faith. Choosing to place our faith in Christ is required. Thus, salvation is conditional. The Apostle John explained this conditional adoption in John 1:12: "But as many as received Him, to them gave He power to become the sons of God, even to them that believe on His name." We become "sons of God" (adopted) as a result of our belief on His name (meeting the conditions). It is not because of an arbitrary predestination by God.

Ephesians 1:11: "In Him also we have obtained an inheritance, being predestined according to the purpose of Him who works all things according to the counsel of His will" (NKJV). Calvinists ask how anyone can argue that we are saved according to our own will when this verse states that we are predestined according to God's purpose and will. Again, such exegesis is based upon theological bias. Leaving aside the fact that Paul's main point is that what was predestined was that we obtain our inheritance through Christ ("in Him"), Calvinists approach the verse with the presupposition that God's will does not include giving people a choice to accept or reject the Gospel. Calvinists make this assumption even though the verse says nothing of the kind. God made man in His image, which includes a free will. This verse does not say God predestines people against their will or that they have no choice in the matter. Calvinists simply assume that it does based on their belief system. Furthermore, we know it is not God's will that any should perish, so willingly predestining people to perish would be against God's will, resulting in God contradicting Himself or being a schizophrenic. If God wills that all be saved, but all are not saved, then it has to be because people are capable of accepting or rejecting His will. Thus, God's will includes humans having free choice. Calvinists do not believe this.

Greek scholar Professor Jack Cottrell offers an additional reason to reject the Calvinistic interpretation of this verse. He explains that the verse is not even referring to individual election but to corporate election. Paul is speaking of the predestination of the two different categories of the human race as commonly distinguished in his day (i.e., the Jews and the Gentiles). This is based on two facts: (1) the sudden shift from first person plural "we" (Jews) in verse 12 to second person plural "you" (Gentiles) in verse 13; and (2) the underlying theme of the letter as expressed in 2:11-3:21 which is God's "eternal purpose" (3:11) of uniting Jews and Gentiles together through Jesus Christ into a single body, the church.

Those who think that corporate election also means individual election of each member of the corporate group are committing the logical fallacy of division. Just because Israel was a chosen nation did not mean that every person in that nation was chosen, individually, for eternal life. Jesus "chose" a group of disciples, but not every individual disciple was saved (e.g., Judas).

Anyone who wants to can sign up for a cruise with Carnival. All are promised a great time. But only those who go on the cruise will visit the Bahamas, eat lavishly, and be thoroughly entertained, because that is what is preplanned. The group is ordained to have a good time. But which individuals will be in the group is not predestined. That is up to each individual to decide if he/she wants to be in the group promised such luxury. In the same way, God has preordained that a certain group of people will go to heaven, but which individuals will be in the group is not predestined. The theme of Ephesians 1 is corporate election, not individual election.

Ephesians 2:10: "For we are God's handiwork, created in Christ Jesus to do good works, which God prepared in advance for us to do." If our good works are prepared in advance, then predestination must be true. So say Calvinists.

This verse is saying the same thing as Romans 8:29 and Ephesians 1:4. God has prepared in advance what Christians should be and do. It is not anyone's individual salvation that is *"prepared in advance"* but the *"good works"* we should do following our conversion.

Do any of these verses support individual predestination?

2 Thessalonians 2:13: "God hath from the beginning chosen you to salvation through sanctification of the Spirit and belief of the truth" (KJV). If the verse had ended with the words "chosen you to salvation" then one could rightly argue for individual predestination. But the verse doesn't end there, nor does any other verse end that way. This verse is explaining that God decided from the beginning *how* people were chosen for salvation, not *who.* They were chosen through the *"sanctification of the Spirit and belief of the truth."* People cannot believe the truth before they are even born, so how could God predestine them through something that hadn't happened yet un-

less He did so by His foreknowledge? People are chosen
for salvation based on God foreknowing they would believe in Jesus. Paul is here giving thanks that the
Thessalonians were not like the people he described earlier in the chapter, those who *refused to love the truth and
so be saved* (verse 10). The Thessalonians chose to believe
the truth, while the others did not. That is why God chose
them for salvation. Their election was conditional.

2 Timothy 1:9: "He has saved us and called us to a
holy life—not because of anything we have done but because of his own purpose and grace. This grace was given
us in Christ Jesus before the beginning of time." Calvinists point out that this verse tells us God saved us "because of His own purpose and grace."

But what is God's purpose and grace? Calvinists assume individual predestination is God's purpose and
grace, but that is not what the verse says. From the
wording, one could just as easily assume (depending
on one's theological bias) that God's purpose and grace
is that we be saved through faith in Jesus Christ. Neither assumption can be proven from the words found
in this verse. So, what do we find to be true from the
actual wording?

For one, we once again find *what* we are saved to –
a holy life. We also find that we are not saved through
works (*anything we have done*). What we do *not* find is
anyone's individual salvation being given to them before the beginning of time. What was given was God's
plan that His grace would be "given us in Christ Jesus."
God predestined that it would be Christ Jesus through
whom His will and grace would come. To assume individual predestination is being taught by this verse
is totally unwarranted.

1 Peter 1:20: "He indeed was foreordained before the
foundation of the world but was manifest in these last
times for you" (NKJV). Whenever Calvinists see the word

"foreordained" they immediately assume it is individual salvation that is foreordained.

But that is just one more of their false assumptions. Christ was foreordained to be the Savior of the world before the foundation of the world. Like 2 Timothy 1:9, nothing in the wording of this verse even suggests that a person's individual salvation was foreordained. The reason Christ was foreordained to be the Savior of the world was because God knew the world would need a Savior. There's only two possible ways God would have known the world would need a Savior. Either He foreknew man would sin, or He predestined man to sin. Which way makes God the author of the very thing He hates (sin)? See Assumption 12 for a discussion on these two views.

Peter writing to Christians tells them, "You are a chosen people" (1 Peter 2:9).

No one questions the fact that Christians are a chosen people. The question is, *Why* are they chosen? They are chosen because they have met the conditions for being chosen – they have put their faith in Christ. Two verses earlier, Peter says the chosen people are *you who believe* (verse 7). Thus, the passage tells us something that Calvinists say we have no way of knowing. It tells us *why* people are chosen (because they believe). The passage in no way teaches individual predestination. If anything, it teaches just the opposite.

Jesus told a parable about a king who invited people to his son's wedding, but they refused to come. So, the king told his servants to gather people from off the streets (highways), both bad and good. The parable was probably meant to teach that the Jews had rejected Christ, so God went to the Gentiles. But even one of those who came to the wedding did not prepare properly. He failed to wear the proper wedding garment and was subsequently cast out. Following this parable, Jesus said, "Many are called, but few are chosen" (Matthew 22:14).

Calvinists assume this verse proves that God chooses who is saved. But Calvinists fail to ask, "Why are they chosen?" Calvinists don't ask this question because they have no idea why God chooses some and not others. Non-Calvinists know people are chosen because they respond positively to the calling. That's what this parable teaches. That's also why only a *few* are chosen, because only a few respond to God's calling. If God chooses for people, why does He only choose a few? Why not choose the majority of the people or, at the very least, half of them? And, if people have no choice, why bother to call those you have not chosen? Doesn't the king know he is wasting his time calling those who will not respond unless he causes them to respond? Is the king unaware of their condition of total depravity? Perhaps the king enjoys teasing people by calling them with no intention of choosing them. Is the king ignorant or just dishonest and cruel? No, God is none of these things, so His calling must be genuine and the reason few are chosen is because few are willing to come to the wedding feast.

There is another point being made by this parable. One of those who came to the wedding failed to meet the conditions required for attending the wedding and so was cast out. Thus, attendance is conditional. One might even suggest that the parable teaches that eternal security is not true because the man cast out was already at the wedding. Such an idea is unlikely as it is probably reading more into the story than Jesus intended. Even less likely, however, is that Jesus intended the parable to teach individual predestination.

Revelation 13:8: "All inhabitants of the earth will worship the beast—all whose names have not been written in the Lamb's book of life, the Lamb who was slain from the creation of the world." Calvinists assume this verse means that the names of the saved were written into the Book of Life from the creation of the world because the beast worshipers' names were not.

There is no exegetical basis for making such an assumption. The verse does not state that any names were absent from the Lamb's Book of Life because God predestined them to be absent. So, one cannot assume that the names of the elect must have been there. The only indication given for why names were not in the Book of Life was because they chose to worship the beast.

If the names of the elect were written in God's Book of Life before the creation of the earth, it is apparent that the angels have never seen the names. Luke 15:10 informs us that, "There is rejoicing in the presence of the angels of God over one sinner who repents." If the angels had seen the person's name in the Book of Life, that would have been the time to rejoice because that is when God decided to save them (according to Reformed Theology), not later when they repent. Even more telling is the fact the angels rejoice over what the sinner does and not over what God did. The verse does not say the angels rejoice over the fact God regenerated a sinner, or the angels rejoice when God saves another one of His elect, or the angels rejoice because God gave faith to one of His elect enabling the sinner to believe. No, the verse says the angels rejoice *over one sinner who repents*. There is nothing in the verse that indicates there was something involved other than the sinner's decision to repent. Rather than supporting the idea that God predestines individuals who have no say in the matter, Luke 15:12 supports just the opposite.

Revelation 17:8: "The inhabitants of the earth whose names have not been written in the book of life from the creation of the world will be astonished." Because this verse says there will be people whose names "have not been written in the book of life from the creation of the world," Calvinists assume that means they were predestined for hell.

But the verse doesn't say *why* their names were not written in the Book of Life. As was the case for Revelation 13:8, their names could have been excluded from the Book of Life for any number of reasons. Because of their theological presuppositions, Calvinists just assume their exclusion is solely because God predestined them to damnation. The context, however, does not indicate that God was the sole reason their names were never written in the Book of Life.

Furthermore, the verse does not even apply to everyone who is lost. Those referred to here are specifically those people who will be on earth during the reign of the beast and, at that time, "all inhabitants of the earth will worship the beast" (Revelation 13:8). In that sense, it was predestined that their names would not be written in the Book of Life from the creation of the world because God foreknew they would take the mark of the beast rather than trust in Christ. It was even prophesied such people would be lost. They do not represent all unregenerate people but specifically those left on earth following the Rapture. Obviously, they are lost but even they are lost by their own failure to choose wisely. Thus, Revelation 17:8 does not support individual predestination. Calvinists force the verse to say something it doesn't.

Most of the above verses that Calvinists often quote can only be used to support individual predestination if you make them say more than they do. This is the same thing Calvinists do with verses that they claim teach eternal security. Adding ideas which are not actually stated in a passage is not done out of good exegesis but out of theological bias.

Assumption #9
God does not Use His Foreknowledge
When Making His Decisions

A PASSAGE ARMINIANS often appeal to as evidence against individual predestination is Romans 8:29-30: "For whom He foreknew, He also predestined to be conformed to the image of His Son, that He might be the firstborn among many brethren. Moreover, whom He predestined, these He also called; whom He called, these He also justified; and whom He justified, these He also glorified." Arminians believe this passage tells us God used His foreknowledge when deciding whom He saves. Calvinists, of course, disagree. They believe God predestined who would be saved and He did not use His foreknowledge when making His determinations.

Sproul made this statement: "In actuality, Romans 8:29-30 militates against the prescient view of election. Paul begins with foreknowledge and then progresses through the 'golden chain' of salvation via predestination, calling, justification, and glorification. The text is elliptical: it does not include the term *all*, but it tacitly implies the word (most translations of the Bible add it)."[66]

After checking over fifty different translations of this text, not one was found to include the word "all." Only The Living Bible (which is a paraphrase) used the word.

Continuing to quote Sproul: "Nevertheless, the sense of the text is that all whom God foreknows (in whatever sense he foreknows them) he predestines. And all whom he predestines he calls. And all whom he calls he justifies. And all whom he justifies he glorifies."[67]

If the text implies the word *all*, then everyone will be saved. The verses would read, "All He foreknew, He also predestined…" Since God foreknows everyone then *all* will be predestined. That would be universalism. Unless God saves everyone, there must be something unique about the people God foreknows that results in their predestination.

Who does God foreknow?

Many believe the Greek word *proginosko* (foreknow) can be used in the sense of fore-loving. Calvinists suggest then that God fore-loved the elect. The problem with such an interpretation is that you can't have an intimate loving relationship with someone who is unborn. So, who is being referred to as those whom God foreknew (fore-loved)?

There are those who contend that the earliest scholars interpreting this passage believed it was referencing those in the Old Testament who did not know Christ. Paul was telling the Jews of his time that those of the past were not lost but were also predestined to be conformed to the image of His Son. The only other usage of the word *proginosko* in the book of Romans is found in chapter 11 verse 2. It reads, "God has not rejected His people whom He foreknew." It is clear that Paul is not talking about the unborn elect here, but His people. It is unreasonable to suggest that in his one other use of the word *proginosko* he is referring to a different group of people entirely.

Leighton Flowers in a "Soteriology 101" blog dated January 7, 2016, stated the following:

> As in Romans 11:2, Paul is simply referring to saints of old in former times who loved God and were known by Him. Paul said, "The man who loves God is known by God" (1 Cor. 8:3). And men like Elijah and those who refused to bow a knee to false gods did love God and thus were known by him in the past. They were foreknown (previously known) by God, as they had an intimate personal relationship with God in the past. There is no reason to add all the esoteric theological baggage of God looking through corridors of time or making arbitrary "sovereign" choices about whom He will and will not love before the world began.
>
> "Foreknow" (or even "forelove") refers to God's intimate relationship with people who loved Him in the past (like Abraham referenced in Rom. 4:22-5:5). There is nothing in this or any other text that supports the concept of a mystical pre-selection of certain individuals out of the mass of humanity in eternity past. It always can simply be interpreted as in reference to those known by God in former times.

In the late 1800s, W.T. Moore, Ph.D. was the Dean (and later became the President) of The Bible College of Missouri. He was a scholar and well versed in Greek grammar. He translated Romans 8:29-30 and agreed that the reference was to Old Testament men and women of faith. He wrote, in part:

> Some of these old heroes are mentioned in the eleventh chapter of Hebrews. To sum up the whole case, this foreknowledge of God is simply his acknowledg-

ment of real historic characters whose faithfulness in the past is referred to as proof that even now all who love God will secure his help and final victory provided they continue in the grace which God has so abundantly provided.

It should be noticed that all this foreknowing, foreordaining, calling, justifying and glorifying is in the past tense Greek aorist and has no reference whatever to the future. The apostle speaks of every act as something already accomplished and makes no reference whatever to the fact that what was done was in the counsels of God before the world was.

The passage makes no reference at all to anything involved in the controversy between Calvinists and Arminians.

Dr. Johnathan Pritchett, of Trinity College of the Bible and Theological Seminary, made the following observation:

> One can't import language from Ephesians or 1 Peter ("before the foundation of the world") or language of foreseen faith into the passage that isn't there just because buzzwords like foreknowledge and predestination have the phrase nearby those words in other epistles written for different occasions in different contexts later than Romans.
>
> What Romans 8:29-30 is saying is that those God foreknew prior to the time of Paul's writing were also predestined to be shaped into the Christ icon, and also named, declared right, and highly honored. What it certainly is not is some chain of individualist redemption... golden or otherwise.

What does God foreknow?

Regardless of whom the verse is referring to, one must

ask, What is it that God foreknew about these individuals? The Bible tells us He foreknew their hearts. In the two previous verses (verses 27 and 28) it says that God *searches the hearts* and knows *them that love God.* God knew those who loved Him in the past (heroes of the Old Testament) and He foreknows those who will love Him in the future. God knows and foreknows everything because He is omniscient. He doesn't have to "look down the corridors of time" to see what happens. He already knows everything that will happen. But Calvinists believe God's foreknowledge of people's hearts was not a factor when He determined who would go to heaven and who would go to hell. In fact, how people respond to the Gospel was irrelevant to His decisions. One has to wonder what purpose God's foreknowledge serves if it is never involved when He makes His determinations.

God predetermined that people who sin would end up in hell. How would God know if a person sinned without the use of His foreknowledge? The only way God could know a person would sin, without active foreknowledge, would be for God to determine that the person sin. This is the only conclusion Calvinism leads to. That means that God sends people to hell for committing sins that He determined they commit. How can such a "god" be called good?

It is no secret what God can do.

On the other hand, if God predestines people to hell based on His foreknowledge of their sin against Him, why would He not use that same ability (prescience) to determine who goes to heaven based on their faith in Him? Even Calvinists admit that God foreknows all things. That would include knowing who will respond in faith to the Gospel. But knowing that is not the reason why God saves some and not others according to Calvinism. Calvinists believe God predestines certain people for salvation and

He gives us absolutely no idea why. He saves for reasons known only to Him and He wants to keep His reasons hidden. In fact, Calvin said we shouldn't even try to understand the heart of God in this matter because such efforts are futile.

> First then, let them remember that when they inquire into predestination they are penetrating into the sacred precincts of divine wisdom. If anyone with carefree assurance breaks into this place, he will not succeed in satisfying his curiosity and he will enter a labyrinth from which he can find no exit... [God] has set forth by His Word the secrets of His will that He has decided to reveal to us. These He decided to reveal in so far as He foresaw that they would concern us and benefit us.[68]

Calvin's statement is yet another huge assumption held by Calvinists. Arminians don't believe God desires to be secretive about His heart, but wants us to know just how great His love is for us. God doesn't hide His motives for doing what He does. He is motivated by love and wants us to know that. Yet, Calvinists believe that God predestines individuals to their eternal fates without giving them a clue as to why. The Bible was not written to keep God's motives a secret but to reveal God and His love. God reveals in the Scriptures all of the following: His motive for, means of, conditions for, and results of salvation. Why then would He not also reveal the who of salvation? Calvinists believe God keeps that a secret, but they don't know why.

John 3:16 (among many other verses) tells us His *motive* in providing salvation for the lost is His love. God "foreordained before the foundation of the world" that Christ would be man's only Savior (1 Peter 1:20 KJV) – this is God's *means* of salvation. In addition, God predetermined that a person must trust in the means (Christ) in order to be saved (Acts 16:31) – this is God's *condition* for salvation. Then we come to the verses like Romans 8:29-30: "For those God foreknew he also predestined to be conformed to the image of his Son – this is one of the many *results* of salvation. Finally, God predestined the *who* of salvation – those individuals who meet God's conditions. He knows who those individuals are because His foreknowledge enables Him to know all things. God has given us all this information about how salvation works, so we don't have to speculate about any of it. Sadly, Calvinists have no idea why God saves some people and not others, even though the Bible tells us why.

Assumption #10
God does not Practice Egalitarian Fairness

IF EVERYONE IS SINFUL and deserving of damnation, then all should be lost. That is called egalitarian fairness (i.e., treating everyone equally in judgment). On the other hand, if some are chosen to be saved, though they are no more deserving than everyone else, then they are not being treated the same as those not chosen. This would not be egalitarian fairness. Calvinists claim God remains just even though He does not practice egalitarian fairness. Robert A. Peterson and Michael D. Williams, in their book, *Why I Am Not an Arminian*, published by InterVarsity Press, even suggest treating all people fairly is simply a Western cultural idea and not a godly one. One wonders if they believe the caste system practiced in Eastern cultures is more godly. On page 134 they write, "Egalitarian fairness – treating all persons the same – may be a cultural ideal of the modern West, but there is no biblical reason to suppose that God shares it."[69]

Really? No biblical reason? What about 2 Chronicles 19:7, Ezekiel 18:25, Acts 10:34-35, Romans 2:11, Ephesians

6:9, Colossians 3:25, and 1 Peter 1:17, just to mention a few of the many biblical passages that tell us God is no respecter of persons when it comes to judgment? What Bible are Peterson and Williams reading? In addition, the Bible is replete with instructions to men not to be respecters of persons in judgment. Deuteronomy 1:17, Proverbs 24:23, Proverbs 28:21, 1 Timothy 5:21, and James 2:9 are just a few examples. Peterson and Williams would have us believe God plays favorites and treats people differently in judgment but tells us not to. It would seem God holds us to a higher standard than He Himself follows.

Yes, there are passages in the Bible that tell us God chose some people over others. The one most often quoted by Calvinists was discussed in chapter 8, the story of Jacob and Esau. As was pointed out in that case, and in every other similar case, those selected were chosen for a specific service – never for salvation. Choosing someone to do a particular job necessitates the rejection of anyone and everyone else from doing it if the job only requires one person. Entering heaven, however, does not require just one person do it. No one has to be rejected over someone else due to a limited number of available spaces. The way God selectively chooses someone for a particular service is not even a metaphor for how individuals enter heaven. Heaven is open to all. God does not discriminate. When it comes to God's judgment of men's souls, the Bible tells us He always demonstrates egalitarian fairness. Consider the following passages from Scripture that are in direct contradiction to what Calvinists like Peterson and Williams would have us believe:

Moses told the judges whom he had appointed over Israel, "Do not show partiality in judging" (Deuteronomy 1:17).

Johoshaphat, king of Judah, appointed judges to bring the people back unto the Lord God of their fathers. Read what he instructed them to do: He told them, "Consider carefully what you do, because you are not judging for mere mortals but for the LORD, who is with you whenever you give a verdict. Now let the fear of the LORD be on you. Judge carefully, for with the LORD our God there is no injustice or partiality or bribery" (2 Chronicles 19:6-7).

In Ezekiel 18:29-30, God challenges His people with the following words: "The Israelites say, 'The way of the Lord is not just.' Are my ways unjust, people of Israel? Is it not your ways that are unjust? Therefore, you Israelites, I will judge each of you according to your own ways, declares the Sovereign LORD. Repent! Turn away from all your offenses; then sin will not be your downfall." The Bible says that God judges "each of you according to your own ways." That means God is just because He practices egalitarian fairness. He is not selective.

Solomon, the wisest man who ever lived (apart from Christ) warned, "To show partiality in judging is not good" (Proverbs 24:23). If it is not good for man to show partiality in judging, why would it be good for God to show partiality?

God practices egalitarian fairness in judgment.

All the Old Testament writers make it clear that God does not play favorites when it comes to judgment. So too do the New Testament writers.

Peter declared in Acts 10:34-35, "I now realize how true it is that God does not show favoritism but accepts from every nation the one who fears him and does what is right."

Paul wrote, "God does not show favoritism" (Romans 2:11).

Colossians 3:25 states, "Anyone who does wrong will be repaid for their wrongs, and there is no favoritism." According to Calvinism, God does show favoritism by not repaying some (the elect) for the wrongs they do. He selects those He loves more than others and exempts them from any punishment, even though this verse says that without exception or favoritism everyone will be repaid for their wrongs. If individual predestination is true, then this verse is a lie. There are only three ways to avoid favoritism – forgive everyone, punish everyone, or allow everyone the opportunity to freely accept Christ's substitutionary death on the cross.

James warns that "If you show favoritism, you sin" (James 2:9). Does God sin if He does not treat everyone equally? Do Calvinists like Peterson and Williams believe God can do nothing wrong even if He sins? Or perhaps God cannot sin even if He does things that would be sin if humans did them.

Moses, the Old Testament prophets, God Himself, Solomon, the Apostle Paul, and other New Testament writers, including Jesus' own disciples Peter and James, make it clear God treats everyone equally in judgment. Even so, Calvinists insist that God selects (predestines) some people for special treatment, even though they are no more deserving of it than anyone else. He gives them eternal life despite the fact they are as sinful as everyone else and equally deserving of condemnation. If individual predestination is true, then God is doing something contrary to everything written about egalitarian fairness by every writer of the Bible, including direct statements by God Himself.

While on earth, Jesus demonstrated how we should treat all people with egalitarian fairness. He did not discriminate against anyone. He healed all who came to Him, whether Israelite or Gentile, Jewish peasant or Roman soldier. Jesus even went to the home of Zacchaeus, a despised tax collector. As a result, Zacchaeus became a Christ follower. Jesus talked with the despised Samaritans, including a woman at a well. If Christ practiced egalitarian fairness while on earth, why wouldn't He (God) also practice it from all eternity? God never changes. He is the same yesterday, today, and forever.

Our hearts tell us that predestination is unjust.

Even most Calvinists admit (if they are honest) it seems unfair of God to send the majority of His creations to hell while excusing others from such a fate, knowing both groups are equally undeserving of salvation. Calvin and Luther themselves wrestled with the idea. Calvin called it *decretum horrible*. In his book, *Bondage of the Will*, Luther wrote,

> It seems an iniquitous, cruel, intolerable thought to think of God… And who would not stumble at it? I have stumbled at it myself more than once, down to the deepest pit of despair, so that I wished I had never been made a man.[70]

Calvinists believe there are only two options to the dilemma. Either God is wrong (and is therefore cruel) or the Christian's sense of fairness is wrong. Obviously, it is not possible for God to be wrong or cruel, so the problem must be with the Christian's belief that God is being unfair. It is every Christian's sense of justice that is wrong. How can every sincere Christian's heart, saddened by such a concept of God, be mistaken? Calvinists say it is because "God's thoughts are not your thoughts, neither are your ways my [God's] ways" (Isaiah 55:8). Does that mean we have no idea what is just even though God tells us what justice is over and over again in His Word? If so, then we have no idea what is good or what is true, despite the Bible's explanations. If Isaiah means what Calvinists contend, then we have no way of knowing anything about God or His ways. What we think is love may be God's idea of hate. His concept of heaven may be our concept of hell. This kind of confusion results from misapplying verses like Isaiah 55:8 to attributes of God that

He has clearly explained to us. Calvinists take this isolated verse and become convinced God is still just, even if He goes against everything He has told us about justice.

If our understanding of justice comes from the Bible but it is not the same way God Himself administers justice, then we can never be sure we are ever being just. And if this is the case for justice, it could be the case for everything else God tells us. Thus, because our understanding of truth is different than God's, we have no way of knowing what is true anymore than what is just. God could be what we would humanly consider dishonest because our thoughts on truth are not God's thoughts. If our thoughts are never God's thoughts, nor our ways God's ways, then we are going to be wrong about everything we believe and do. And the Bible is of no help.

The real problem with Calvinists' conclusion that God can be just even if we think He is being unjust rests with their inability to see a third option to the issue. For them it comes down to an either/or question of who is right in the matter – God or man.

Another Option

There is, however, a third possibility, which Calvinists will not consider. The third option is that their theology of predestination is the thing that is really wrong. If predestination isn't true, then God need not be cruel, nor Christians mistaken in their moral sensibilities about the injustice involved in a God who doesn't practice egalitarian fairness. There is a reason Christians feel uncomfortable with Calvin's view that God sends men to hell for committing sins He ordained them to commit. The reason for their discomfort is because their God-given sense of justice tells them such behavior is unjust. If God is love (which He is) and Christians are correct in their God-given sense of justice (which they are) then it must be Calvin's theology of individual predestination that is untrue.

Assumption #11
God Cannot be Sovereign if Humans have Libertarian Free Will

CALVINISTS DO NOT BELIEVE humans have libertarian free will because they are convinced such freedom would restrict God's sovereignty. They insist that if people can freely choose to accept the Gospel that means they have the power to determine God's decision regarding their salvation. Thus, God does not sovereignly make the decision. Sproul wrote the following: "I have often heard it said, 'God's sovereignty is limited by human freedom.' In this statement God's sovereignty is not absolute. It is bounded by a limit and that limit is human freedom."[71]

Funny, I am over seventy years old and I have never heard that statement; yet, Sproul claimed he heard it often. We have obviously run in different circles. The statement itself is totally false. Human freedom in no way keeps God from being totally sovereign. We have such freedom because God in His sovereignty chose to give us free will. If God were unable to give us free will then He would neither be omnipotent nor sovereign.

There is an interesting illustration by Augustine that was later adopted by James Montgomery Boice and is today often quoted by Calvinists. The story goes like this: An Arminian is in heaven and is asked how he got there. The Arminian answers, "Well, I hate to say this in heaven, because we are supposed to be spending our time here glorifying and praising God, but since you ask, I have to reply that the reason I am here and that other person is not here is that I had faith, and he did not. I chose to believe. I, by my own power, received Jesus Christ as my Savior."[72]

The illustration is used in an attempt to show how pride is inevitable if one is able to freely choose to receive Christ. The issue of pride was addressed in Assumption 7. The illustration is also quoted, however, in an attempt to demonstrate how human choice means people are saved through their own power usurping God's power. Both attempts are misleading. The use of the word "power" is more than just misleading. It is dishonest. We have no power to save ourselves or to cause God to save us. Because He is God, He can do whatever He chooses without any regard for mankind. The fact He gives us a choice about our eternal destiny does not mean we have any power over God. If He wanted to, He could still send us to hell even after we placed our faith in Christ. Giving us the choice simply means God is not going to use His power to force us into trusting Jesus. He wants us to love and trust Him the same way He loves us – volitionally.

A father lets his son choose.

If a loving father allows his son to choose whether or not he wants a bicycle for his birthday, the father is still in control of what the boy actually receives. The son has no power over what the father ultimately decides because the father could override the boy's choice. From beginning to end, the father is in control of the situation. The father is not controlled by the son's decision. He is simply demonstrating his love for the son by not forcing him to accept a gift he does not want.

The same is true with the Heavenly Father's decision to give us a choice as to whether or not we desire to follow Christ. Could He force us to? Certainly! Could He reject us even if we did wish to follow Him? Again, the answer is Yes. The fact that He desires for us to volitionally follow Jesus takes absolutely nothing away from His power, nor does it give us power over God's will. Sometimes it appears that Calvinists think God is so insecure that He would be threatened if people could freely choose Christ. Before the world began, God's will regarding salvation was determined and it included giving us the choice to accept or reject it. We were not even born at the time, so we certainly had no power in determining how salvation would work. It was the sole decision of the sovereign God. He offers us a choice because He loves us and wants us to respond in kind. He wants us to love Him because He first loved us (1 John 4:19), not because He predestined us to.

Calvinists disagree. They argue that if salvation is not possible unless a person decides to trust in the atonement then a person's faith is the final determining factor. Calvinists do not believe anything is determined by anyone other than God. But even if we make such an assumption that only God determines (and never allows) everything that happens, why couldn't one of the things God determined be that humans have free will? That would mean that people are free to decide if they want to trust in the atonement because God determined they would have that freedom. So, even the idea (assumption) that God predetermines everything does not preclude free will.

206 | FIVE REASONS TO BELIEVE IN CALVINISM, FIFTY REASONS NOT TO

Human logic shouldn't take precedence over the Scriptures.

As was pointed out previously, so much of Reformed Theology is based on logic rather than the Scriptures. Calvinists reason, "If God cannot save us unless and until we decide to allow Him to, then we are the first cause and God the second." In other words, if God's actions are at all conditioned upon ours, then our choice is the cause and God's choice is the effect. In order for God to be truly sovereign, His actions cannot be conditioned upon anything or anyone.

What such "logic" fails to take into consideration is that if the first cause is only able to make choices because the second cause gives him/her that ability to choose, then the second cause is really the first cause. In other words, God is still sovereign even if He allows us to make choices. This is true because He could take away our ability to choose at any time. To put it another way, free will and free grace are not mutually exclusive. Free will is only available to us due to God's free grace.

God took away our desire for Him.

If God has sovereignly predestined everything, then total depravity was ordained by Him. God determined what the consequences of sin would be, and He decided to make total depravity the consequence. According to Reformed Theology, God not only punished Adam for his sin by removing him from His presence (which only makes sense, given God's holiness), but He also took away from Adam (and all humankind) any desire to trust God or even to know Him. If that is true, then Adam and Eve had no feelings of loss following their Fall and did not miss the intimate relationship they once had with God in the Garden of Eden. That would be the case if total depravity means no one has a desire to return to God or to have a relationship with Him. In addition, such total depravity means no man or woman since the Fall has desired to have a relationship with God because God took that desire away from everybody.

Calvinists might argue that it was not God but Adam who caused his desires to change. But that is inconsistent with their view of God's sovereignty. Again, Reformed Theology contends that God ordained everything. That would include what emotions, feelings, and desires people have. If that is true, then He was the one who removed Adam's (and everyone else's) desire for God. If only God can cause the sinner to desire God, then only God can cause the sinner to reject God. Whatever man's condition became as a result of Adam's sin, it was determined by God and God alone, according to Calvinism, because God determines everything. Man sinned, but God (not man) decided what the consequences of that sin would be. Thus, the sovereign God took away from everyone any desire to trust God, yet He sends people to hell for not having any desire to trust Him. In addition, He tells them to believe in the Lord Jesus in order to be saved knowing full well they can't because He took that desire away. This is the behavior of the God Calvinists believe in.

Infidelity

In a marriage relationship, if one partner is unfaithful it does not mean a permanent destruction of the love relationship is inevitable. The offended party may choose to forgive the unfaithful partner and allow the relationship to be restored (see the book of Hosea). Unconditional love is willing to take the unfaithful person back if he/she sincerely seeks forgiveness and genuinely desires to have the relationship restored. This will only take place, however, if the offending partner realizes what a valuable thing he/she has lost (the relationship) and is willing to seek forgiveness of the faithful partner. It's hard to believe Adam and Eve did not do that. Calvinists are convinced they did not because they wanted only to sin. They were so corrupted by their one act of disobedience that they had no further longings for God or His love.

If Calvinists are correct in saying only God can cause a person to want God, then it follows that only God can cause a person to not want God. Thus, God caused Adam and Eve to no longer want anything to do with Him. Far worse, God sends the majority of people He created to hell for being in a condition He Himself ordained. Is this a God of love?

Jesus told us to forgive those who trespass against us. That's not how it works with God, however, according to Reformed Theology. Instead, God decided to retaliate against those who have scorned Him by making sure they would never again seek His forgiveness. God wanted to make sure the breakup was permanent. He then picks a select few for restoration even though they have no desire to have the relationship restored.

Commanding the Impossible

According to Calvinists, God took away from people their desire to seek God, to repent and to ask God for forgiveness, or even to accept His offer of restoration. Even though the Bible tells fallen people to do all of these things, no one ever will because God took all these desires away from mankind after the Fall. Thus, when John the Baptist told his hearers to repent, he should have saved his breath because he was asking them to do the impossible.

Likewise, when Peter said, "Repent, then, and turn to God, so that your sins may be wiped out" in Acts 3:19, he was asking people to do something they were totally incapable of doing due to total depravity. If you have no will, you have no way.

Was Christ sincere when He said, "Unless you repent, you too will all perish" (Luke 13:3)? He must have known repentance was never going to happen due to total depravity. What purpose then is there in telling people what they must do to avoid perishing if they will never do it?

Jesus said, "If your brother or sister sins against you, rebuke them; and if they repent, forgive them" (Luke 17:3). Obviously, Jesus thought it was possible for people who are rebuked to repent of sins they commit against other people. Apparently, it is only sins committed against God that people are unable to repent of. Why then bother to rebuke anyone for such sins?

Isaiah, too, urges everyone to do the impossible when he writes, "Seek the LORD while he may be found; call on him while he is near. Let the wicked forsake their ways and the unrighteous their thoughts. Let them turn to the LORD, and he will have mercy on them, and to our God, for he will freely pardon" (Isaiah 55:6-7). Was Isaiah unaware of total depravity?

Remember what Acts 17:27 tells us all men should do: "they should seek the Lord, if haply they might feel after him, and find him, though he be not far from every one of us" (KJV). Why tell people to do something Calvinists claim is not even a possibility for the natural man to do? Even more deceptive is to promise people they can find the Lord if they do something they will never do. If total depravity means that the unsaved will never seek God (as Calvinists claim) then such a promise is both dishonest and serves no purpose other than to tease. This is not something God does.

Joshua, in asking the Israelites to serve God, tells them to "choose for yourselves this day whom you will serve" (Joshua 24:15). This is very cruel of him, if he knows what Calvinists know – that they really can't choose. Only God can choose for them.

Luther's View

From Genesis to Revelation, the Bible implores us to choose correctly. Calvinists claim all these pleas are not genuine because man is incapable of choosing correctly. Luther, for example, in his book *The Bondage of the Will*, says such commands as "choose you this day whom ye will serve" are only intended to show us we can't follow them, rather than to cause us to try.[73] He appeals to Romans 3:20 to show how the law was not written for us to keep (because we can't), but to give us the knowledge of our sins.

What Luther neglects to point out, however, is God has a good reason for telling us we cannot keep the law. It is to show us we need to look for another way to God, because commandment-keeping won't get us there. It is this very knowledge of our sins and our total impotence that causes us to realize our need for a Savior. When we learn we are incapable of keeping the law (as Romans 3:20 tells us) we realize our need to seek salvation in another way (through faith). Like all Scripture, this passage serves a good purpose. In contrast, learning we are incapable of choosing God does nothing for us.

Who even needs to be informed of this inability? If God causes the elect to choose Him even though they have no desire to do so, they certainly don't need to be informed they can't choose Him. It would appear then the non-elect need this information, but why? The only thing such knowledge could accomplish for them (other than to be tormented by it) would be to cause sinners to sin all the more. After all, if you are trapped forever in sin, you might as well make the most of it. If you can't choose God, then indulge yourself in the only thing you can do – sin. Maximize the enjoyment you can get out of the only thing you will ever have, and hope God changes His mind and makes you one of His elect. Even if you are unsure whether or not you are one of the elect, you still needn't worry about enjoying sin to the maximum, because if you are one of God's elect, you will be saved anyway. If you are not, there is nothing you can do but sin. No amount of sin will make any difference as to your eternal destiny, so have at it and hope God chooses you for salvation.

God wants you to realize you can't keep the Commandments so you will turn to Christ for salvation. To whom does He want you to turn when He informs you that you can't choose God – Satan? Nothing good results from telling people to choose God in order to show them they can't, unless you either want people to sin more, or you enjoy causing them total despair, or both. It is deceitful, cruel, and leads to nothing profitable. The true God is not like that. It must hurt God to see there are Christians who believe that He *is* like that.

Luther's claim that God implores us to choose, even though He knows we can't, arguably makes God out to be a deceiver and his request a ruse. But there is an even more convincing argument against Luther's view (i.e., his attempt to explain Joshua 24:15 in a way that fits Reformed Theology). People *do* choose to serve God. Joshua himself said, "As for me and my house, we will serve the Lord." By his own volition, Joshua chose correctly. Thus, Luther's claim (assumption) that the biblical pleas to choose God are not meant to be followed because no one can, is proven to be false by Joshua himself as well as everyone else who has chosen wisely.

The Bible tells us to choose.

The Bible records many people who made the right choice with no mention of their supposed inability to do so, or that God first gave them the faith to do so, or that God regenerated them beforehand, or that God did anything prior. Indeed, the Bible gives sole credit to the individual.

Abel offered a better sacrifice to God than Cain because Abel chose to do so (Genesis 4:4-5). Abraham left Haran to follow God because he chose to do so (Genesis

12:4). Moses refused to enjoy the pleasures of sin for a season in Egypt because he chose to esteem the "reproach of Christ greater riches than the treasures in Egypt" (Hebrews 11:24-27). The Israelites avoided the death angel because they chose to put the lamb's blood over their doorposts (Exodus 12:28). Those who were spared death from snake bites were those who chose to look up to the brass snake that Moses had made (Numbers 21:9). Joshua chose whom he would serve (Joshua 24:15). Ruth chose to go with Naomi and make Naomi's God her God (Ruth 1:16). David said he chose the way of truth (Psalms 119:30). All these people made the correct choice and were rewarded for it. Making the wrong choice is also possible, but the results are different. Jeremiah said the people who hearkened not to walk in God's ways had chosen death rather than life (Jeremiah 7:23-24, 8:3). Whether they chose life or death, the Bible says it was the individuals who made the choice. Nowhere does it say God enabled them to make the right or wrong choice.

In the New Testament, we find a centurion who chose to seek Jesus for the healing of his servant (Matthew 8:5-6). Jesus marveled at the great faith of the centurion (verse 10) and said, "Thou hast believed, so be it done unto thee" (verse 13 KJV). And his servant was healed at that moment. Jesus wasn't amazed at the faith God had given the centurion. He was amazed at the centurion's faith. After four men chose to bring a man with palsy to Jesus and Jesus saw their faith, He said, "Thy sins be forgiven" (Matthew 9:2). It was their faith, not God's faith, that Jesus responded to. A woman "who lived a sinful life" chose to come to Jesus and wash his feet. Afterwards, Jesus tells her, "Your sins are forgiven. Your faith has saved you; go in peace" (Luke 7:37-50). Nowhere in the passage does it say the woman was regenerated before she chose to come to Jesus. Nor was she given faith to believe. It was her faith that resulted in her sins being forgiven. Over and over again, Jesus stated that it was the person's own faith that resulted in their being changed. In no instance is there a statement about God doing something previous to a person's decision to believe or that such belief was the consequence of God predestining it.

From Genesis to Revelation, the Bible tells us to choose life rather than death. And the offer of life is to anyone who chooses to accept it. "Let the one who is thirsty come; and let the one who wishes take the free gift of the water of life" (Revelation 22:17).

Anyone can come.

Jesus said similar words without any apparent concern over God being less than sovereign as a result. Jesus said, "Let anyone who is thirsty come to me and drink" (John 7:37). What Jesus says in this verse contradicts four of Reformed Theology's basic tenets. Number one is *total depravity*. Jesus gives no indication that people cannot come to Him of their own free will. In fact, by telling them to come to Him, He indicates just the opposite. He makes it clear that He expects them to do what He asks, so they must be capable of doing it. Number two is *limited atonement*. By using the word "anyone" Jesus is offering to quench the thirst of all who come to Him. Number three is *unconditional election*. Jesus said His offer was to those who meet the condition of coming to Him. Number four is *individual predestination*. Those who drink are not elected before they come to Jesus. They must first meet the condition of coming to Him before they are given drink.

Was Jesus sincere in His John 7:37 offer? According to Reformed Theology He was *not*. He makes the offer knowing no one would be willing to actually take Him up on His offer because of total depravity. He leads them to believe they can come to Him of their own free will when, in fact, they cannot. More than just being insincere, Jesus was being dishonest. According to Calvinism, Jesus knew no one would ever receive drink by coming to Him on the basis of His request alone. They must be regenerated first. Thus, He promises something to people He has no intention of giving them. Knowing what Jesus is like, we should trust Him to be sincere in His offer. We should conclude that He actually believed people could come to Him. A belief in total depravity, limited atonement, unconditional election, and individual predestination means Jesus was not sincere in making statements like this. Even worse, it makes it hard to believe Jesus when He said He is the Truth (John 14:6).

God is patient.

The Apostle Peter tells us, "The Lord is not slow in keeping his promise, as some understand slowness. Instead he is patient with you, not wanting anyone to perish, but everyone to come to repentance" (2 Peter 3:9). The reason God is patient with us is because he is waiting for us to choose. He wants "everyone to come to repentance." If we will never choose correctly, then God is futilely wasting his time patiently waiting for something that will never happen. Thus, God is doing something for no reason, and He knows it.

Calvinists claim that 2 Peter 3:9 refers to the elect rather than the lost. God is waiting for all the elect to repent because He doesn't want any of them to perish. The King James Version of this verse reads, "The Lord is longsuffering to us, not willing that any should perish, but that all should come to repentance" (KJV). Sproul tried to avoid the obvious interpretation of this verse by arguing, "That verse has a restrictive word in it, which is the word us. The word any, therefore, refers to 'any of us.' Since 2 Peter is written by a Christian believer to Christian believers and for Christian believers, it is likely that us refers to Christian believers and not human beings (universally).[74] Thus, God is not willing that any of his elect should perish."[75]

If the word *us* refers only to Peter and the Christians he is writing to, then Peter is needlessly stating the obvious. Obviously, if predestination is true, God is not willing that any of His elect should perish. That would go without saying. In this particular case, according to Sproul, Peter is assuring the Christians he is writing to that none of them will perish. But there is a much bigger problem with Sproul's interpretation when you include the words Peter uses at the end of the verse. Peter says the Lord is waiting (longsuffering) until all come to repentance. If Peter is writing to Christians, as Sproul alleges, they have already come to repentance. In that case, God would be patiently waiting for them to do something they have already done. The *us*, therefore, must refer to lost human beings (universally) and not to Peter and the Christians he is writing to. But if the verse is talking about the unregenerate, then Reformed Theology has a problem, because it says God doesn't want *anyone to perish, but everyone to come to repentance.* That is why Sproul tried to interpret (re-interpret) the verse. He wanted it to fit in with Reformed Theology. But there is yet another problem the verse presents for Sproul. According to Calvinism, God causes people to repent by His irresistible grace. If that is true, there is no need for God to be patiently waiting for people to come to repentance because He causes people to repent whenever He wants. So, the only one He would need to be patient with would be Himself.

A related verse (Romans 9:22) asks, "What if God... bore with great patience the objects of wrath, prepared for destruction?" Do Calvinists expect us to believe that this verse too is talking about the elect (those who are objects of God's wrath and are "prepared for destruction")? The only reason God would need to be patient with people is because the choice is theirs. He is patiently waiting for them to make a decision for Christ. He is not patiently waiting on the elect.

Paul says that God's kindness and patience is intended for the lost (not the elect). Paul asks the question, "Do you show contempt for the riches of his kindness, forbearance and patience, not realizing that God's kindness is intended to lead you to repentance?" (Romans 2:4) The word "intended" means it may or may not actually happen. While God wants his patience and kindness to cause people to repent, it would appear from the context that it failed here as these people show contempt for it all rather than repent. How can that be true if the verse is referring to the elect who repent? If all these verses refer to the elect, who are saved through God's irresistible grace, there is no need for God to be patient. Patience is only required when you are waiting for someone else to make a decision, not when you have already made the decision for them.

God asked Moses, "How long will these people treat me with contempt? How long will they refuse to believe in me?" (Numbers 14:11) If God has already decided everything then this question to Moses is ridiculous. The people would believe when God preordained they would believe. The question to Moses is a legitimate one only if the people are the ones who decide when they will believe, and not God.

We must choose.

Romans 2:6-8 tells us, God "will repay each person according to what they have done." To those who by persistence in doing good seek glory, honor and immortality, he will give eternal life. But for those who are self-seeking and who reject the truth and follow evil, there will be wrath and anger (NIV). The choice of what we do is not God's, but ours. It is the consequences of our choice (not the choice itself) that are in God's hands. And he will judge with egalitarian fairness, as verse 11 goes on to explain: "For God does not show favoritism." God judges everyone the same way based on what they have chosen to do (accept or reject the truth).

Despite all the Scriptural calls for people to choose and all the biblical examples of people choosing to put their faith in God, Calvinists are certain God chooses for us. *The Westminster Confession of Faith* declares, "God from all eternity, did, by the most wise and holy counsel of His own will, freely, and unchangeably ordain whatsoever comes to pass."[76] Thus, there is not a thing humans can do other than what God has already ordained them to do. Humans then are just going through the motions of doing what God has predestined. As someone has said, "We are puppets forced to play our part in the play in the way the puppeteer decides." Furthermore, even if we should be the object of the puppeteer's affection, we have absolutely no ability to respond to his love except in the exact way he has already predetermined.

A Calvinist once told me that God's determinism of our lives does not make us puppets because humans (unlike puppets) have self-consciousness. That fact makes the situation even worse. Unlike puppets, we are fully aware that we are being manipulated by strings designed to force us into accomplishing God's will. It would be better to be a puppet unaware of what was happening to us.

Calvinists do not believe God can be sovereign if humans have libertarian free will. But there is no basis for such a belief. The Early Church Fathers believed God was sovereign, yet they also believed humans had free will and could choose between good and evil.

What did the Early Church Fathers believe?

Ignatius of Antioch, who died no later than AD 110, was likely a disciple of both Apostles Peter and John. Ignatius was martyred in the Coliseum in Rome where he was forced to fight wild beasts. Seven of his letters have survived to this day. He believed in free will as evidenced by statements he made, such as the following:

> If anyone is truly religious, he is a man of God; but if he is irreligious, he is a man of the devil, made such, not by nature, but by his own choice.[77]

Irenæus (AD 130 - 202) was also a martyr and was taught by Polycarp (AD 69 - 155). Polycarp had been a disciple of John. About AD 180 Irenæus wrote against ideas that would later become aspects of Calvinist and Reformed Theology in its denial of the free will. The following is a direct quote from his work *Against Heresies*:

> Men are Possessed of Free Will, and Endowed with the Faculty of Making a Choice.[78]

Justin Martyr (c. AD 100/114– c. AD 162/168) was another early Christian apologist who was martyred by beheading. He wrote:

> Man acts by his own free will.[79]

> We have learned from the prophets, and we hold it to be true, that punishments, chastisements, and rewards are rendered according to the merit of each man's actions. Otherwise, if all things happen by fate, then nothing is in our own power. For if it be predestined that one man be good and another man evil, then the first is not deserving of praise or the other to be blamed. Unless humans have the power of avoiding evil and choosing good by free choice, they are not accountable for their actions— whatever they may

be... For neither would a man be worthy of reward or praise if he did not of himself choose the good, but was merely created for that end. Likewise, if a man were evil, he would not deserve punishment, since he was not evil of himself, being unable to do anything else than what he was made for.[80]

God, wishing men and angels to follow His will, re-solved to create them free to do righteousness; pos-sessing reason, that they may know by whom they are created, and through whom they, not existing for-merly, do now exist; and with a law that they should be judged by Him, if they do anything contrary to right reason: and of ourselves we, men and angels, shall be convicted of having acted sinfully, unless we repent beforehand. But if the word of God foretells that some angels and men shall be certainly punished, it did so because it foreknew that they would be unchangeably [wicked], but not because God had created them so.[81]

Clement of Alexandria wrote:

Neither praise nor condemnation, neither rewards nor punishments, are right if the soul does not have the power of choice and... if evil is involuntary.[82]

Archelaus wrote the following:

All the creatures that God made, He made very good. And He gave to every individual the sense of free will, by which standard He also instituted the law of judg-ment... There can be no doubt that every individual, in using his own proper power of will, may shape his course in whatever direction he pleases.[83]

Methodius wrote:

Those [pagans] who decide that man does not have

free will, but say that he is governed by the unavoidable necessities of fate, are guilty of impiety toward God Himself, making Him out to be the cause and author of human evils.[84]

Tertullian (AD 155 – c. 240) was a prolific early Christian author from Carthage in the Roman province of Africa. He wrote:

So in the Creator's subsequent laws also you will find, when He sets before man good and evil, life and death, that the entire course of discipline is arranged in precepts by God's calling men from sin, and threatening and exhorting them; and this on no other ground than that man is free, with a will either for obedience or resistance.[85]

It was not until Augustine, about 400 years after Christ, that individual predestination became an accepted theology within the church community. Not only did these Early Church Fathers not believe in individual predestination, but they also rejected a belief in limited atonement. In 1882, James Morrison wrote in *The Extent of Atonement* about an English Bishop, John Davenant (1572-1641), who was present at the Synod of Dort in 1618. Morrison quoted Bishop Davenant as writing:

It may be truly said before Augustine and Pelagius, there was no question concerning the death of Christ, whether it was to be extended to all mankind, or to be confined only to the elect. For the Fathers... not a word (that I know of) occurs among them of the exclusion of any persons by the decree of God. They agree that it is actually beneficial to those only who believe, yet everywhere confess that Christ died in behalf of all mankind...

Augustine died in AD 429, and up to his time, at least, there is not the slightest evidence that any Christian ever dreamed of a propitiation for the elect alone. Even after him, the doctrine of limited propitiation was but slowly propagated, and for long but partially received.[86]

Even Calvinist writers themselves acknowledge that the Early Church Fathers did not ascribe to the doctrine of individual predestination. Quoting Loraine Boettner:

> It may occasion some surprise to discover that the doctrine of Predestination was not made a matter of special study until near the end of the fourth century... They of course taught that salvation was through Christ; yet they assumed that man had full power to accept or reject the gospel.[87]

Biblical historians and scholars know that the closer one gets to the original source, the more likely one is to get accurate doctrine from those who were there. The reverse is also true – the farther away you get from those who were there, the more likely errors will develop in doctrine. Yet, Calvinists assume the Early Church Fathers, many of whom studied under the original disciples, did not understand the basic Christian doctrine of salvation.

Historical development of Calvinism

So, when did Reformed Theology become a major belief system in the Church? We know the Reformation took place between AD 1517 and AD 1648, long after the Early Church Fathers had died, but Calvinism's roots can be traced further back than Luther and Calvin. Calvin developed much of his theology from the works of Augustine (AD 354 – AD 430). Augustine's ideas grew out of a desire to incorporate the thinking (logic) of secular philosophers with the theology of Christianity. As a result, many of his amalgamations contained logic taken from Greek scholars such as Plato. A major source for

Augustine's ideas was the writings of the great scholar, Aristotle, particularly his work entitled *The Metaphysics*. Aristotle called metaphysics "first philosophy" and speculated on what God was like.[88]

One of Aristotle's positions on God was that He was immutable (unchangeable). According to Aristotle, to be unchangeable means God cannot be influenced. In order to avoid being influenced, God must also be unfeeling. Apparently, the thinking was if God had feelings, He could be influenced and, if he could be influenced, He would not be immutable. It is not surprising then that Augustine's concept of a sovereign God was one who could not be influenced by the desires of men. He got the idea from Aristotle. It is here an understanding of the all-encompassing love of God was lost. The love of God was no longer a two-way relationship with give and take. It now became entirely one-sided. God did everything without any involvement or influence from man. Both the love of God and His relationship with man became secondary to the sovereignty of God.

From Augustine's immutable God, Calvin created his theology of a sovereign God with whom humans have no influencing interaction. God became a deterministic deity unmoved by what men may desire or choose. In fact, God chooses for them. He decides if a man is saved, even if the man has no desire to be saved. Man has no choice. As *The Westminster Confession of Faith* states, men are "altogether passive" in the matter.[89] Prior to AD 400, it was pagan philosophers such as the Gnostics who taught a God of determinism.

So, history shows that Calvin's concept of individual predestination came from Aristotle by way of Augustine. Despite its untimely development, Calvinists are convinced that individual predestination is what the Bible teaches. They believe that centuries after the Bible was written one man, Augustine, was finally able to give

Christians the real truth of the Gospel. And he did so by studying the works of pagan Greek philosophers like Plato and Aristotle. Why would anyone think this later theology, developed by such a scenario, is more trustworthy than the one held by the Early Church?

Assumption #12
God Ordained Evil

OF ALL THE ASSUMPTIONS Calvinists accept as true, this one maligns the character of God the most. If what the Confession says is true, that God ordained 'whatsoever comes to pass,' then God ordained sin and evil. Some Calvinists balk at this idea, but it can't be avoided if one believes God ordained everything. Honest Calvinists admit that they believe God created evil. God desired for man to fall into sin. God wanted sin to come into the world.

Sproul wrote, "Yes, God created sin."[90]

Edwin Palmer wrote:

All things that happen in all the world at any time and in all history come to pass because God ordained them, Even sin - the fall of the devil from heaven, the fall of Adam, and every evil thought, word, and deed in all of history. It is even biblical to say that God has foreordained sin.

No, he has foreordained everything 'after the counsel of his will': the moving of a finger, the beating of

a heart, the laughter of a girl, the mistake of a typist–
even sin.[91]

Calvinists point out that there is no Scripture that says
God ordained everything *except* sin. But such a statement
would be unwarranted if sin was not an ordained thing.
In fact, such a statement would actually be false if sin
was something God allowed to occur rather than ordained. It is also true that there is no Scripture that says
God ordained everything *including* sin. More convincing, however, is the fact that there is no Scripture that
makes the statement, "God ordained sin." Conversely,
Calvinists argue there is no Scripture that states, "God
did *not* ordain sin." But there is a reason for the absence
of such a statement. The reason is because no writer
thought it necessary. There is no need to state the obvious. The writers took for granted that God is good and,
therefore, He would not deliberately create something so
horrible and destructive. It would be a given that God
would not ordain what He hates. It goes without saying.

Joseph

Calvinists do have a verse that they point to, claiming
it teaches that God ordained evil. It is found in the Old
Testament in the story of Joseph. After the brothers sold
Joseph into slavery, Joseph said to his brothers, "You intended to harm me, but God intended it for good" (Genesis 50:20 NIV). Calvinists claim that because the verb
(hšb) in the verse applies to both the brothers and God
that means they both did the sin. But the verb is not the
action itself (the sin) but the intention of the action. What
the brothers intended the action to result in and what
God intended the same action to result in were different.
But the action itself (the sin) was committed by the brothers, not God. God does not sin. What the brothers did
was "intended" by them for evil. Then the verse says,

but God "intended" it (what the brothers did and not what God did) for good. God used the evil that the brothers did (which He foreknew they would do) to accomplish His purpose. We must keep in mind that God is omniscient. He foreknew what the brothers would do (not what He would do) and used it (what the brothers would do) to accomplish a different purpose (His purpose). Allowing evil to occur is not the same as doing evil or even ordaining it.

It would be similar to a person erecting a building for the purpose of using it as an overpriced luxury hotel in order to get rich. Just after it is erected, however, another person takes over the building and turns it into a shelter for homeless people. One person intended the construction of the building for a greedy purpose, while the other person intended the same construction of the building for a good purpose. The question, however, is who actually erected the building? The building was intended to be used for two different purposes, but only one person constructed it. And it was *not* the person who used the building for good even if he knew ahead of time what the actual builder intended to use the building for. Knowing that someone was going to build the building for greed does not mean the person who used the building for good was responsible for the building itself. Joseph's brothers did evil, but God used *their* evil for good. Using evil for good, however, is not the same as doing the evil.

An additional reason for rejecting Calvinists' interpretation of Genesis 50:20 is found in the fact that the verse is an historical account of what one person said. The intent of the verse is not to teach theology but to give an account of the words Joseph spoke to his brothers. As was stated earlier, a sound theology cannot be built on the historical accounts of Scripture alone. This is especially true if the historical accounts are not supported by what is taught in the didactic passages. Genesis is a book of history. The number of didactic passages teaching that God is just as responsible for evil as Joseph's brothers is exactly zero. If Reformed Theology's interpretation of Joseph's statement is correct, then there should be at least one didactic passage stating that truth. Moreover, if God is the creator of sin and evil, there should be numerous verses stating that fact and the verses should all be accompanied by words of comfort. Without such comfort, we would be left with the very terrifying truth that God is the one who created sin and evil simply for His good pleasure. Of course, that is the God Calvinists believe in.

Yes, the Bible tells us God is sovereign, but that is not the same as telling us He created evil. God ordained all things, including Satan and man, who created evil through their libertarian free will, which God also ordained. Thus, God allowed evil to come into existence by creating what He did (beings with free choice). God wanted beings to be able to volitionally love Him because He knew you can't force people to love you. Of course, giving people free choice means they can also choose to reject you and sin against you, which is what mankind has repeatedly done.

Guilty but Not Guilty

If God ordained the evil acts that Joseph's brothers committed (and all evil acts), then God is directly responsible for sin. Of course, Calvinists do not want to admit that is what their theology teaches. So, while they maintain that God ordained evil they also, at the same time, maintain that God cannot be held accountable for evil. Huh? What? Obviously, Calvinists do not want to blame God for the existence of sin even though He ordained it, so they created a differentiation between "efficient" cause and "ultimate" cause. Man is the *efficient* cause of sin and hence is responsible; but God is the *ultimate* cause, so He is not responsible. Seriously? Only someone with a theological bias could believe that the ultimate *cause* of sin is not responsible for its existence. God can only avoid being responsible for sin if He is the ultimate *non-cause*.

More than just allowing sin, Calvinists argue that God can, as the primary cause of sin, foreordain its commission by secondary or proximate causes (moral agents) without Himself being guilty. How is that possible? If God hadn't ordained sin, sin would never have come into existence. So, He is directly responsible, regardless of how He makes sin happen or whom He involves in making sin happen. To say otherwise is ludicrous.

This attempt to exonerate God is like saying David wasn't responsible for the death of Uriah because David wasn't the one who actually murdered Uriah. David just ordained that his murder would take place. It was actually Joab who placed Uriah in harm's way. And even Joab wasn't the killer, but the enemy soldiers were. Actually, the real reason Uriah was killed was because it is the nature of warriors in battle to kill those that oppose them. So, David wasn't the efficient cause of Uriah's death. He was only the ultimate cause. So, David wasn't responsible for Uriah's death. Please! This argument is just a terrible and desperate attempt to avoid the obvious. The only ones who would accept such a ridiculous excuse for God's behavior are those who are willing to believe anything to avoid the truth that Reformed Theology makes God into a monster. Calvinists are willing to come up with and believe absurd ideas like this, which are not found in the Bible, rather than abandon their theology. Their philosophy seems to be, Create and believe whatever it takes to make it work. As someone has pointed out, "Calvinists often use language like this designed to distance God's direct causal role in evil implied within his deterministic language. The result is asserting [A] and [NOT A] simultaneously, resulting in doublespeak." If God isn't responsible for evil, why did He hold David responsible for doing the very same thing that God does – ordaining sin but not directly committing the sin (2 Sam. 11:27)?

Since Calvinism is a 5-Point system, Calvinists are philosophically pre-committed to make every Scripture that contradicts a point in the system fit their narrative regardless of how absurd such an interpretation may be. Because of the necessity to keep their entire *golden chain of salvation* held together, Calvinists are very vulnerable to circular logic.

No, God did not ordain evil.

The best way to absolve God from the sin of creating evil isn't by concocting lame excuses, but by reading the Bible and discovering that He didn't do any such thing. In the Bible, God Himself declares that He did not ordain evil.

Jeremiah 7:30-31:

> The people of Judah have done evil in my eyes, declares the LORD. They have set up their detestable idols in the house that bears my Name and have defiled it. They have built the high places of Topheth in the Valley of Ben Hinnom to burn their sons and daughters in the fire—something I did not command, nor did it enter my mind.

Jeremiah 19:3-6:

> Hear the word of the LORD, you kings of Judah and people of Jerusalem. This is what the LORD Almighty, the God of Israel, says: "Listen! I am going to bring a disaster on this place that will make the ears of everyone who hears of it tingle. For they have forsaken me and made this a place of foreign gods; they have burned incense in it to gods that neither they nor their ancestors nor the kings of Judah ever knew, and they have filled this place with the blood of the inno-

cent. They have built the high places of Baal to burn their children in the fire as offerings to Baal—something I did not command or mention, nor did it enter my mind.' So, beware, the days are coming, declares the LORD, when people will no longer call this place Topheth or the Valley of Ben Hinnom, but the Valley of Slaughter.

Jeremiah 32:35:

They built high places for Baal in the Valley of Ben Hinnom to sacrifice their sons and daughters to Molek, though I never commanded—nor did it enter my mind—that they should do such a detestable thing and so make Judah sin.

Not only does God say that He did not decree these sins, He also says that these sins didn't even enter His mind. God here is not denying *knowledge* of their sin, but he is denying that it ever entered His mind to *command* it. The question is, How can God foreordain something He did not decree or that never even entered His mind? No, God did not ordain evil.

James tells us that God never tempts anyone (James 1:13). If God is not the cause of temptation, yet temptation happens, how can God be sovereign over everything? If it is because He causes someone or something else to tempt man, He is being disingenuous when He says it's not really Him that does it. Neither Satan nor man can be held responsible for the creation of evil if God foreordained that they do it. The only way anyone can be held responsible for evil is to say they sinned by their own free will.

Man was created with a free will, as was Satan.

God has a will and He created man with one as well, for He created man in His (God's) own image. That's why

Adam and Eve were able to disobey God by eating of the forbidden fruit. They used the free will God had given them to choose incorrectly and foolishly. Nothing is said in the Bible about them or anyone else losing their free will as a result of the Fall.

Satan also has a will (2 Timothy 2:26). Satan's will is to destroy people (1 Peter 5:8). If God's will is always done on earth as it is in heaven, then Satan's will is really God's will. That means that it is God's will to destroy people even though the Bible indicates that Satan's will and God's will are in opposition to each other.

In 1 Tim. 2:25-26, Paul tells Timothy how to teach those who have an incorrect doctrine. Paul says, "Opponents must be gently instructed... that they will come to their senses and escape from the trap of the devil, who has taken them captive to do his will." Not God's will but the devil's will. They are not the same.

The devil is the prince and god of this world (John 12:31). He seeks to hinder the Gospel; see Matt. 13:19, 2 Cor. 4:4, 1 Thess. 2:18. Why would God want to hinder the Gospel? God's will is that the Gospel be preached to the entire world (Matt. 28:18). Yet, according to Reformed Theology, He ordained Satan to hinder the Gospel from being preached. Does that make any sense? God ordains everything for a purpose. What purpose would God have for ordaining something that hinders His will from taking place?

Some Christians teach that evil has no purpose. That's not true. Evil has a definite purpose, which is to thwart the will of God. Satan (not God) first created evil and Satan's purpose in doing so was to thwart God's plans. You find this in the story of Job when God allowed (not directed) Satan to attempt to destroy Job. You also find it during Christ's days in the wilderness when Satan tried to thwart Jesus from going to the cross. Why would God want to thwart His own will? That's what Calvinists are

232 | FIVE REASONS TO BELIEVE IN CALVINISM, FIFTY REASONS NOT TO

saying when they say God ordained evil. The purpose of Satan and evil is to seek and to destroy mankind and God's kingdom. If God ordained evil, then He ordained something that attempts to destroy both His kingdom and mankind. That's not God's nature and it means God ordained things designed to hinder His will from happening. That makes God both evil and schizophrenic. Despite all the futile attempts made by Calvinists to avoid such a conclusion (e.g., proffering compatibilism), their theology cannot avoid it. The only way to avoid the conclusion that God Himself is evil is to realize that Satan (who is the very personification of evil) created evil through his libertarian free will that God gave him.

Are sin and evil really good and not bad?

In the very beginning, God said everything He made "was good" (Genesis 1:4, 12, 31). If everything God made is good then, according to Calvinists, sin and evil are actually good and not bad, because they came from God. Conversely, if sin is not good, then God created something that was not good. If sin is a good thing that God ordained, why then does He become angry with what He ordained?

Lorenzo Elijah Heighway comments:

> To a Calvinist, "sin and evil" are good because it *originates* from God. Conversely in Arminianism, all "sin and evil" are conceived *outside* of God, independent of God (consider Jeremiah 32:35 for instance), as God uses the "sin and evil" of others to *salvage* good from the bad. The "bad" is not a "means to an end," as it inherently is with Calvinism, but "bad" within Arminianism is something that God works around. It is something He never liked (He hates sin), never wanted, never intended, and best of all, never needed. But in Calvinism, God absolutely *does* need it, and

that's a significant difference. God would have been just as blessed (and I would argue, far more), had Adam and Eve *never fallen*. Calvinists cannot say this. In Calvinism, God absolutely needs "sin and evil," while in Arminianism, "sin and evil" doesn't stop God whatsoever.[92]

If God could not display His full glory without sin, then He is less than sovereign because He needed evil to accomplish His will. The God of Arminianism needs nothing. On the other hand, if God didn't need sin to display His full glory, then He Himself is evil because He could have accomplished His will another way (without creating evil), but He didn't. The same is true for God's creation of humans. According to Reformed Theology, God creates humans and then sends the majority of them to hell for His glory. If God must ordain the preponderance of mankind to eternal suffering in order to get glory for Himself, then God *needs* men to get what He wants. If He does not need people and is able to receive glory in a different way, then He is monstrously cruel because this is the way He has deliberately chosen to receive self-glorification.

The end does not justify the means. This is particularly true of God, because He could devise any means He wished to accomplish His will. But, according to Calvinism, He chose to ordain sin to accomplish His ends. The good purposes that result from sin justify His creating sin. Such a God is anything but good. Only evil beings deliberately ordain evil when they could avoid doing so, especially if they do so primarily for themselves.

Calvinists argue that *allowing* evil to occur is just as bad as *ordaining* it, but that's not true. The Father of the prodigal son allowed his son to leave. Does that mean that the father was complicit in his son's resulting debauchery? There is a world of difference between creating something evil and allowing others to create something evil. In the first case, you must be evil yourself. In the second case, you (or, in this case, God) remains good because even though He knows evil is inevitable due to Satan and man's wrong choices, He also knows it is necessary in order for love to be volitional. God allows evil to occur because He wants people (with free will) to choose to avoid evil by accepting Him and His remedy for it. Yes, He could force people to follow Him, stop sinning, or anything else He wanted them to do, but He wants them to choose Him of their own free will. True love can only occur when someone volitionally chooses to love.

The Master Chemist

It must be conceded that God did create the conditions that made evil possible. That is, He gave other beings the awesome power of choice. By doing so, He also gave them the power to create evil. It is not unlike a chemist who creates two chemicals that, if used separately, can do nothing but good. At the same time, he is aware that mixing the two chemicals would create a poisonous explosion and warns his assistant never to mix them together.

One day the assistant, overcome with curiosity as to whether the chemist is telling the truth, decides to disobey the strict command and mixes the chemicals. After the fire-fighters sort through the debris, whom do they blame for the poisonous explosion, the master chemist or the foolish assistant? If only the assistant had trusted the master chemist and obeyed his warning, the explosion would not have happened.

The same is true for evil. God created other beings such as angels and humans (good things). He also created and gave to them the power of choice (another good thing). He warned them, however, that they should not use their power of choice unwisely by disobeying Him. Satan (and subsequently all humans) used the power of choice to disobey God's commands and thus created evil. Sin and all of its ugly results then came into existence ("exploded onto the scene," if you will) not at the hand of God, but as a result of the disobedient choices made. We cannot blame God for what we ourselves have created. Granted, God, as the master chemist, knew the serious risks involved in giving us the gift of choice, but He knew that love required it. If He wanted to force His creations to love and trust Him, He would have created slaves or robots but not people. God desired to create people in His own image with the capability of responding volitionally to both His love and His commands. As a result, He also had to create us with the potential for rejecting both His love and His commands (warnings). He took the risk, completely aware that the "explosion" would occur and that we would disobey. He also knew He would have to do something to take care of the "mess" at great price to His only Son. But that's how great His love is for us.

Calvinists reject the above illustration because they believe God ordains everything and what He ordains happens. Humans only do what God has ordained them to do. Thus, sin happened because God wanted it to happen. It was no accident. But the illustration does not portray sin as an accident. The illustration portrays sin as something humans did and not God. God foreknew sin would occur, but He did not ordain it.

Foreknowledge

Calvinists argue that a theology that believes God foreknew sin would occur and did nothing to stop it faces the same quandary as Reformed Theology. Allowing sin to come into existence makes God just as culpable as He is for ordaining sin. In making such a statement, Calvinists demonstrate that they misunderstand the meaning of foreknowledge. God's foreknowledge is foreknowledge of what *will* happen, not what *might* happen. Therefore,

God can't use His foreknowledge to see what is going to happen and then act to make sure it doesn't happen, as that would make God's foreknowledge incorrect (i.e., not foreknowledge). God can foreknow events without being responsible for their occurring. Recall the illustration of the man sitting on top of a mountain and foreseeing two automobiles below about to have a head-on collision. Foreseeing is not the same as causing. Nor is creating good things wrong, even if they are used for bad. This truth can be better understood when one examines how God demonstrates His will.

God's Natural Laws

God demonstrates His sovereign will in three different ways. One way God has demonstrated His will can be found in His *natural laws*. These are the laws He put into effect in order for creation to function. In other words, the law of gravity keeps us from floating up into outer space and the sun comes up every morning to provide light and heat to keep us from freezing to death. Of course, the sun enables a great number of things to happen in nature (e.g., plants to grow, produce chloroform, give off oxygen, etc.). The point is, it is God's will that natural laws exist.

But it is critical to understand that God is not bound by natural laws. Because He created them, He is above them and can change them anytime He pleases. In fact, He has done so on a number of occasions. Jesus and Peter walked on water defying the law of gravity. God stopped the sun from moving for the Israelites so they could defeat their enemies (Joshua 10:13). It should be noted that it was because Joshua asked God to hold back the sun that He did it. Verse 14 reads, "the Lord hearkened unto the voice of a man" (KJV).

After Isaiah informed Hezekiah, who was very sick, that the Lord said he would die and not live (2 Kings

20:1), Hezekiah prayed and asked God to let him live (verse 3). God then told Isaiah, who had already left Hezekiah's house, to return and tell Hezekiah He had heard his prayer and seen his tears and, as a result, would add fifteen more years onto his life (verses 5-6). Hezekiah then asks Isaiah what sign will God give to show He would heal him (verse 8). Isaiah says the Lord will either turn the sun forward ten degrees or turn it back ten degrees (verse 9). Hezekiah tells Isaiah turning the sun forward ten degrees was no big deal, so he asks that the sun be turned back ten degrees (verse 10). Verse 11 says, "And Isaiah the prophet cried unto the Lord: and he brought the shadow ten degrees backward, by which it had gone down in the dial of Ahaz" (KJV).

Several things should be observed from these passages. The most obvious is that God can intervene and change the way His natural laws operate. He can even eliminate a law if He should wish to. Because God created natural laws, He can change or even remove any or all of them. If He could not, He would not be sovereign. While His natural laws can change whenever He wishes them to, He remains the same yesterday, today, and forever.

Apart from a few rare interventions by God, even His natural laws remain very consistent. Obviously, if God changed the natural laws on a regular basis there would be chaos. If we could not depend on the sun coming up every morning, the world would soon be in shambles. If God periodically removed the law of gravity from the earth, none of us would remain alive very long. Thus, natural laws are crucial to sustaining order on our planet and are an important part of God's will for us during our earthly stay. For that reason, our response to God's natural laws is to plan.

Farmers plant seed in the spring because they expect to have a harvest in the fall. They do not plant in the middle of the winter (at least not in cold climate areas), because the ground is too hard, the weather too cold, and the plants will not grow. Nature requires them to plan on planting in the Spring. A person does not jump out of an airplane without a parachute (unless committing suicide) because the law of gravity plunges people to earth so fast and hard they will die. So, the person jumping from an airplane plans ahead by having a parachute. For the most part, we can depend on the laws of nature to remain constant, so our response is to plan accordingly.

God's Immutable Will

A second way God demonstrates His will is through His *immutable will*. This is the area of God's will that never changes. God's immutable will includes His commands. If God commands there be light, then there will be light. If God tells the Red Sea to part, it will part. His immutable will also includes His plans which cannot be changed regardless of the circumstances. No one, for example, could stop Christ from dying on the cross. Not even Satan himself can prevent what God has predestined. God ordains certain things to happen and they happen, period – end of story. Our response to God's immutable will is to trust and obey. Knowing God is omniscient, loving and just, we should trust Him and accept His will rather than Satan's will or our own will.

The challenge for Christians is to discern what the will of God is. This becomes particularly difficult, if not impossible, if God does not always tell us what His will really is. Even worse, according to Calvinists, God tells us things that are the exact opposite of His real intentions. For example, there are verses that tell us God does not want anyone to perish. But, according to Calvinists, He actually desires the exact opposite. These verses include the following:

> "Do I take any pleasure in the death of the wicked? declares the Sovereign LORD. Rather, am I not

pleased when they turn from their ways and live?" (Ezekiel 18:23)

"I will judge each of you according to your own ways, declares the Sovereign LORD. Repent! Turn away from all your offenses; then sin will not be your downfall. Why will you die, people of Israel? For I take no pleasure in the death of anyone, declares the Sovereign LORD. Repent and live!" (Ezekiel 18:30-32).

"As surely as I live, declares the Sovereign LORD, I take no pleasure in the death of the wicked, but rather that they turn from their ways and live. Turn! Turn from your evil ways!" (Ezekiel 33:11).

"Who will have all men to be saved, and to come unto the knowledge of the truth" (1 Timothy 2:4 KJV).

"The Lord is not slow in keeping his promise, as some understand slowness. Instead he is patient with you, not wanting anyone to perish, but everyone to come to repentance" (2 Peter 3:9).

Does God mean what He says?

Arminians take God at His word. They believe God is telling the truth when He says it is not His desire for anyone to perish. Thus, the reason people perish isn't because God decreed them to, but because He gives them the choice to accept or reject His Son. Calvin, on the other hand, taught that "God by his eternal and immutable counsel determined once for all those whom... it was his pleasure to doom to destruction."[93] How does one reconcile a God who claims to take *no pleasure in the death of the wicked* with a God who (at the same time) takes pleasure in dooming men to destruction?

Decretive Will and Revealed Will

Calvinists attempt to reconcile the conflict by claiming God has two kinds of wills, a revealed will and a decretive will. What God might *reveal* to be His desired will is sometimes different from what He has *decreed* to actually happen. In other words, despite what God may say He wants to have happen, that's not necessarily what will happen. That's because God has a different will that He doesn't reveal to anyone. His decretive will has also been called His hidden or secretive will. Thus, God can say He wills all to be saved (His revealed will), but doesn't save everyone for reasons known only to Him (His decretive or secretive will). Naturally, His decretive will takes priority over His revealed will.

Basically, in their attempt to avoid the obvious conflict, Calvinists have created a God who says one thing but does another. If that is true, then the verses previously quoted are more than just confusing. They are deceptive because we are left thinking God wants all men to be saved when, in fact, He takes pleasure in dooming the majority of men to destruction. Even worse, we have no way of knowing for sure anything God tells us is His decretive will or merely His revealed will. As a result, we are left wondering if God means what He says. What good does it do for God to reveal something to us that is not really the case?

Sproul has stated that "The Bible is not to be interpreted arbitrarily. Fundamental rules of interpretation must be followed to avoid subjectivistic or fanciful interpretation, rules developed by the science of hermeneutics."[94] But the way Calvinists interpret the aforementioned verses fails to follow the fundamental rules of interpretation that Sproul exposits. Sproul also stated that "God is not the author of confusion. He does not contradict himself."[95] But what Calvinists claim is true of these verses makes God do exactly that. The idea that God has

GOD ORDAINED EVIL | **241**

two conflicting kinds of will is sheer double-talk. Cottrell does a great job of explaining how Calvinists make God contradict Himself when he writes:

> How shall we evaluate this attempt to explain the inconsistency between God's so-called decretive will and his revealed will? We certainly can accept the idea of "mystery" and "multiformity" in God's will. What we are asked to accept here, though, goes far beyond mystery and manifoldness. In this Calvinist explanation we are dealing, plainly and simply, with contradiction. A basic law of logic (and logic is grounded upon and derived from God's own nature) is the law of non-contradiction. This law says that no statement can be both true and not true, in the same sense, at the same time. But the Calvinist says that it IS God's will that all the lost be saved, and it is NOT God's will that all the lost be saved. Assigning the first desire to one level of God's will and the second to another level of his will does not remove the contradiction: it is the same God in both cases, and the desire is sincere in both cases. The same God decrees things to happen that he does not desire to happen, things that are the opposite of what he desires.
>
> The problem here is that if God is free to transcend the laws of logic (i.e., to go against his own nature) in this one area, how can we trust anything he says about anything else? What is left of Titus 1:2, which says that God "cannot lie" (NASB)? Or of Paul's declaration in Romans 3:4, "Rather, let God be found true,though every man be found a liar, as it is written, 'That You may be justified in Your words, and prevail when You are judged" (NASB)?[96]

Martin Luther said the following:

> Neither a conclusion nor a figure of speech should be admitted in any place of Scripture. On the con-

trary, we must everywhere adhere to the simple, pure, and natural meaning of the words. For if everyone is allowed to invent conclusions and figures of speech according to his own whim... nothing could to a certainty be determined or proved concerning any one article of faith that men could not find fault with by means of some figure of speech. Rather we must avoid, as the most deadly poison all figurative language which Scripture itself does not force us to find in the passage.[97]

It's too bad that Luther didn't practice what he preached. When interpreting the verses listed previously, he did not *adhere to the simple, pure, and natural meaning of the words.*

Sproul said literal interpretation *(sensus literalis)* seeks the plain sense of Scripture and to focus on one meaning.[98] Sproul advocates for this principle but does not apply it when interpreting the texts under consideration. Applying *sensus literalis* allows us to take God at His Word (i.e., He desires all men to be saved because He desires all men to be saved). The reason all men are not saved is due to their own rebellious hearts and not because God has a secret plan for the lost. This explanation doesn't require God to be secretive or to say things He doesn't really mean. It allows the verses to be understood by *sensus literalis.* Look at the verses again:

"Do I take any pleasure in the death of the wicked? declares the Sovereign LORD. Rather, am I not pleased when they turn from their ways and live?" (Ezekiel 18:23) This verse tells us God is pleased when people do what Calvinists claim they are incapable of doing due to total depravity. If nobody will ever turn, then God apparently will never be pleased.

"I will judge each of you according to your own ways, declares the Sovereign LORD. Repent! Turn away from all your offenses; then sin will not be your downfall. Why will you die, people of Israel? For I take no pleasure in the death of anyone, declares the Sovereign LORD. Repent and live!" (Ezekiel 18:30-32) This passage tells us that God is not selective in whom He saves but judges each "according to their own ways." In addition, we find God asking people to do something (repent) that they will never do according to Reformed Theology. Why would God ask people to do the impossible? Finally, we find God asking an even more ridiculous question (if Reformed Theology is true), "Why will you die?" Doesn't God know they will die because they are not of His elect?

"As surely as I live, declares the Sovereign LORD, I take no pleasure in the death of the wicked, but rather that they turn from their ways and live. Turn! Turn from your evil ways!" (Ezekiel 33:11) Once again, we find God asking people to turn from their evil ways knowing full well they can't because of total depravity. According to Reformed Theology, God promises that if the people will "turn from their ways," they will live even though He knows such turning is impossible. If God were honest, He would tell the people, "You won't turn, so I am going to turn some of you against your will, and I will be sending the rest of you to hell. In fact, I planned to do that long before I made these pleas for you to repent. That's been my plan from the beginning even if I did say I take *no pleasure in the death of the wicked.*"

God is He "Who will have all men to be saved, and to come unto the knowledge of the truth" (1 Timothy 2:4 KJV). If Reformed Theology is true, this verse should read, "Who will have *some* men to be saved." As it stands, this verse is lying because God doesn't want all men to be saved.

"The Lord is not slow in keeping his promise, as some understand slowness. Instead he is patient with you, not wanting anyone to perish, but everyone to come to repentance" (2 Peter 3:9). He is being patient with *everyone* because He doesn't want *anyone* to perish.

Do any of these verses give us a reason to conclude that God doesn't really mean what He says? Are we to conclude that what God reveals in these verses to be His will isn't to be accepted at face value because He has a secret will that contradicts what He tells us is His will?

God's Conditional Will

Calvinists had to invent a secret will that contradicts the will that God reveals to us because God's revealed will contradicts some of the beliefs found in Reformed Theology. So, rather than abandon their theology, they created a God who tells us things that aren't actually true. The real reason Calvinists can't accept God's words as they are written is because Calvinists do not believe in God's *conditional will*. This is the third way in which God demonstrates His will. This is not a secretive or contradictory kind of will but rather a different way God displays His will. God desires all men to be saved but because of His conditional will, He allows men to choose. Men end up in hell, not because God predestined them to be there, but because they choose to ignore His love and refuse to accept Christ's atonement. They fail to meet the conditions (repentance and faith) God requires for forgiveness and salvation. God's conditional will allows people to ignore His commands (at their own peril, of course). But He does not ordain their disobedience. If He did, then He could not justly hold them accountable.

In the same way, God does not thrust His will on passive humans to make them into believers. His conditional will allows people to choose for themselves. The Bible is full of examples of God's conditional will as evidenced by all the "if – then" scenarios found throughout the Scriptures. For example, in 2 Chronicles 7:14 God promises, "*If* my people, who are called by my name, will humble themselves and pray and seek my face and turn from their wicked ways, *then* I will hear from heaven, and I will forgive their sin and will heal their land." God will act to forgive only if all the conditions are met. His conditional will allows people the freedom of choice. This does not, however, mean God is limited by the acts of His people. He is still sovereign and could force forgiveness, if He wanted to, but He leaves the decision in the hands of the people. In this case, like many others, God has chosen to enact His conditional will.

God changes His mind.

This aspect of God's will explains how God can change His mind. This does not mean God makes mistakes. It means God decides something for a particular situation and then decides something different when the circumstances warrant it. What God does is conditional.

In Numbers 14:12, God is so provoked by the unbelief of the Israelites that He declares to Moses, "I will strike them down with a plague and destroy them." Moses intercedes with these words, "In accordance with your great love, forgive the sin of these people, just as you have pardoned them from the time they left Egypt until now" (verse 19). The very next verse reads, "The Lord replied, 'I have forgiven them, as you asked'" (verse 20). God responded to Moses' request. God changed His mind as a result of Moses' prayer. David affirms this truth in Psalm 106:21, 23: "They forgot the God who saved them... So he said he would destroy them — had not Moses, his chosen one, stood in the breach before him to keep his wrath from destroying them." If it hadn't been for Moses, God would have destroyed the Israelites. God responds to men's requests (prayers). His will is often conditioned upon human prayers.

Does the wording indicate that the fix was in before Moses ever prayed or that God changed his mind as a result of Moses' prayer? If God had already predestined everything, why would the Bible give the impression Moses' prayer made a difference in what God did? Was David wrong when he declared "had not Moses stood in the breach" the Israelites would have been destroyed? We cannot ignore the words themselves simply because they do not fit our theological narrative.

Jeremiah is full of situations where God changes His mind. In chapter 26, verse 13, Jeremiah even promises the people of Israel that God will change His mind, if they will only obey Him. The prophet urges Israel to obey with the words, "Therefore now amend your ways and your doings, and obey the voice of the Lord your God; and the Lord will repent him of the evil that he hath pronounced against you" (KJV). The word *repent* is not used here to mean a turning from sin (God does not sin), but a turning or changing of the mind. Jeremiah is saying that God plans to bring something very harsh to the people, but He will change His mind and not bring such judgment on them, if they amend their ways. Thus, His will, in this situation, is determined by what the people decide to do. His will, in this case, is conditional.

No one in the Bible understood Divine determinism.

If God has already predestined everything without using his foreknowledge, why didn't anyone in the Bible realize it? For example, after giving birth, Hannah said, "For this child I prayed; and the Lord hath given me my petition which I asked of him" (verse 27). Hannah was obviously unaware that her prayers were not the reason she was given a child. It was because God predestined that she would (according to Reformed Theology). And God seems content to leave her in her state of cluelessness. The Bible says that "the Lord remembered her" (Hannah) and "she bare a son" (1 Samuel 1:19-20). It doesn't say God remembered what He ordained. It says God remembered Hannah's pleas and responded by giving her a son. How can that be true if everything has already been predestined without the use of foreknowledge?

The psalmist yearns for God to "listen to my cry, for I am in desperate need" (Psalms 142:6). Apparently, the psalmist was also unaware that it's too late for him to pray because everything has already been decided. David said the Lord had "given him his heart's desire" and had not "withheld the request of his lips" (Psalms 21:2). Obviously, David didn't realize the request of his lips had nothing to do with what God gave him. What David received was decided before David was even born, and it was not based on what God foreknew David would pray.

If anyone should have understood predestination it would have been Jesus. Yet, he told his disciples to pray for God's will to be done on earth as it is in heaven (Luke 11:2). Did he not know it was already being done? And why did he weep over Jerusalem (Luke 19:41) if God's perfect will for the Jews was being done? He should have rejoiced instead because God's secret will was being accomplished. Did Jesus not know that God has two kinds of wills— revealed and decretive?

If man has no say in his situation, why did Jesus say that he wanted to gather the children of Jerusalem under his wings, but they would not (Luke 13:34)? Isn't God sovereign? Or are people able to resist God's will and grace? Jesus rebukes people for being "slow of heart to believe" (Luke 24:25). Why rebuke people for being slow to believe if they have no faith to believe? According to Reformed Theology, God must give people the faith to believe. Is God slow to give people faith? So much of the Bible becomes confusing and contradictory, if not absurd, if one accepts the Reformed Theology of individual predestination. The only way to make sense of it is to understand God's will is sometimes conditional. God's conditional will explains how Satan and people can commit evil without God ordaining such evil. God can foreknow events without being responsible for their occurring because He allows things to happen by His conditional will.

Pray

We see then that the appropriate response to God's conditional will is to pray. The fact that God is sovereign over all doesn't mean He cannot respond to human desires or prayers. Suppose I decide to buy my wife a dress and I know she wants a red dress because that is the color she needs to match her shoes. Does her desire mean that I cannot buy her a dress of any color I want? That's a rhetorical question. The reason I don't buy a blue dress when she desires a red one is not because I am not sovereign enough to do what I please. (This analogy should not be interpreted to mean I believe I am sovereign over my wife or that my wife could not buy a dress on her own. I use it here merely as an illustration). The point is, my wife's desire does not limit me in any way. The reason I buy her a red dress is because I love her and want to meet her need of a red dress. In the same way, God responds to our prayers because He loves us and wants us to know He will meet our every need. In doing so, nothing is taken away from His sovereignty.

Imagine a husband who decides not only what dress color his wife must wear but decides everything else the wife is allowed to have or do. She has absolutely no influence in anything he decides for her. In fact, he decided everything for her before they were even married. The desire of the husband is to control a robot rather than to have a thinking, feeling wife. By taking away the wife's free will, the husband prevents the two of them from having a volitional interactive relationship. The wife needn't bother asking for anything because everything has already been decided. The only way the wife is going to love such a husband is to be somehow forced to do so. If the wife is not under some type of hypnotic spell, she is going to be miserably sad. So, the husband must secretly cause her to like his style of sovereignty. This is the kind of husband Calvinists portray God to be.

Loving relationships involve a willingness on the part of both parties to respond to each other's longings. Does God have to respond to our prayers? No, but He does so because He loves us. That's how true love works. It's hard to imagine how anyone can fully appreciate God's love until one understands how it is expressed through His conditional will. By dismissing this mutual interaction of God and man, Calvinists miss a wonderful part of our relationship with the Lord.

The Dangers in Limiting God's Will

There is danger in believing God only demonstrates His will in one way. If we accept only one of the three areas of God's will as the whole, we not only limit God's will, but we end up believing a heresy. For example, if we see God's will only as Natural Laws, we will fail to see the supernatural and become humanists. If we look only to God's Conditional Will, we end up with magic or trying to make God into our personal Santa Claus. Our prayers should primarily be a time for us to seek God's will, and not a time for us to attempt to get God to do ours. Prayer should be an intimate time when we develop our relationship with the Lord. As has been often stated, "Seek the giver more than the gifts." And finally, if we accept all of God's will to be His Immutable Will – as Calvinists do – we will fail to fully understand how much God loves us and we will be left with nothing but fatalism.

Calvinism is not a belief in fatalism.

Calvinists will protest the idea that Reformed Theology is a belief in fatalism. To them such a notion is one of the many straw men that critics of Calvinism make. Calvinist C. Michael Patton, for example, states, "A fatalistic worldview is one in which all things are left to fate, chance, and a series of causes and effects that has no intelligent guide or ultimate cause. Calvinism believes that God (not fate) is in control."[99]

That may be how Patton defines fatalism, but according to Webster's dictionary, the word is defined as "the belief that all events are predetermined and hence inevitable."[100] Whether you believe events are predetermined by fate, chance, or God does not change the fact that they are all inevitable. That is exactly what Calvinism teaches. The non-elect have no choice as to what their ultimate fate will be, because it has already been predetermined and hence, it is inevitable. Merriam-Webster defines fatalism as "the belief that what will happen has already been decided and cannot be changed."[101] Again, that is exactly what Calvinism teaches. God has already decided, and it cannot be changed. This is the very definition of fatalism according to Webster.

Even if we use the term *determinism*, rather than *fatalism*, to allow for the existence of God, it doesn't help. The non-elect are in the same circumstances. Semantic word games do not improve their lot. If they are helpless to do anything to escape hell, then they are in a fatalistic situation, even if it is at the hands of God.

The Stanford Encyclopedia of Philosophy states that "philosophers usually use the word [fatalism] to refer to the view that we are powerless to do anything other than what we actually do."[102] Once again, that is exactly what Calvinism teaches as a result of their view of total depravity. Sinners are powerless to do anything other than sin. When the word fatalism is understood properly, there is no avoiding the fact that Calvinists teach it, even if they claim they do not. It is not a straw man. By denying the existence of God's conditional will, Calvinists are consigned to teaching fatalism.

Aspects of God's will	Right Response	Wrong Response (any one aspect alone)
Natural Laws	Plan	Humanism
Immutable Will	Trust	Fatalism
Conditional Will	Pray	Magic

Assumption #13
Reformed Theology Cannot be Disputed

R. C. SPROUL STATED that "Reformed theology applies the doctrine of God relentlessly to all other doctrines, making it the chief control factor in all theology. Reformed Theology is unique in that way."[103]

That statement is merely another false assumption. Reformed Theology is hardly unique in making God the chief control factor in one's theology. What the Early Church Fathers taught was not man-centered. Having a theology that is God-centered is certainly commendable but holding to the one you are convinced is the only correct one does not make it unique. Nor should a God-centered theology simply view His creations as basically superfluous. Reformed Theology's primary teaching about humans is that they are totally depraved, incapable of seeking God, exist only to glorify God, and can only do what God has already decided they will do. But that's not God's primary view of humans. He places a much higher value on them. For example, the reason Jesus came and went to the cross was because He loved people so much. He was willing to suffer and die in order to provide atonement for His lost creations. The purpose then of salvation was primarily man-centered. God doesn't need saving. It is humans who do. Christ didn't die for Himself. He died for humans because He loved them. So, in that sense, any theology that teaches salvation's purpose is only God-centered fails to understand who it is that needs saving. God is at the center of everything, but He designed salvation specifically for lost humanity. Christ's loving sacrifice on the cross was man-centered, not self-centered.

Even more arrogant than believing Reformed Theology is unique because it is the only one that applies the doctrine of God relentlessly is the statement by Lorraine Boettner. He decreed, "there are no valid arguments to refute predestination/Calvinism."[104] Calvinists like Boettner are not ignorant of the many scholarly refutations of Calvinism. They simply are convinced that they alone are capable of determining what constitutes a valid argument. Only arrogance would lead someone to make such a boastful declaration.

Sadly, pride is often a hallmark of Calvinists. The intellectual prowess required to understand Reformed Theology can easily lead one to think more highly of himself (and his theology) than he ought to think. It's hard to remain humble when you are convinced your theology is far superior to everyone else's. This is especially ironic when you consider Calvinists' claim that it is the non-Calvinists who are full of self-conceit as a result of their belief in conditional election.

The Synod of Dort

One reason many Calvinists are convinced their theology is superior is because they believe the historical Church rejected Arminianism at the Synod of Dort. In 1618-19 the Synod of Dort was convened and adopted a high Calvinistic statement which included the supralapsarian position of Beza. Although Arminius him-

self had called for an open forum, he was not in attendance, having died previous to the convention. Those who
were in attendance included over a hundred Calvinists
and only thirteen Remonstrants (Arminians).[105] When the
Remonstrants voiced their opposition, they were dismissed from the proceedings and were not allowed to vote
on any of the issues. The Synod was a totally stacked
deck. It is of no surprise then that the Synod condemned
Arminianism as heretical. As a result some 200 Remon-
strant ministers were ousted from their pulpits. Some were
banished and persecuted until 1625.

Calvinists still appeal to the decisions made during the
Synod of Dort as being authoritative declarations for the
Church to accept as truth. The truth is the Synod of Dort
was a totally one-sided affair with all voting attendees
having already decided what their vote would be. The
attendees came to Dort having already made up their
minds that the positions of Arminius were false. Many
had written prior statements clearly delineating their
views. Thus, the Synod of Dort was a mere charade.

Nevertheless, Calvinists suggest that the Synod of
Dort's conclusions represented the view of the Christian
Church as a whole and should be accepted as such. In
the 1959 edition of the *Psalter Hymnal*, you find the following: "Having been condemned by the Synod of
Dordrecht (Dort) in 1618-1619, Arminianism is indeed a
heresy." Even though it was ardent Calvinists who decided Arminianism was a heresy, Calvinists proffer the
Synod's findings as the definitive truth.

A second reason many Calvinists are convinced their
theology is superior is because they read great theologians who write very scholarly defenses of Reformed Theology and conclude that such brilliance has to be correct.
Furthermore, they listen to the arguments given by many
ardent Arminians and find them to be based more on
emotion than on scholarly exegesis. Sadly, most

Arminians are not well equipped to defend their views from an understanding of the Greek usage of words or solid hermeneutics. Thus, Calvinists conclude Arminians do not have sufficient knowledge to rightly divide the Word. Unfortunately, in most cases Calvinists are correct about the lack of knowledge possessed by the average Arminian. That does not mean, however, that all Arminians are incapable of giving a scholarly exegesis in refutation of Reformed Theology. There have been and continue to be a large number of greatly educated intellectuals who have done exactly that. Sadly, however, the average Arminian is not schooled in this rich heritage.

This brings up a third reason many Calvinists are convinced their theology is superior. They are persuaded Calvinism presents the correct interpretations of Scriptures because they only read books that support Reformed Theology. As a result, they are never challenged to broaden their thinking. Some Calvinists believe that reading Arminian books is a waste of time because such books are logically inferior or have nothing new to say. Such arrogance assumes one already knows it all or, at the very least, one knows enough that he/she doesn't need to consider anything that differs from the truth that he/she believes in. Such exclusivity differs little from that of Jehovah's Witnesses or any other authoritarian group. Try as I might, I have never been able to convince a Jehovah's Witness to read the book, *30 Years a Watchtower Slave*. In the same way, I have never been able to convince a Calvinist to read any of my books. As long as people are absolutely certain they have the ultimate truth, it becomes almost impossible to open their minds to anything different. Such is the allure of Calvinism.

Are there any good reasons to reject Calvinism?

With that said, let me conclude this book by offering what I consider to be fifty valid reasons (arguments) to reject Calvinism. Obviously, Calvinists like Boettner would not view them as valid. I'll leave it to the readers to decide if they think they are.

1. Calvinism originated with Augustine who lived decades after the Bible was written. It was not taught by the Early Church Fathers. In fact, many of the Early Church Fathers left writings that taught concepts that Augustine would later claim were not true. A belief in libertarian free will is just one example of Early Church theology that Augustine viewed as unbiblical. Acceptance of Reformed Theology requires one to believe the Early Church Fathers were wrong and it wasn't until Augustine came along that the proper interpretation of the Bible was first discovered.

2. Augustine developed his ideas from the writings of pagan Greek philosophers, such as Plato and Aristotle, who taught that God is unemotional and is never influenced by man. By contrast, the Bible tells us that Jesus (God in the flesh) was very emotional. He became angry, He was sad, and He wept. He was also influenced by people. Jesus responded to every hurting person who sought Him in faith. He did not pick out a select few to heal and ignore the majority of those who came to Him. All who desired healing were healed. Unlike the God of the secular Greek philosophers, Jesus was compassionate and was influenced by and responded to people and their faith in Him. In order to accept Calvinism, one must believe in what pagan philosophers thought God was like over what God revealed Himself to be like.

3. Calvinists hold to the belief that God cannot be sovereign if humans have libertarian free will. Such a belief is easily shown to be untrue. God is sovereign regardless of what abilities He may decide to give to mankind. God created man in His own image. There is no biblical reason to assume that His image did not include the ability to choose.

4. Calvinists insist that God cannot be sovereign if His decisions are conditioned upon what man decides or does. Yet, the Bible is replete with examples of God's actions being conditioned upon what people decide to do (e.g., 2 Chronicles 7:14).

5. Calvinists believe all unregenerate hearts are the same. Their hearts are filled only with evil and they hate God. The Bible, on the other hand, tells us differently. Not only are people's hearts different (e.g., Cain and Abel), but God tests men's hearts to see the differences in them. When God finds hearts that have integrity, He is pleased (1 Chronicles 29:17). If Calvinism is true, then God's search for integrity is a futile waste of His time because no heart has any integrity.

6. Calvinists claim that not a single unregenerate person ever seeks God, yet the Bible is full of examples of people who did. Furthermore, the Bible is full of exhortations for people to seek God while He may be found. If Calvinism is true, then such exhortations serve no purpose because they will never be followed. So, once again, God is wasting His time when He tells people to do something they will never do.

7. According to Calvinism, God also wastes His time when He tells the unregenerate to repent, because they will never do that, either.

8. In the same way, God is wasting His time when He asks non-believers to believe. Reformed Theology leaves one wondering why God would spend so much time requesting people to do things they will never do.

9. If God knows sinful humans cannot seek Him, repent of their sins, or place their faith in Christ, His requests for them to do these things are disingenuous, making God less than honest.

10. Calvinists believe man lacks the faith needed to trust in the atonement, yet nowhere in all of Scripture do you find such a statement. Nor does the Bible indicate any-

where from Genesis to Revelation that man lost his ability to believe in God as a result of the Fall.

11. Calvinists claim God must give the unbeliever the faith needed to repent, yet there is no such wording found anywhere in the Bible. Furthermore, whenever the Scriptures tell of anyone trusting Christ there is no mention of them first receiving the needed faith from God to do so.

12. According to Calvinism, God must give people a second kind of faith in order for them to trust in Christ. But the Bible doesn't teach that there are two kinds of faith. There is only one definition given for faith in the Bible (Hebrews 11:1). Furthermore, that definition includes the same kind of faith everyone has. Where one's faith is placed differs, but the faith is the same.

13. In order to accept Calvinism, one must believe that human faith and human works are the same. The Bible teaches that they are not the same. Works will not be counted for righteousness while faith will.

14. Calvinists believe that if we are saved by human faith then pride is inevitable. The Bible says otherwise (Romans 3:27). Nowhere in all the examples detailing people of faith (e.g., Abraham, Noah, Joshua, Caleb) are any of them said to have become proud because they trusted God. There is no biblical or experiential evidence that faith results in pride.

15. In order to avoid contradiction with their theology of total depravity, Calvinists are required to believe that regeneration comes before faith. They must do so despite the absence of any direct statement in the Bible giving that sequence of events, and despite the multitude of verses that specifically declare the exact opposite *ordo salutis*.

16. If the unregenerate lack the faith to trust in Christ, the only ones God should expect to follow His commands to believe would be the regenerated. Yet God makes His requests to believe to the unregenerate. Additionally, not a single person who is said to have believed is said to have

been regenerated prior to their belief. Nor is regeneration said to have taken place prior to all those who sought
the Lord. Of all the people Christ told their sins were forgiven, not one is said to have been regenerated first. In
not a single instance (not even one time) is the word
palingenesias (regeneration) even mentioned when someone is said to have chosen to obey God or to follow Christ.
Everything in the wording of all these stories indicates
that it was the individuals themselves who made the decisions they did.

17. If Calvinism's concept of total depravity is true then
Joshua wasn't being completely honest when he stated
that he and his family will choose to serve the Lord. He
should have been more forthright and said that it was
God who caused him to make such a choice. Statements
like Joshua's shouldn't be accepted at face value if Calvinism is true.

18. If the only reason a person believes is because
God gives them a special kind of faith to do so, why is
the individual praised by God for having such faith?
Why does the Bible say the faith that some people ex-
hibited (e.g., Abraham) was counted for righteousness?
According to Calvinism, it should have said it was the
faith that God gave these people that was counted for
righteousness. The Bible says people please God when
they have faith. According to Calvinism, however, God
is pleased with Himself because it was His faith and
not the individual's faith that resulted in His being
pleased.

19. According to Calvinism, God offers eternal life to
all, knowing full well He has no intention of giving it to
the vast majority of people. In fact, He never intended to
give eternal life to most people from the very beginning.
Thus, such offers are not only dishonest, but cruel. Making such offers to the non-elect serves no purpose, except
to taunt.

20. In His parables, Christ made it clear that salvation was conditional. A great number of other passages in the Bible make that clear as well. Despite all the Scriptural evidence, Calvinists insist that salvation is unconditional. The reason they believe in unconditional election is because logic requires it to be true if their concept of total depravity is true. They are forced by logic to accept the concept despite the fact the Bible teaches salvation to be conditional.

21. Calvinism teaches that the atonement is limited, while the Bible states over and over again that Christ died for all. A belief in Calvinism requires twisting the meaning of a great many verses that deal with the inclusiveness of Christ's atonement in order to make the verses say something other than what they do. Such twisting of Scripture is also required for other concepts held by Calvinists (e.g., eternal security).

22. The idea of a limited atonement was first introduced by Augustine four hundred years after Christ. Even then it was not generally accepted. It took much time and effort before Christians were convinced of the idea (brainwashed?). Calvinists believe the early Christians were wrong regarding the atonement. It wasn't until centuries later that one man finally got it correct. Prior to Augustine, the entire Church was mistaken.

23. Calvinists claim God's saving grace cannot be resisted, yet the Bible is full of examples of people who did precisely that. Furthermore, God warns people not to resist His grace. Why would He do that if people can't resist it even if they wanted to? Calvinism's God senselessly warns people not to do something that is impossible for them to do.

24. According to Calvinism, sinful man cannot volitionally respond to God's love. If that is true, then it is because God did not predestine lost men to have such a will, because God predestines everything according to

Calvinism. Yet God sends people to hell because they lack the will which He refused to give them.

25. Calvinists maintain that no one desires to be saved. As a result, God must reprogram a person's will before they will respond positively to the Gospel. Fortunately for some, God does reprogram the will of a select few (the elect) for salvation even though they have no desire to be reprogrammed. Calvinists, nevertheless, maintain that no one becomes a Christian against their will. Huh? By contrast, Jesus never selectively reprogrammed anyone. Instead, He offers His love and rest to *all* who are *"weary and heavy burdened"* (Matthew 11:28). In addition, He often told people it was their faith that saved them, with no mention of God first reprogramming them. Throughout Scripture people made choices to trust God without any indication they were unable to make such a choice without first being regenerated.

26. According to Calvinism, God does not practice egalitarian fairness, even though the Bible is full of admonitions for us to practice it. The Bible also tells us that God Himself does not show partiality (i.e., He practices egalitarian fairness). The Bible tells us God judges each according to his deeds (Romans 2:6). A belief in individual predestination makes such Scriptures untrue.

27. If God has already predetermined everything, then to tell us we can ask anything of Him is really only an unloving ruse. He's already made up His mind, so prayer requests are useless. We are children with no ability to genuinely interact with the Father because our relationship with such a sovereign God is all one-sided.

28. According to Calvinism, one cannot lose his salvation, yet the Bible is full of warnings to Christians about that very possibility. If Calvinism is correct, then the Bible is warning Christians to avoid something that could never happen. Furthermore, there is case after case of Chris-

tians who are said to have fallen away. Non-Christians have nothing to fall away from.

29. Calvinism's view of God's sovereignty requires that everything be predestined by God. Man is only doing what God has already decided he will do. Man is going through the motions of an uncreative robot designed to do exactly what it has been programmed to do. But if God preordained everything, then why does He become angry when people and nations disobey Him? Are they not doing exactly what He preordained them to do? Did God create men for the purpose of making Himself angry?

30. If Calvinism is correct that God sends the majority of people to hell to demonstrate His justice and only sends a small minority of people to heaven to demonstrate His love, then His desire from all eternity was to demonstrate more of His justice than His love. This does not square with the Bible telling us God is love. It should tell us God is more justice than love.

31. Calvinists believe God created man in His own image primarily for self-glorification. Jesus, on the other hand, did not demonstrate that while He was on earth. His desire was always to give rather than be given to. Jesus was far more concerned with loving others than He was with receiving glory from others. Jesus did not view man's primary reason for existence to be for glorifying God but for loving Him and others. He even declared those to be the two greatest commandments. At best, glorifying God comes in as a distant third in importance.

32. When Calvinists do discuss God's love, they teach that He has two kinds, one kind for the lost and another kind for the elect. Nowhere in the Bible does it teach that God's love is anything less than perfect agape love. Calvinists are required to come up with a God with dual loves in order to justify their belief in limited atonement.

33. Even if one could justify God having two kinds

of love, how could love of any kind let most of those you have created in your own image be cast into hell for all eternity if only you have the ability to keep them from such a fate? Furthermore, if you did have such an ability and did not exercise it, how could you claim you did not wish for anyone to perish if the choice is totally yours? A good shepherd seeks to save *all* his lost sheep. Calvinism's God is content with selecting a few and sending the rest to be tortured forever for committing sins He Himself ordained they commit. This is not love by any definition. To send people to hell for your own good pleasure is sadism.

34. Extreme love is not demonstrated in dying for those whom you know (from before the world began) are your children. Almost any good parent would be willing to die for their children. Extreme love is found in giving up your life for lost souls even if they do not respond in kind – who may not be your own precious children. The love of Jesus is extreme. The love of Calvin's God is not.

35. It is in recognizing the length to which the Father is willing to go to save (the giving of His only begotten Son) that can break the hearts of sinners and cause them to seek His forgiveness. Calvinists don't believe anyone can be moved by Christ's death on the cross or respond volitionally to His great love. No, God must change the will of the elect before they can repent. Such involuntary repentance is not genuine but a mere sham to accomplish God's will.

36. The Father doesn't force the prodigal son to return. By contrast, Calvinism's God must use His irresistible grace to bring the prodigal home because the son has no desire to be there. Of course, the only prodigals brought home are those the Father predestined to bring home.

37. Love is a volitional act. If God chooses who will be saved on some basis other than knowing ahead of time who will volitionally respond to His love, the only way to

264 | FIVE REASONS TO BELIEVE IN CALVINISM, FIFTY REASONS NOT TO

guarantee the ones chosen will love Him is to require them
to. Such a forced response is not love at all. To suggest
that being chosen by God automatically results in love
toward Him is not a biblical teaching. The entire history
of Israel demonstrates that being chosen by God results
more often in a turning away from God than it does in
loving Him.

38. Calvinists contend that God has kept His reasons
for saving some and not others a complete secret. Yet,
there is not a single verse in the Bible that even hints that
such is the case.

39. If I am no different than every other sinful human
being on the earth, yet am one of the lucky few who are
not punished for it, love would result in great mourning
for those who were not so lucky. But Calvinists see no
reason for weeping because God is glorified by sending
people to hell; we should rejoice in that.

40. Love was not the central teaching of Calvin, nor is
love the primary emphasis of Reformed Theology, despite
the Bible declaring that, of all the things that abide, the
greatest is love (1 Cor. 13:13). The one thing the Bible
makes clear to us, above everything else, is *not* that we
must fully understand God's sovereignty and our total
depravity. Instead, our number one priority is that we
love God with all our hearts, souls, and minds (Matthew
22:37), and that we love our neighbors as ourselves (Matthew 22:39). This is not, however, what is found to be the
number one priority in Calvin's writings or in the writings of most Calvinists. While *grace* (love?) is a recurring
theme, it is very exclusive unless you believe sending the
lost to hell is an act of grace.

41. Calvinists believe God wanted sin to occur. That's
why He ordained it, but He is not responsible for it. Do
Calvinists even listen to what they are saying?

42. Even though God hates sin, Calvinists believe He
wanted every sick and twisted evil there is to take place.

Despite all the hurt and damage that sin causes, God still wanted sin to infect every single human being for His glory. At the same time, Calvinists declare Him to be a *good* God. What?

43. God said what He created was good. If that is true and God created evil, then evil must be good under the theology of Calvinism.

44. According to Reformed Theology, God needed humans and sin in order to display His glory. At the same time, Calvinists say God is sovereign and in need of nothing. Both contentions cannot be true. If God is truly sovereign and in need of nothing, then He didn't need sin to display His glory. And if He didn't need sin in order to accomplish His purposes but ordained it anyway, then He is Himself evil.

45. Calvinists attempt to get around all the verses that tell us God wants all to be saved by telling us God doesn't really mean that. He actually has another desire (will) that contradicts what He reveals to be His will. While He may tell us He wants something to happen, He really has a decretive will that is opposite to what He claims (reveals) in the Bible to be His will. The idea that God has two opposing wills is a sheer concoction by Calvinists to avoid the truth of unlimited atonement. If God has two wills that are not compatible, then we have no way of knowing for sure whether we are doing God's will. This is especially true if the only will we know is what God claims (reveals) is His will which may not be congruent with His decretive will.

46. All of the verses that Calvinists appeal to in support of their theology can be exegeted differently. In many cases, the alternate exegesis actually refutes Calvinism. In some cases, the exegesis by Calvinists can be clearly shown to be influenced by presuppositions and theological bias when an honest observation is made.

47. When the interpretation Calvinists deduce from a

particular verse contradicts other verses in the Bible, Calvinists make heroic but futile attempts to avoid the contradiction. They offer convoluted thinking (e.g., God ordained all things, but He is not responsible for their existence), they create things not found in the Bible (e.g., two kinds of faith, two kinds of love possessed by God, two wills desired by God that actually oppose each other— a revealed will that is opposite to His decretive or hidden will), they claim that logic demands their interpretation be correct even if the simple wording given in the text says otherwise, they excuse the problem by claiming God's ways are not ours, or they blame the problem on our inability to understand the Word of God. When all else fails, they simply call the contradiction a mystery.

48. Some beliefs held by Calvinists are impossible to reconcile with other beliefs they accept as true (e.g., God's sovereign determinism and man's responsibility). Rather than question the accuracy of their theology, however, Calvinists simply accept both ideas as true. When the absurdity of such a position is pointed out to them, Calvinists respond by saying, "It is better that one's theology suffer from philosophical problems than exegetical ones." It does not occur to Calvinists that it is far better to have a theology that suffers from neither.

49. Like cults whose followers call themselves Christians (e.g., Mormonism), Calvinism is so complicated that it requires extra-biblical sources to even begin to understand it. Even John 3:16 cannot be understood as it stands (see epilogue for details). A great deal of additional exegetical explanation is required to correctly understand what the words in this verse really mean.

50. Finally, as explained in this book, belief in Calvinism requires followers to accept a huge number of dubious assumptions, including all five points of the TULIP.

Any one of the above fifty arguments could be viewed as a good reason to reject Calvinism. All of them combined represent more than ample evidence that there are, indeed, many valid arguments to refute Calvinism, despite what Calvinists like Lorraine Boettner may proclaim.

Epilogue
Faith in Jesus is Simple

CALVINISTS WILL NO DOUBT CLAIM that much of what is written in this book represents the author's misunderstandings of Reformed Theology. This should come as no surprise as Calvinists are constantly decrying the fact that critics of Reformed Theology don't really understand it. This makes one wonder if the reason is because their theology is too complicated for the average person to comprehend.

The Apostle Paul writing to the Corinthians was concerned they might have their minds corrupted from the simplicity that is in Christ (2 Corinthians 11:3). Rather than simplicity, just the terms alone needed to adequately describe Calvinism are many and complicated. They include the concepts of monergism, semipelagianism, compatibilism, efficient cause and ultimate cause, common grace and irresistible grace, general calling and effectual calling, sublapsarianism and infralapsarianism, desiderative will and decretive will, federal headship, *ordo salutis*, and on and on. It's hard to imagine any two people agreeing on what all these words actually mean. If it should happen, it would be

due to years of study by both parties in concert. How then can the average Christian be expected to understand the teachings of Reformed Theology?

Paul said Christ sent him to preach the gospel, "not with wisdom of words, lest the cross of Christ should be made of none effect" (1 Corinthians 1:17 KJV). Paul was not against deep theological study, but he was against making the Gospel more complicated than it is, resulting in the cross becoming ineffective. Given the complexity of Calvinism, it's no wonder critics cannot comprehend it. Even Calvinists themselves admit they don't always understand their own theology. In a sermon entitled *The Ultimate Security of Our Salvation*, Calvinist John MacArthur confesses that he doesn't understand how God can predestine everything and still hold man accountable for what he does. He just accepts it. Below is a quote from that sermon:

> Now you say, "I don't understand that. It doesn't seem to jive with my own choice." I told you, you wouldn't. And if it makes you feel any better I don't understand it either and I've been going over this thing for years and the longer I study it the more I'm aware of the fact that my knowledge doesn't increase. I still don't understand it as much as I didn't understand it the first time I heard it. I just believe it and I'm happy to believe what I don't understand.[106]

These words remind me of a priest who was asked why the Bible says to call no man "father." The priest replied, "The more I read the Bible the less I understand it." What a sad comment.

The reason MacArthur and the priest don't understand certain verses is because they completely contradict what they believe. They know the verses must be true, but because they don't fit in with their particular theology, they assume it is a matter of them not understanding it. It doesn't occur to them that the problem is with their errant theology. In MacArthur's case, his errant theology is Calvinism.

Calvinists believe sovereign determinism and human responsibility are both true. That is equivalent to saying that if God cuts the head off of a sheep, the sheep is responsible for its own death. Seriously? If God has predetermined every action humans make but still holds them responsible for what they do, then He is an unjust and evil God. If God is a just and good God, then it is impossible for Him to hold people responsible for what they do unless they have been given libertarian free will. Because Calvinists do not believe God has given anyone such free will, they are forced to accept the impossible. They admit there is an obvious contradiction in what they believe, but they assuage themselves by claiming it must be due to man's limited understanding. That is like saying that when the Scriptures talk about an olive and a fish, the two are the same thing. It is merely a lack of understanding that prevents anyone from realizing they are identical. No, a fish and an olive are not the same. It is an "either/or" reality. The inability to reconcile the two cannot be chalked up to a lack of understanding. The same is true of the incompatibility of sovereign determinism and human responsibility. They cannot both be true if God is loving and fair. It is an "either/or" reality. To say they are both true is to say the Bible contradicts itself.

It should be true that the more one reads the Bible the better one understands it. The Spirit of truth guides us into all truth. To say God has written the Word in ways that make it impossible for Christians to understand (especially about something as critical as the Gospel itself) is to say that it was impossible for God to have done a better job of explaining how salvation works. He was unable to make it understandable for people. A person's theology of the Gospel should not require him/her to be content with illogical contradictions and confusion.

There was a time when the Catholic Church discouraged the laity from reading the Bible. The concern was they would not be able to correctly interpret it because they lacked the necessary training. The Lord, on the other hand, prefers revealing truth to children over the wise and learned (Matthew 11:25). Rather than requiring one be an intellectual with a degree in theology, God desires for even the least intelligent among us to be able to comprehend the Gospel and His will by simply reading the Scriptures. Calvinism requires much more.

Mormons consider themselves to be Christians. It is impossible, however, to read the Bible alone and understand what it means to be a Mormon. A person must read other material such as the Book of Mormon and/or be taught by the followers of the Church of Jesus Christ of Latter-Day Saints. It is equally true one cannot read the Bible alone and understand what it means to be a Calvinist. One must read other Calvinist teachings, such as *The Westminster Confession of Faith*, and/or be taught by followers of this particular theology. I am not suggesting Calvinism and Mormonism are the same, but I am suggesting that neither is what a person comes away with if one has only the Bible to read. They both require extra-biblical sources.

One should trust what the majority of people understand from reading the Word alone, rather than what scholars may teach from extra-biblical sources. This is particularly true when there is conflicting opinion among the academics, which there certainly is with the topic of election. A good example of the conflict can be found in the book *Perspectives on Election — Five Views* edited by Chad Owen Brand and published by Broadman and Holman Publishers. Five theologians (each with a Ph.D.) present five totally different views on the subject. It can be depressing to think God would make the Bible so difficult to understand that even the most learned among us cannot agree on what God is teaching. No, the Bible is not a book written by scholars for scholars, but a book written by common folks for everyone and anyone to read and understand. God shares His truth with all who seek it – educated or uneducated, king or peasant, high intelligence quotient or low.

It really is simple. "For God so loved the world that he gave his one and only Son, that whoever believes in him shall not perish but have eternal life." Calvinists don't accept this at face value. They claim there are a lot of nuances that the average reader doesn't understand. For example: God actually has two kinds of love (one kind for the elect and one kind for the non-elect); the word *world* doesn't mean everyone in the world but people from all different nations; and no one believes in the Son unless God gives them a special kind of faith that He only gives to the elect after He has regenerated them; so the word *whosoever* isn't a universal term but is restricted to the elect only. The verse is much more complicated than it appears. According to Calvinists, a more honest rendering of John 3:16 would be, "For God so loved [not the world but] the elect from all different nations whom He loves differently from the way he loves the non-elect that he gave his one and only Son for the elect alone, that by regenerating the elect and then giving them the faith they needed, they would believe in him and not perish but have eternal life unlike the non-elect who have been ordained to persist in unbelief and will perish."

To its credit, Reformed Theology corrected (reformed) many of the doctrinal heresies held by the Catholic Church prior to the Reformation. It correctly moved away from salvation by works, for example, and taught what is called the priesthood of the believer.

Unfortunately, in their efforts to correct errors in the Church, the Reformers created errors of their own.

Appendix A

CALVINISTS CONTEND THAT the Greek verbs used in 1 John 5:1 prove that faith follows regeneration. They argue that the verb for believe is in the present tense: "Everyone who believes that Jesus is the Christ..." It's also a participle; a more literal translation is, "Everyone believing that Jesus is the Christ..." The second verb for "born" is perfect tense: "...has been born of God." The perfect tense carries with it the idea of past action with continuing results. Being born of God produces results continuing into the present. When the present participle, believing, is coupled with the perfect tense verb, being born of God, faith is the result of being born again. The voice is passive; God alone accomplishes this birth. Faith is the result of regeneration; regeneration produces, and hence precedes, faith.

Daniel D. Musick refutes such an interpretation as follows:

> This interpretation is unwarranted from the tense of the Greek verbs. There are at least two examples in John's writings where, rather than the present tense participle resulting from the perfect tense

verb, the perfect tense verb results from the present tense participle.

One example is John 3:18. "Whoever believes (present participle) in him is not condemned (perfect tense)." Believing removes, and hence, precedes, not being condemned. Expressed positively: "Whoever believes (present participle) in him is justified (perfect tense). Believing is not the result of having been justified; rather, faith precedes justification.

A second example is 1 John 5:10: "Whoever does not believe (present participle) God has made (perfect tense) him a liar, because he has not believed in the testimony that God has borne concerning his Son." The perfect tense, making God a liar, is a result of the present participle, not believing.

The most you can conclude from the Greek present participle and the perfect tense verb is that the actions occur contemporaneously. There is regeneration and there is faith. The Greek tenses do no more to establish the order of salvation than the conjunction "and" in the previous statement.

Most Calvinists also resort to the use of the Greek word, gennaô, to be born. They teach that whenever this word occurs as a perfect verb, it produces a range of results expressed as present participles, of which faith is one.

"If you know that he is righteous, you may be sure that everyone who practices righteousness has been born of him" (2:29).

"No one born of God makes a practice of sinning, for God's seed abides in him, and he cannot keep on sinning because he has been born of God" (3:9).

"Beloved, let us love one another, for love is from God, and whoever loves has been born of God and knows God" (4:7).

"Everyone who believes that Jesus is the Christ has

been born of God, and everyone who loves the Father loves whomever has been born of him" (5:1).

According to Daniel Spratlin, "We can make two observations from these texts. First, in every instance the verb "born" (gennaô) is in the perfect tense, denoting an action that precedes the human actions of practicing righteousness, avoiding sin, loving, or believing."

"Second, no evangelical would say that before we are born again we must practice righteousness, for such a view would teach works-righteousness. Nor would we say that first we avoid sinning, and then are born of God, for such a view would suggest that human works cause us to be born of God. Nor would we say that first we show great love for God, and then he causes us to be born again. No, it is clear that practicing righteousness, avoiding sin, and loving are all the consequences or results of the new birth. But if this is the case, then we must interpret 1 John 5:1 in the same way, for the structure of the verse is the same as we find in the texts about practicing righteousness (1 John 2:29), avoiding sin (3:9), and loving God (4:7). It follows, then, that 1 John 5:1 teaches that first God grants us new life and then we believe Jesus is the Christ."[107]

If this were the only passage in Scripture that references regeneration and faith, I would favor the later reformed position, but I could not be dogmatic about it. It's the strongest argument of many Calvinists, but it is not without its problems.

1. The raw text of 1 John 5:1 carries more weight than the context of word association; in exegesis context is king, but sentence structure trumps context. Let's examine the two verses above side by side:

"Whoever believes (present participle) in him is not condemned (perfect tense)." John 3:18. (A then B)

276 | FIVE REASONS TO BELIEVE IN CALVINISM, FIFTY REASONS NOT TO

"Everyone who believes (present participle) that Jesus is the Christ has been born (perfect tense) of God." 1 John 5:1. (B then A)

2. From John's use of gennaô it would be appropriate to suggest that regeneration might precede faith, but to write, "It follows, then…" is to grasp an opinion that rests on thin ice. The conclusion is unwarranted.

3. John's uses of gennaô nowhere preclude the possibility of faith preceding regeneration. You can argue for regeneration preceding faith, but you can't argue against faith preceding regeneration.

4. John's use of the verb gennaô allows for at least four scenarios in which faith precedes regeneration.

First, a sinner believes, he's born again, and he continues in the present believing. John's reference could be to the ongoing faith of those who have been born of God.

Next, if faith and regeneration occur simultaneously, there's no time gap between faith and regeneration. Everyone who believes has been born again and everyone who has been born again believes. It's impossible to be born again and not believe; it's impossible to believe and not be born again.

A third scenario has to do with John's terminology. He uses the phrase "born of God" to designate "Christians," a term he never uses. The phrase, "born of God" can be substituted with the term, "Christian." Look at how the emphasis shifts.

Everyone who practices righteousness is a Christian. (2:29)

No one born of God keeps on sinning because he is a Christian. (3:9)

Whoever loves is a Christian. (4:7)

Everyone who believes that Jesus is the Christ is a Christian. (5:1)

John is not laying out here an *ordo salutis*. He is characterizing Christians, those who have been born again.[108] It's inappropriate to force results from the perfect tense.

Consider this fourth scenario.

Everyone who believes that Jesus is the Christ has been born of God. (1 John 5:1)

Everyone who believes that Jesus is the Christ has been justified. Is this true?

According to later reformed *ordo salutis*, being born of God precedes faith which precedes justification (Rom. 5:1). If the same grammatical structure that places being born of God before faith can also allow justification after faith, then the grammatical structure of the verse does not really address the order of salvation. John could have been writing from the same time-order orientation.

5. The broader context of John's writings. John would not teach here that regeneration precedes faith and elsewhere present faith as a condition for life. "These are written so that you may believe that Jesus is the Christ, the Son of God, and that by believing you may have life in his name." (John 20:31) You cannot have life without regeneration; birth is the beginning of life; it is part and parcel of life: faith then life (regeneration the beginning of life and continuing through eternity). Calvinists separate regeneration life from eternal life: regeneration life then faith then eternal life.

John's statement here not only supports the view that faith precedes regeneration, but it also precludes the possibility of regeneration preceding life. John 3:15-16: "And as Moses lifted up the serpent in the wilderness, so must the Son of Man be lifted up, that whoever believes in him may have eternal life. For God so loved the world, that he gave his only Son, that whoever believes in him should not perish but have eternal life."

The argument from the Greek tenses is without merit. When examined in the context of John's first letter, the argument from John's use of gennaô is, at best, tenuous. When examined in the context of other writings, the belief that regeneration precedes faith is without merit and it is precluded by clear Biblical statements contradicting that view.

Calvinists' belief that regeneration precedes faith is based on faulty exegesis, a vapid hermeneutic, altered definitions and Scriptures taken out of context. On this issue they clearly abandon *sola scriptura*.

Most Calvinists present Biblical support for their belief that regeneration precedes faith, but none of it is conclusive. They have no Biblical texts connecting faith and regeneration in a grammatical structure that prescribes an order that supports their view. Neither do these Calvinists have any words from Scripture which preclude the possibility of faith preceding regeneration.

In contrasts to these Calvinists we do find in Scripture passages that support the teaching that faith precedes regeneration, and these are conclusive. There are Biblical texts connecting faith and regeneration in a grammatical structure that supports this view. And we find in Scripture at least five passages that preclude the possibility of regeneration preceding faith (John 3:14-18, 6:40, 20:31; Colossians 2:12, and 1 Timothy 1:16).

The only reasonable conclusion from Scripture is that faith precedes regeneration.[109]

In other words, to deny the truth that faith precedes regeneration is to deny the Scriptures.

Appendix B

PROF. JACK COTTRELL'S EXEGESIS of Acts 13:48:

We can see how the usual translations of Acts 13:48 support the Calvinist view: only those appointed (ESV, NIV, NASB, NKJV) or destined (NRSV) or predestined (Weymouth) or ordained (KJV, ASV) or chosen (TEV) for eternal life actually became believers.

The question is this: how can this be reconciled with the Arminian (non-Calvinist) view? The key lies in the form of the main Greek verb, tassô. The basic meaning of this verb is "to place, to order, to appoint, to ordain, to determine, to arrange in order." As it appears in this text, the verb form is the participle tetagmenoi. It is simply assumed that this is the PASSIVE form of the verb, thus: "to be appointed, to be ordained, to be destined." What is often forgotten is that in the Greek language, often the passive and the middle form of verbs are spelled exactly the same way. That is the case here. The word tetagmenoi can also be the MIDDLE form of the verb. Here is the main point: that is how it should be understood in Acts 13:48.

What does this verse mean, then? The middle voice

of a verb in Greek is sometimes used in a reflexive sense. The idea is that the action of the verb is something performed by the subject (not by someone else upon the subject), but in such a way that the action is directed back toward the subject or the self. Understanding that the verb means "to place, to set, to arrange in a certain order or position," we can see that the statement in 13:48 can quite validly be taken thus: "As many as arranged themselves unto (eis) eternal life believed," or "As many as turned themselves toward eternal life believed," or "As many as disposed themselves toward eternal life believed."

Why should we accept this approach to the verb — i.e., as middle voice rather than passive? For two reasons. First, it agrees with the general overall teaching of Scripture, that turning toward God is a matter of free will and personal responsibility, not something unconditionally and irresistibly caused by God.

Second, this agrees with the context, where the Jews' response to the gospel is being contrasted with that of the Gentiles. In Acts 13:13-41 Paul preached a powerful Sabbath sermon in the Jews' synagogue at Antioch. Many of the Jews were so impressed that they asked for an encore the next Sabbath (vv. 42-43). Then on "the next Sabbath almost the whole city gathered to hear the word of the Lord" (v. 44). This crowd obviously included many Gentiles, because "when the Jews saw the crowds, they were filled with jealousy and began to contradict what was spoken by Paul, reviling him" (v. 45). This provoked Paul and Barnabas to speak this judgment upon the Jews: "It was necessary that the word of God be spoken first to you. Since you thrust it aside and judge yourselves unworthy of eternal life, behold, we are turning to the Gentiles" (v. 46). This verse is important because it shows that the exclusion of the Jews from the ranks of the saved was their own choice, not the result of some predestining activity of God. The Jews specifically judged themselves unworthy of eternal life.

This is exactly the opposite of the Gentiles' reaction, especially when Paul and Barnabas applied Isaiah 49:6 to themselves: "I have made you a light for the Gentiles, that you may bring salvation to the ends of the earth" (v. 47). Verse 48 then describes the reaction of the Gentiles to this preaching. It was in fact just the opposite of the Jews' reaction: "And when the Gentiles heard this, they began rejoicing and glorifying the word of the Lord." Then follow the crucial words: and as many as set themselves toward eternal life believed. How did they set themselves toward eternal life? By hearing and heeding the word of God (see Rom. 10:17). We cannot ignore the symmetrical contrast between the reaction of the Jews in v. 46 and the reaction of the Gentiles in v. 48. Whereas the Jews rejected the gospel and judged themselves to be unworthy of eternal life (v. 46), the Gentiles received it gladly and embraced the message of eternal life (v. 48). In both cases the decision was a matter of free choice. There is no support for Calvinism in v. 48.[110]

Notes

Chapter 1

1. Michael Horton, *For Calvinism* (Grand Rapids: Zondervan, 2011), p. 193.
2. Ibid., 137.
3. Ibid., 193.
4. Brian McLaren, *A Generous Orthodoxy* (Grand Rapids: Zondervan, 2004), 188.

Chapter 2

5. These thoughts were adapted from a message by Elder Aylett Raines, *A Refutation of Hereditary Total Depravity*.
6. John Piper, notes entitled *Total Depravity*, written for the Bethlehem Baptist Church in Minneapolis, MN, in 1998.
7. R. C. Sproul, *What is Reformed Theology?* (Grand Rapids: Baker Books, 2008), 184.
8. Edward White, *Life In Christ: A Study Of The Scripture Doctrine On The Nature Of Man, The Object Of The Divine Incarnation, And The Conditions Of Human Immortality* (London: Elliot Stock, 62, Paternoster Row, 1878), 306-307.
9. Sproul, *What is Reformed Theology*, 153.
10. R. C. Sproul, *Before the Face of God: Daily Guide for Living from Ephesians, Hebrews, and James* (Grand Rapids: Baker Book

House; Ligonier Ministries, 1994), 36.

11. *Kittel Theological Dictionary of the New Testament*: Abridged in One Volume, Gerhard Kittel and Gerhard Friedrich, editors (Grand Rapids: Eerdmans Publishing Co., 1985), 227.

12. Galyn Wiemers, *Examining John 6:44*, Posted by Generation Word Bible Teaching Ministry, Saturday, August 1, 2009. http://www.generationword.com.

13. Sproul, *What is Reformed Theology?*, 119.

14. Grant R. Osborne, "Exegetical Notes on Calvinist Texts," in *Grace Unlimited*, ed. Clark H. Pinnock (Minneapolis: Bethany Fellowship, Inc., 1975), 167-85.

15. Lorraine Boettner, *Man's Totally Helpless Condition* in *The Reformed Faith* (Phillipsburg, New Jersey: P & R Publishing, 1983).

16. For those readers who might wonder if I believe in total depravity, I say, If by total depravity, Christians mean we are all sinful, separated from God, unable to save ourselves, and in desperate need of the Savior, then I do, indeed, believe in total depravity. What I do not believe in is total depravity as defined by Reformed Theology.

I further believe that a person's faith comes in response to God's revelation of Himself, which He has done in many ways including through creation itself. It is every person's choice as to whether or not they put their faith in that revelation regardless of the amount they may have. Today, we have God's revelation of Himself through His Word (the Bible). Romans 10:17 tells us faith comes by hearing the word of God. It does not say faith comes by way of predestination. That is why it is so important for Christians to share the Gospel.

Chapter 3

17. Sproul, *What is Reformed Theology?*, 128.

18. Dr. Jerry L. Walls and Dr. Joseph R. Dongell, *Why I Am Not a Calvinist* (Downers Grove: InterVarsity Press, 2004), 77.

19. Albert Barnes, *The Whole Bible: Notes on the Whole Bible*, "Commentary on Psalms 118," written in 1834.

20. J. I. Packer and O. R. Johnston's translation of Luther's *Bondage of the Will* from German and Latin to English, (Grand

Rapids: Baker Books, 2012), Packer makes this statement in the introduction on page 59.

21. Grant Hawley, *The Guts of Grace: Preparing Ordinary Saints for Extraordinary Ministry* (Allen, Texas: Bold Grace Ministries, 2013), p. 124.

22. Dr. Jerry L. Walls and Dr. Joseph R. Dongell, *Why I Am Not a Calvinist* (Downers Grove: InterVarsity Press, 2004), p. 78.

23. Ibid.

24. Sproul, *What Is Reformed Theology?*, 195.

25. John MacArthur, *Faith Works* (Dallas: Word, 1993), p. 62.

26. Daniel D. Musick, "Faith Precedes Regeneration," 2012, http://danmusicktheology.com/faith-precedes-regeneration. Designed by Erich Musick, 2002. (Used by permission of the author)

Chapter 4

27. Arminius, *Works*, "Examination of Perkins's Pamphlet" 3:333. Cf. F. Leroy Forlines's juxtaposition of "influence and response" and "cause and effect" in *Classical Arminianism*, 3:426.

28. Walter A. Elwell, *Evangelical Dictionary of Theology* (Grand Rapids: Baker, 2001), 115.

29. Sproul, *What is Reformed Theology?*, 166.

30. Millard J. Erickson, *Christian Theology*, Second Edition (Grand Rapids: Baker, 2007), 851.

31. Robert Lightner, "For Whom Did Christ Die?" *Walvoord: A Tribute*, ed. Donald K. Campbell (Chicago: Moody Press, 1982), 166.

32. John Calvin: *Commentary on the Epistle to the Colossians* (Grand Rapids: Baker, 1979), 148.

33. Sproul, *What is Reformed Theology?*, 176.

34. Ernest DeWitt Burton, "The Epistles of John", *The Biblical World.* (University of Chicago Press, 1896). 7 (5): 367.

35. John Calvin: *Institutes of the Christian Religion*, Book 3, Chapter 7, Section 2210. First published in 1536.

36. Ibid., III: xxiii.

37. *Westminster Confession of Faith*, Ch. 3:1.

38. John Piper, "Why God is Not a Megalomaniac in Demanding to Be Worshipped," accessed July 30, 2012,

www.desiringgod.org/resource-library/conference-mes-
sages/why-god-is-not-a-megalomaniac-in–demanding-
to-be-worshipped.

39. Jonathan Edwards, *The End for Which God Created the World*, quoted by John Piper, "God's Passion for His Glory" (Wheaton, IL.: Crossway, 2006), 151.

40. John Calvin, *Institutes of the Christian Religion* (1536), first edition.

41. John Calvin, quoted in Colleen McDannell and Berhard Lang, *Heaven: A History* (New York: Vintage Books, 1988), 155.

42. *The Westminster Confession of Faith*, Chapter II, Section 1, Article 6.011 (Westminster Assembly, 1646).

43. John Calvin, *Genesis*, Calvin's Commentaries, vol. 1 (Grand Rapids: Baker, 1979), 248-49.

44. Austin Fischer, *Young, Restless, No Longer Reformed: Black Holes, Love, and a Journey In and Out of Calvinism* (Eugene: Cascade Books, 2014), 40.

45. Gregory Boyd, *Is God to Blame? Beyond Pat Answers to the Problem of Suffering* (Downers Grove, IL: InterVarsity, 2003), 35.

46. Fischer, *Young, Restless, No Longer Reformed,* 47.

47. Ibid., 46.

48. John Wesley, Sermon 128, *Free Grace*, preached at Bristol in 1740.

49. Fischer, *Young, Restless, No Longer Reformed,* 24-25.

50. Loraine Boettner, *The Reformed Doctrine of Predestination* (Grand Rapids: Eerdmans, 1957), 160.

Chapter 5

51. Sproul, *What is Reformed Theology?,* 153.

52. Ibid., 159.

Chapter 6

53. *Grace for All: The Arminian Dynamics of Salvation*, Clark H. Pinnock and John D. Wagner Editors, Resource Publications, (Eugene, OR: An Imprint of Wipf and Stock Publishers, 2015), 42.

54. Paul T. Butler, *The Gospel of John: A New Commentary, Workbook, Teaching Manuel* (Joplin, Mo.: College, 1961), 112.

55. Alan P. Stanley, *Salvation Is More Complicated Than You Think: A Study on the Teachings of Jesus* (Colorado Springs: Authentic, 2007), 165–166.

56. *Grace for All: The Arminian Dynamics of Salvation*, Clark H. Pinnock and John D. Wagner Editors, Resource Publications, (Eugene, OR: An Imprint of Wipf and Stock Publishers, 2015), 42.

57. Robert Shank, *Life in the Son*, (Minneapolis, Minnesota: Bethany House Publishers, 1960), 60.

58. *Grace for All: The Arminian Dynamics of Salvation*, Clark H. Pinnock and John D. Wagner Editors, Resource Publications, (Eugene, OR: An Imprint of Wipf and Stock Publishers, 2015), 42.

59. Sproul, *What is Reformed Theology?*, 216.

Chapter 7

60. G. C. Berkouwer, *Divine Election* (Grand Rapids: Eerdmans Publishing Co., 1960), 42.

61. R. C. Sproul, "Why Did God Save Me?" https://www.monergism.com/thethreshold/articles/onsite/sproulwhy.html

Chapter 8

62. J. Vernon McGee, *Thru the Bible Radio Broadcast* by J. Vernon McGee on Exodus 7.

63. Shank, *Life in the Son*, 184.

64. Brian Abasciano, *Acts 13:48, Election, Greek Grammar, Translations*. Posted by The Society of Evangelical Arminians (SEA), March 12, 2015.

65. Ibid.

Chapter 9

66. Sproul, *What is Reformed Theology?*, 143.

67. Ibid.

68. John Calvin: *Institutes of the Christian Religion*, Book 3, Chapter 11, Section 1.

Chapter 10

69. Robert A. Peterson and Michael D. Williams, *Why I Am Not an*

Arminian (Downers Grove: Inter Varsity Press, 2004), 134.

70. Martin Luther, *The Bondage of the Will*, (Westwood: Fleming H. Revell, 1957), 217.

Chapter 11

71. Sproul, *What is Reformed Theology?*, 26.

72. James Montgomery Boice, *Whatever Happened to the Gospel of Grace?* (Wheaton, IL.: Crossway, 2001), 167. Original illustration by Augustine of Hippo.

73. Luther, *The Bondage of the Will*, 158.

74. Sproul, *What is Reformed Theology?*, 170.

75. Ibid., 171.

76. *The Westminster Confession of Faith*, Ch. 3:1.

77. Ignatius of Antioch, *Epistle to the Magnesians*, Vol. 1, Chapter V.

78. Irenæus, *Against Heresies* Book IV Chapter XXXVII, (37).

79. Justin Martyr, *Second Apology*, 7.

80. Justin Martyr, *First Apology*, Chapter XLIII, (43).

81. Justin Martyr, Chapter CXLI, (141).

82. Clement, *Miscellanies*, Book 1, Chapter 17.

83. Archelaus, *Disputation With Manes*, pp. 32, 33.

84. Methodius, *The Banquet of the Ten Virgins* Discourse 8, Chapter 16.

Sources for the quotations of the Early Church Fathers (footnotes 72-79) were taken from *Ante-Nicene Fathers*, ed. Philip Schaff (Grand Rapids: Christian Ethereal Library, 1885).

85. Tertullian, *Against Marcion*, Book II, <u>Chapter V</u>.

86. James Morrison, *The Extent of Atonement*, (London: Hamilton, Adams, and Co., 1882), 117.

87. Lorraine Boettner, *The Reformed Doctrine of Predestination* (Phillipsburg, NJ: Presbyterian and Reformed Publishing Co., 1932), 365.

88. Aristotle, *Metaphysics*, Book XII or Lambda, 350 BC.

89. *The Westminster Confession of Faith*, Chapter X (Westminster Assembly, 1646).

Chapter 12

90. R. C. Sproul, Jr., *Almighty Over All* (Grand Rapids: Baker Books, 1999), p. 54.

91. Edwin Palmer, *The Five Points of Calvinism* (Grand Rapids: Baker Books, 1999), p. 25.

92. Arminianism also has a "Problem of Evil" — Examining Calvinism. www.examiningcalvinism.com/files/Complaints/Charge_POE.html.

93. John Calvin: *Institutes of the Christian Religion*, Book 3, Chapter 7, Section 2210, 1536.

94. Sproul, *What is Reformed Theology?*, 55.

95. Ibid., p. 56.

96. Jack Cottrell, *How Do Calvinists Explain 2 Peter 3:9?*, Posted on April 3, 2010.

97. Martin Luther, *What Luther Says: An Anthology*, ed. Edwald M. Plass, 3 vols. (St. Louis: Concordia, 1959), 1:93.

98. Sproul, *What is Reformed Theology?*, 57.

99. C. Michael Patton, Parchment & Pen Blog (Credo House Ministries, March 4, 2010).

100. *Webster's College Dictionary* (New York, New York: Random House, Inc., 2001), 449.

101. *Merriam-Webster's Essential Learner's English Dictionary* (2010), 435.

102. Hugh Rice, "Fatalism", *The Stanford Encyclopedia of Philosophy* (Winter 2010 Edition), Edward N. Zalta (ed.), URL: http://plato.stanford.edu/archives/win2010/entries/fatalism/.

Chapter 13

103. Sproul, *What Is Reformed Theology?*, 23.

104. Lorraine Boettner, *The Reformed Doctrine of Predestination*, Christian Classics Ethereal Library (Grand Rapids: Eerdmans Publishing Co., 1932), 234.

105. Martin Mulsow, Jan Rohls, *Socinianism and Arminianism: Antitrinitarians, Calvinists, and cultural exchange in seventeenth-century Europe* (2005), p. 38.

Epilogue

106.Sermon by John MacArthur: *The Ultimate Security of Our Salvation (Romans 8:29-30)* given on October 02, 1983.

Appendix A

107. Daniel Spratlin, "Does regeneration precede faith", accessed July 8, 2012. http://carm.org/does-regeneration-precede-faith.

108. Joe Holden, "Faith Precedes Regeneration" 1John 5:1 "Who Are in the Faith," accessed August 12, 2012. http://www.youtube.com/watch?v=JBvl8TMdSo4.

109. Daniel D. Musick, "Faith Precedes Regeneration," 2012, http://danmusicktheology.com/faith-precedes-regeneration. Used by permission of the author.

Appendix B

110. Jack Cottrell, *Acts 13:48 and Calvinism,* Posted on December 23, 2011 (Notes). Used by permission of the author.

About the author

Gil VanOrder, Jr. received a B.A. degree in psychology from Houghton College and studied in a Masters' program at Fuller Theological Seminary before moving to Hawaii, where he directed a homeless shelter for seven years. He has served for over twenty-five years as a youth evangelist, including work with Youth for Christ and Young Life.

Today, he lives in the area of Atlanta, Georgia, with his wife, Sandee. The two have been married for over fifty years and have two children and five grandchildren. He and his wife are members of Sugarloaf United Methodist Church in Suwanee, Georgia.

In addition to *50 Reasons Why I Rejected Calvinism*, Gil has written several other books, including *Jesus or Mohammed: Love or Law* which compares the founder of Christianity with the founder of Islam showing the profound differences between the two. Another book entitled *Jesus Loves Allah* grew out of Gil's personal experiences working with urban youth involved in a racist Muslim cult. Gil recounts in this book some of his dramatic encounters with angry black teenagers who viewed white people as the devil. Also, from his experiences as an evangelist to teenagers, Gil wrote the book, *Blindfolded: Why We Can't See God*, in which he shares some of his observations of today's cultural thinking. In this book, Gil exposes obstacles that block our vision of the Almighty. In his book, *8 Ways to Show Your Kids You Love Them*, Gil shares lessons he learned as a father of both a son and a daughter.

Eric Liddell said in the movie *Chariots of Fire* that when he ran, he felt God's pleasure. Gil says when he writes he feels God's pleasure. He's convinced this particular book was written with a great deal of leading by the Spirit of God.

You may contact the author at vogil@vanorders.net.

Made in the USA
Middletown, DE
29 March 2020